Hamlet Lives in Hollywood
John Barrymore and the Acting Tradition Onscreen

Edited by Murray Pomerance and Steven Rybin

EDINBURGH
University Press

Edinburgh University Press is one of the leading university presses in the UK. We publish academic books and journals in our selected subject areas across the humanities and social sciences, combining cutting-edge scholarship with high editorial and production values to produce academic works of lasting importance. For more information visit our website: edinburghuniversitypress.com

© editorial matter and organization Murray Pomerance and Steven Rybin, 2017
© the chapters their several authors, 2017

Edinburgh University Press Ltd
The Tun—Holyrood Road
12 (2f) Jackson's Entry
Edinburgh EH8 8PJ

Typeset in 11/13 Monotype Ehrhardt by
Servis Filmsetting Ltd, Stockport, Cheshire

A CIP record for this book is available from the British Library

ISBN 978 1 4744 1139 4 (hardback)
ISBN 978 1 4744 1140 0 (webready PDF)
ISBN 978 1 4744 1141 7 (epub)

The right of the contributors to be identified as authors of this work has been asserted in accordance with the Copyright, Designs and Patents Act 1988 and the Copyright and Related Rights Regulations 2003 (SI No. 2498).

Contents

List of Figures   v
The Contributors   vii
Acknowledgments   xi

Introduction   1
Steven Rybin and Murray Pomerance

1. The Pre-Bard Stage Career of John Barrymore   10
   Philip Carli

2. Dangerously Modern: Shakespeare, Voice, and the "New Psychology" in John Barrymore's "Unstable" Characters   22
   Michael Hammond

3. The Curious Case of *Sherlock Holmes*   35
   Colin Williamson

4. John Barrymore's Introspective Performance in *Beau Brummel*   47
   Martin Shingler

5. "Keep Back your Pity": The Wounded Barrymore of *The Sea Beast* and *Moby Dick*   59
   Dominic Lennard

6. From Rome to Berlin: Barrymore as Romantic Lover   71
   Douglas McFarland

7. The Power of Stillness: John Barrymore's Performance in *Svengali*   85
   Diane Carson

8   Prospero Unbound: John Barrymore's Theatrical Transformations
    of Cinema Reality   98
    George Toles

9   A Star is Dead: Barrymore's Anti-Christian Metaperformance   109
    Kyle Stevens

10 Handling Time: The Passing of Tradition in *A Bill of Divorcement* 123
    Daniel Varndell

11 John Barrymore's Sparkling *Topaze*   135
    Steven Rybin

12 "Planes, Motors, Schedules": *Night Flight* and the Modernity of
    John Barrymore   145
    Will Scheibel

13 Barrymore and the Scene of Acting: Gesture, Speech, and
    the Repression of Cinematic Performance   157
    Barry Langford

14 "I Never Thought I Should Sink So Low as to Become an Actor":
    John Barrymore in *Twentieth Century*   169
    William Rothman

15 Barrymore Does Barrymore: The Performing Self Triumphant in
    The Great Profile   183
    R. Barton Palmer

Works Cited   195
Index   200

Figures

1.1 John Barrymore with Constance Collier in *Peter Ibbetson* — 11
2.1 Barrymore as Richard III in John G. Adolfi's *The Show of Shows* — 23
2.2 Barrymore as the sinister Tsarakov in Michael Curtiz's *The Mad Genius* — 31
3.1 Moriarty meets Holmes (John Barrymore) for the first time in *Sherlock Holmes* — 43
4.1 John Barrymore thinking his character's thoughts in *Beau Brummel* — 53
5.1 Barrymore on romantic display as Ahab Ceeley in *The Sea Beast* — 63
5.2 Ahab (John Barrymore) is restrained by shipmates as his limb is torturously cauterized in Lloyd Bacon's *Moby Dick* — 66
6.1 Don Juan de Marana (John Barrymore) attempts to seduce the virginal Adriana in *Don Juan* — 72
6.2 A shameful Marcus (John Barrymore) realizes he is about to lose the woman he most desires in *Eternal Love*. — 75
6.3 In *Arsène Lupin*, the clever and sophisticated Lupin (John Barrymore) discovers a naked woman in his bed — 78
6.4 The upper-class Baron (John Barrymore) flirts with the modern working girl in *Grand Hotel* — 81
7.1 Svengali (John Barrymore) taking control of Trilby in *Svengali* — 93
8.1 Barrymore's Larry Renault gazes absently at his ghostly mirror image in *Dinner at Eight* — 106
9.1 In *A Bill of Divorcement*, viewers meet Hilary through a portrait that showcases the profile for which John Barrymore was famous during his silent-screen days — 113

9.2 Larry Renault carefully organizes the setting and lighting for his final repose in *Dinner at Eight* — 119
9.3 Costume, lighting, and blocking collude to picture Barrymore/Mercutio as a star within the world of *Romeo and Juliet* — 120
10.1 A piano tutorial in *A Bill of Divorcement* — 131
11.1 John Barrymore, sparkling under the influence, in *Topaze* — 140
12.1 Cold and mechanical, resistant to "tears and hysterics," Rivière is John Barrymore at his most ruthlessly antiromantic in *Night Flight* — 146
13.1 The spectacle of degradation in *The Beloved Rogue* — 162
14.1 Six delicious moments from *Twentieth Century* — 170
15.1 In *The Great Profile*, Evans Garrick first appears in the film with his cheeks heavily rouged, still dressed for his role in the studio production of *Macbeth* — 187

The Contributors

Philip Carli is a cultural historian, musicologist, silent-film accompanist, and conductor based in Rochester, New York where he is Adjunct Faculty at the Eastman School of Music and the University of Rochester. He has been the resident musician for the George Eastman Museum in Rochester since 1989 and has played for, and lectured on, silent film all over the world, most notably for twenty-six editions of Le Giornate del Cinema Muto in Pordenone, Italy where he has also contributed program articles and, in 2014, curated a series of films covering the silent productions starring the Barrymore siblings Lionel, Ethel, and John, as well as their uncle Sidney Drew.

Diane Carson, Professor Emerita, St. Louis Community College, is codirector/producer of the documentary *Other People's Footage: Copyright & Fair Use* (2016). She is past president of the University Film and Video Association, and served as Film Specialist for the UFVA American Documentary Showcase to Indonesia, Myanmar, Vietnam, and Kazakhstan. She is coauthor of *Appetites and Anxieties: Food, Film and the Politics of Representation*, (2014) and has contributed to anthologies on Clint Eastwood, Preston Sturges, and John Sayles, and South Korean film. She has contributed to and coedited anthologies on contemporary film performance, feminist film analysis, and multicultural media and pedagogy.

Michael Hammond is Associate Professor in Film at the University of Southampton UK. He is the author of *The Big Show: British Cinema Culture and The Great War* (2006, reprinted 2010) and coeditor of *Silent British Cinema and the Great War* (2013). He is currently working on a British

Academy-funded research project on the impact of the Great War on the aesthetic practices of the Hollywood studios between 1919 and 1939.

Barry Langford is Professor of Film Studies at Royal Holloway, University of London. His publications include *Film Genre: Hollywood and Beyond* (2005) and *Post-Classical Hollywood: Film Industry, Style and Ideology since 1945* (2010). He has published widely on Holocaust film, cinema and the city, 1970s Hollywood, and the theory of screenwriting. He is also a professional screenwriter whose credits include the six-part drama series *The Frankenstein Chronicles* (2015). He is currently preparing *Darkness Visible*, a monograph on Holocaust film.

Dominic Lennard is an Associate Lecturer in the Pre-degree Programs at the University of Tasmania. He is the author of *Bad Seeds and Holy Terrors: The Child Villains of Horror Film* (2014).

Douglas McFarland is retired Professor of English and Classical Studies at Flagler College, Saint Augustine, Florida where he taught Renaissance literature, Latin, and Greek. He has published on sixteenth-century English and French literature as well as numerous articles and chapters on film. He is coeditor (with Wesley King) of *John Huston as Adaptor* (1917).

R. Barton Palmer is Calhoun Lemon Professor of Literature at Clemson University where he also directs the World Cinema program. Palmer is the author or editor of more than forty volumes devoted to various film and literary subjects, including *Thinking in the Dark: Cinema, Theory, Practice* and *Shot on Location: Postwar American Cinema and the Exploration of Real Place*, and he serves as the general editor of book series at six academic publishers. He is also the editor of the *South Atlantic Review* and the *Tennessee Williams Annual Review*.

Murray Pomerance is Professor in the Department of Sociology at Ryerson University and the author, editor, or coeditor of numerous volumes. His most recent books are *The Man Who Knew Too Much* (2016), *A King of Infinite Space* (2017), and *Moment of Action: Riddles of Cinematic Performance* (2016). He edits "Horizons of Cinema" at SUNY Press and "Techniques of the Moving Image" at Rutgers University Press.

William Rothman is Professor of Cinema and Interactive Media at the University of Miami. He received his PhD in Philosophy from Harvard University where he taught film for many years. He was founding editor of the "Harvard Film Studies" and "Cambridge Studies in Film" series.

His own books include *Hitchcock—The Murderous Gaze*, *The "I" of the Camera*, *Documentary Film Classics*, *Reading Cavell's* The World Viewed: *A Philosophical Perspective on Film*, and (as editor) *Cavell on Film*, *Jean Rouch, Three Documentary Filmmakers* and (as coeditor) *Looking with Robert Gardner*.

Steven Rybin is Assistant Professor of Film Studies in the English department at Minnesota State University, Mankato. He is the author of *Gestures of Love: Romancing Performance in Classical Hollywood Cinema* (2017) and editor of *The Cinema of Hal Hartley: Flirting with Formalism* (2016) among other books, book chapters, and articles.

Will Scheibel is Assistant Professor in the Department of English at Syracuse University. He is the author of *American Stranger: Modernisms, Hollywood, and the Cinema of Nicholas Ray* (2017) and coeditor, with Steven Rybin, of *Lonely Places, Dangerous Ground: Nicholas Ray in American Cinema* (2014).

Martin Shingler is Senior Lecturer in Radio & Film Studies at the University of Sunderland, UK. He has published numerous essays on Bette Davis, is coauthor of *On Air: Methods and Meanings of Radio* (1998), *Melodrama: Genre, Style & Sensibility* (2004) and author of *Star Studies: A Critical Guide* (2012). He is also the coeditor of the BFI *Film Stars* series and is currently writing *When Warners Brought Broadway to Hollywood, 1923–39*.

Kyle Stevens is Assistant Professor of Film Studies at Appalachian State University. He is the author of *Mike Nichols: Sex, Language, and the Reinvention of Psychological Realism* and coeditor (with Murray Pomerance) of the two-volume collection *Close-Up: Great Screen Performances*. His essays have appeared in *Cinema Journal*, *Critical Quarterly*, *Film Criticism*, *World Picture*, as well as several collections. He is also editor-in-chief of *New Review of Film and Television Studies*.

George Toles is Distinguished Professor of Literature and Film at the University of Manitoba. He is author of *Paul Thomas Anderson* and *A House Made of Light: Essays on the Art of Film*. For twenty-five years, he was Guy Maddin's screenwriting collaborator. The feature films he wrote or coauthored include *Archangel*, *Careful*, *Twilight of the Ice Nymphs*, *The Saddest Music in the World*, *My Winnipeg*, *Brand Upon the Brain*, and *Keyhole*. George has written daily mininarratives for Facebook—in the inchoate genre he calls Status updates—since 2008.

Daniel Varndell is an interdisciplinary scholar working in English Literature at the University of Winchester, UK. He is the author of *Hollywood Remakes, Deleuze and the Grandfather Paradox* (2014) and his most recent publications include work on Hal Hartley and Michael Haneke. He is currently working on a new monograph on torture and etiquette in film performance.

Colin Williamson is an Assistant Professor of Film and Screen Studies at Pace University (New York City). He is the author of *Hidden in Plain Sight: An Archaeology of Magic and the Cinema* (2015), and has published articles and essays in *animation: an interdisciplinary journal*, *Leonardo*, *Journal of Arts, Sciences, and Technology*, *The Moving Image*, and *Thinking in the Dark: Cinema, Theory, Practice* (2015).

Acknowledgments

We extend sincere gratitude to all of the editors and project managers at Edinburgh University Press, including especially Gillian Leslie, Richard Strachan, Rebecca Mackenzie, and Eddie Clark; also to our copy-editor, Neil Curtis. The care and consideration we have received from the Press have been considerably more than encouraging. The contributors, too, have each gone far beyond the call of authorial duty in warmth, collegiality, and generosity, some of them laboring intensively even during illness to help us bring this project through on time. Collegial and institutional support, a great boon for any teacher and scholar, has been received from the English department at Minnesota State University and the Faculty of Arts at Ryerson University. The individuals nearest and dearest to us, Jessica Belser, Nellie Perret, and Ariel Pomerance, have unfailingly given support, encouragement, and love during this and all of our projects.

Introduction

Steven Rybin and Murray Pomerance

When at 10.20 p.m., May 29, 1942, he died at Hollywood Presbyterian Hospital in the company of his brother Lionel, his lifelong friend Gene Fowler, John Decker, and the actor Alan Mowbray, John Barrymore was only sixty years old. His liver and kidneys ravaged by alcoholism, he had been partially comatose for seventy-two hours. The *Los Angeles Times* saw fit to mount him to its topmost headline, "John Barrymore Taken by Death," an elevation that allowed him posthumously to supersede George Marshall's planned invasion of France. That he was imagined to have been "taken by Death" rather than, less Olympically, dying as mortals do, signals the monumental quality of the regard in which he was held by those who admired him. This was not merely a "great performer," not merely an onstage and onscreen presence shining with all the brilliance of astute training and preparation for an august craft; it was an almost superhuman being who, in the end, had to be reached out for and seized away, so tenaciously did his spirit and courage hold on to his wounded living force. In "taking" Barrymore, Death was stealing from us all.

He picked up the nickname "The Great Profile" (around the time of *Beau Brummel*), a tag with resonance. After all, any part of a body might gain prominence in imagery: Georgia O'Keefe's hands in the photography of Alfred Stieglitz; Fred Astaire's feet. And, as to faces, any screen actor might choose to suggest or request that the cameraman bias his view to one side: no one's face has two identical sides, and it is to the actor's career benefit that he take steps to ensure, as much as possible, an appealing view for potential ticket buyers' ongoing fascination. But other actors, turning only one side to the camera (a celebrated case was Claudette Colbert), did not (and do not) get named a "great profile," they are merely seen in profile, and to better effect. Barrymore was being coined. In the deep thoughts of his viewers, he was receiving the respect and adoration that had also bathed the identity of the Roman emperors, and that for Barrymore was iconized even while he lived on coinage of his own country. Barrymore, of course, lived far from Rome, to be categorically correct in Benedict Canyon, that is, Beverly Hills, not Hollywood.

The profile, as we conventionally recognize it, is an iconography of the head and, with every replication, echoes Guy Davenport's seminal idea of Western society's connection of fatality with the head (25 ff.). It is the head that stands for the life and the personality; the head that signifies and interprets; the head that knows the world. Davenport quotes Benjamin: "To inhabit means to leave traces" (32). Barrymore inhabited his face, and the face onscreen is the cumulative total of the nuances of his habitation. For Hollywood, from very early days, the head was reduced to the face, a fountain of recognizability, so that from facial portraits, broadcast small in newspaper advertisements and gigantic on billboards, audience allegiance could be marshalled and stimulated. Barrymore's head was a signal faciality, his aquiline nose, eyelashes, and etched lips an assemblage of expressive organs beyond the pale. It needed hardly to be spelled out for his viewers that the profile triply enunciated: the eyes would *see and take in* what was present in the scene, what the viewer, too, was seeing and taking in, and would thus affiliate Barrymore with those who adored him. When another character reacted to a situation through feeling, he would detect and evaluate, as would we, yet on a higher plane, the plane occupied by imperial faces in profile. The nose would sense, would taste the atmosphere of the moment. The lips would taste the most private realities of his lovers; and would form the words that, so eloquently and crisply articulated by Barrymore—he was a master of the powers of speech—gave body to the voice *nonpareil* in the history of cinema. Garbo, Richard Burton, Orson Welles had voices of this magnitude historically—voices that resonated through time; but speaking, they did not quite manage to command and engender the moment as Barrymore did.

He was more than a person with a job in the theater and in Hollywood, then; had ascended into a supreme status, even above power figures, as a figurehead in a kind of pantheon. Washington . . . Lincoln . . . Barrymore. This is not to suggest that onscreen he made exclusive use of the profile, for he showed himself in every possible way. But this actor showing himself was thought, in America's deep thoughts, a profile, not a man: an etching, an iconographic line. Everlasting. Barrymore "had a wonderful edge," John Gielgud reflected thirty years after the death (Kobler 208). If he had been a quintessential performer on the stage, he was immortalized by his performances onscreen.

Yet the kind of acting Barrymore did for the camera was hardly endemic to moving pictures. Born in an age of high capital, technological innovation, urbanization, and itinerant showmanship, moving pictures derived, as much articulate scholarship has shown, from many earlier forms, photographic and non-photographic, scientific as well as popular, including among others magic-lantern shows, fairs, peep shows, and vaudeville performances (see Gunning; Gaudreault, ed.; Williamson for just some sources). The narrational film as we know it goes back to the earliest years of the second decade of the twentieth century, with the work of D. W. Griffith (for example, *The Lonedale Operator* [1911]), but moving images in the service of chained tableaux—story-like forms—of course go back further (consider Georges Méliès's *Voyage à la lune* [1902; see Solomon] and Edwin S. Porter's *The Great Train Robbery* [1903]). What might generally be called the "fictional film," by which can be meant the moving picture originating in, or owing allegiance to, a known literary source, stems from the 1910s and the 1920s, and a great deal of the burgeoning production of those early years was based on classical dramatic forms—Scott, Shakespeare, Poe, Stevenson; or on mythic tales, such as the Arabian Nights. By the mid 1920s, elaborate and dramatically intensive film productions of classical literary forms were common, and the need had now regularly to be satisfied for skilled performances of celebrated figures from the pages of great novels and plays. While acting, strictly identifiable as such, had been employed in moving-picture production since at least 1910, the call finally went out for performers who, even more than expressing facially in close-ups (Lillian Gish), positioning themselves balletically in comedy (Buster Keaton), or posing heroically in action (Douglas Fairbanks), could use the body and, after 1927, the voice to galvanize audiences' attention to the character and his tribulations inside a visually (and then acoustically) unfolding tale. More than a body that showed itself, and moved, the actor gained emotive and dramaturgical weight. Cinema backed away some from the artful and ingenious constructions Griffith had used to visualize performance—the emphatic use of close-ups, for just one example—and began, in the most theatrical of ways, to stage its dramatic action. Movies became infatuated with the stage.

JOHN BARRYMORE, STAGE AND SCREEN

Few figures in the history of American screen acting are as essential to our understanding of the medium's theatrical roots as John Barrymore. An actor renowned for playing the screen lover—he was born February 15, 1882, just hours past Saint Valentine's Day—Barrymore would become, throughout his career, the exemplar of performative range in both the theatrical and cinematic arts of the 1910s, 1920s, and 1930s. His statuesque profile and commanding physical and vocal presence serve well in staged tragedy; his roles as both Peter Ibbetson in the 1917 production of the same name and as Hamlet in 1922, among other performances, established Barrymore as the peerless stage tragedian of his era. But the actor's start in theater was mainly in light comedies, a fact reflected as he later on cajoled laughter from appreciative film audiences as the impresario Oscar Jaffe in 1934's screwball masterpiece, Howard Hawks's *Twentieth Century*, the most hilarious of his screen comedies (and, in our biased view, one of the funniest movies ever made). Yet he was also capable of stunning pathos, drawing tears in Edmund Goulding's *Grand Hotel* and George Cukor's *Dinner at Eight*. Revisiting Barrymore in the twenty-first century gives us the opportunity to discover once more his versatility, his passion, his humor, and his way of wooing (us, and his characters' onscreen paramours), fascinations that come alive every time one of his films is viewed.

Yet for students and scholars encountering Barrymore (and his era) for the first time, it is worth remembering that the performative journey Barrymore invites us to take leads to a different kind of reality. The world Barrymore draws us into, through his gestures, expressions, and movements, could not be further from most of the kinds of films and performances movies now give us. We live in the early twenty-first century with a Hollywood cinema obsessed with various forms of "you-are-there," often militaristic, realism and with flattering its audience with "relatable" characters whose lives, we are to take it, are just like ours, or just like those of people we might meet in everyday life. To *not* be realistic is, for many viewers who pass over a contemplation of film performance lightly and quickly, a fatal flaw. But John Barrymore enchants us away from—is, indeed, above—reality, and he enthralls us through his magical and thoughtful performative craft, rather than through his everydayness. In her important work on the actor, Marian Keane suggests this ability to invoke a beautiful artifice is one of this actor's special gifts: "Barrymore's ability to conceive a reality beyond what anyone's, including his own, ordinary senses deliver, or beyond what others in the worlds of his films can know, means he is considered mad by others in many of his films" (192). This is a madness that is sometimes made literal, as in *Dr. Jekyll and Mr. Hyde* (1920) or *Svengali* (1931), among other films. Yet, even when Barrymore's characters go mad (literally or metaphorically), we should take this as a sign of his exemplary performative control: he takes us beyond our routine inhabitations of life, and convinces us of his characters' belief in the possibility of an alternative reality. His theatricality, at its grandest, transcends everyday life (or opens a cinematic door to another kind of living). All of this magic he conjures for us through his mastery of gesture and expression. The ongoing treasure of a Barrymore performance is the reminder it gives that cinema, and performance in cinema, are, in fact, at their best artistic astonishments rather than mere documents of existence.

A POWERFUL PERFORMANCE

Despite the actor's penchant for carefully controlled performative magic, Barrymore also works to draw us inside the minds of his characters, and in ways that inspire contemplation and thought. Early signs of this thoughtfulness could be glimpsed in Barrymore's stage work prior to taking on Shakespeare and other roles associated with great actors, as Philip Carli shows in our first chapter. Here, we get a glimpse of Barrymore's "cerebral and inventive" creativity as well as his dazzling physical presence in his early stage performances, work which is often overshadowed in discussions of his later acting in Shakespeare. Audiences of both theater and film in the 1910s and the 1920s, of course, came with their own preconceptions of what a "realistic" stage play, or film, should be, and Barrymore's work had to negotiate these expectations. As Michael Hammond discusses at length here, these years were the age of psychological realism and theater's gradual transition away from the symbolic heights of Victorian melodrama. During the time of Barrymore's first triumphs on the stage, the psychoanalytic postulates of Sigmund Freud began to shift expectations of what an audience might expect to receive, in terms of communicable narrative content, from both stage and film characterization: how dark a characterization could conceivably be, and dark in what ways. Barrymore's career underwent a related and attendant shift as the actor transitioned from his work in theatrical and filmic comedies in the 1910s to a series of more complex characterizations of subtle shade and texture. The nascent expressionism of many early Barrymore films during the 1920s—most emblematically *Dr. Jekyll and Mr. Hyde* in the first year of that decade—balances grounded psychology (the rationalism of Jekyll) with the more ostensive flair for the theatrical (the villainy of Hyde). Often, however, the marvel of Barrymore's expressivity in films arrives through the way in which he reverses or complicates our expectations about what an actor might find himself doing in relation to a particular film technique (such as camera placement). As Colin Williamson shows in his chapter here on Barrymore's performance in *Sherlock Holmes*, it is often Barrymore's close-ups that are most grand, most worthy of detailed and impassioned study: rather than only drawing us closer to a psychological interiority or "realism," Barrymore's close-ups, and the beautiful face he figures within them, are grand attractions in themselves, both expressing a character's thoughts and emotions and demonstrating the delightful possibilities of cinema as a medium complex and mysteriously attractive in the possibilities of presentation it bequeathed to actors.

So because film gave us the mystery of a Barrymore close-up, viewers got closer to Barrymore through the medium of cinema. While viewing Barrymore today, in our later age of image ubiquity and instant accessibility, it can be difficult to remember that actors were once not so available: to see Barrymore onstage one would have to have lived in the right city at the right time, and to see Barrymore at his best one would have to attend the right performance. As it did with all screen actors, cinema slowed Barrymore's image to become viewable by audiences around the world: both practically, in the opportunity the art of film gave viewers to see a Barrymore who had otherwise been restricted to a smaller, privileged few paying to see him on the physical stage; and also emotionally, in that seeing Barrymore's inimitable profile on a giant movie screen offered viewers the opportunity to wonder and dream at what the former matinee idol might be thinking and feeling. What Barrymore poses for us during such moments of wonderment are often questions regarding the mystery of acting itself, as Martin Shingler explores in his contribution to the book on the introspective qualities of the Barrymore star vehicle *Beau Brummel*. As the Barrymore character thinks, we see Barrymore, too, performing a kind of thinking about his performance: we are drawn closely inside both character and actor at once. At other times, Barrymore prompts us into contemplation of masculinity and its various cultural and contextual meanings. Though previous scholars have emphasized the way in which Barrymore's screen image was feminized by worshipful female audiences (see Studlar), Barrymore's manliness could also open up questions regarding different kinds of vulnerabilities. As Dominic Lennard teaches us in his contribution to this volume, Barrymore's characters were often wounded, pitiful men, as his performances as disabled or stigmatized figures in films such as *The Sea Beast* (1926) and *Moby Dick* (1930) gamely show us a figure of masculine strength grappling with its softer, or more exposed, side.

Of course, the introspective, at times feminized, and occasionally vulnerable characters Barrymore played are so effective and memorable precisely because Barrymore himself has few shortcomings as an actor: his ability to elicit pity for a character's limitation is every bit the product of the performer's own awe-inspiring power. Some of our authors take this strength, the sheer authority of a Barrymore performance, as their muse. Barrymore's performative transcendence was perhaps never more evident than in his role as a lover, particularly at the height of his physical beauty in 1920s cinema. He played the screen lover in numerous films, including *Beau Brummel*, *Don Juan* (1926), *Eternal Love* (1929), *Arsène Lupin* (1932), and *Grand Hotel* (1932). Few viewers who have seen *Grand Hotel*, especially, can ever forgot the way in which Barrymore gazes upon the ballet dancer Grusinskaya, played by Greta Garbo, and the ways in which the eyes and hands of each actor form an implicit gestural study of the beauty and mystery of the other. But Barrymore never settled into a single type of onscreen lover. His seductive roles are, collectively, a microcosm of his expansive versatility, as Douglas McFarland demonstrates here in a chapter that explores the thematic and performative connections which bind various and always distinctive Barrymore lovers. Sometimes, the Barrymore lover's passion could take villainous turns: his evil Svengali, in the film of the same title, is driven by a kind of twisted love, and, as Diane Carson shows in her analysis of the film in this volume, Barrymore's characterization in *Svengali* is as powerful as any of his more benevolent film characters.

Indeed, central to Barrymore's versatility is this sense that, with each subsequent role in films, the theatrical Barrymore reveals new ways of revealing the human face behind the illusory mask. This is the central theme of George Toles's contribution to this book, which takes Barrymore to be "the supreme embodiment of theatre on film" in his perpetually magical transcendence of the inherent boundaries and limits of each role he played.

THE MODERN BARRYMORE

The initial decades of Barrymore's career on film and in theater prompt us also to consider the relationship between the traditional theater and the new cinema. Here we think about the ways in which Barrymore plays repeatedly with the power of his theatrical persona in front of what was, in the first half of the twentieth century, the astonishing new power of the motion-picture camera. Another surprise in store for any first-time viewer of Barrymore's films today is that he is always, not despite but indeed because of his peerless theatricality, a thoroughly and perpetually modern figure of cinema—indeed, much more modern and "new" today, in his way, than in so many contemporary performers who tend to limit the possible range of their theatricality to the demands of a kind of psychological realism that insists we meet the character as an ordinary fellow, or a regular guy, or a "pal." The modernity of Barrymore is located in his tendency to draw us into an acute awareness of his grand theatricality: if Barrymore is larger than life, he is so in a highly self-reflective fashion and, in privileged instances, his approach to performance could work against received traditions in unexpected ways.

One of those received traditions is, of course, the standard procedures of classical Hollywood itself: one of the marvels of Barrymore's career on film is that it thrived even as the Hollywood machine worked tirelessly to rid itself, in the late 1920s and early 1930s, of any actor who could not conform, in vocal comportment, to the new demands of the nascent technology of sound film. If Barrymore is remembered today for his grand poses in the silent tableaux of his early and mid 1920s films, it is also his voice that we often recall when thinking of his later screen work. In his chapter on Barrymore's three "meta-performances" for George Cukor (a director who is no stranger to the theme of stardom in movies), Kyle Stevens suggests that the actor's work with that filmmaker poses its own critique of Hollywood's "foundational myths of Hollywood stardom," in particular, those myths that frame the "born-again" star of the newly speaking sound cinema in grandly celestial terms. If these films demonstrate the Barrymore figure's implicit rejection of traditional Hollywood myths, they might also suggest a more balanced tension between tradition and modernity. Daniel Varndell suggests that Barrymore the actor, at his best, served to pass secrets from one generation or tradition to a new tradition or generation—but these "secrets" that Barrymore bequeaths, through his screen work of the early 1930s and Cukor's *A Bill of Divorcement* in particular, are often inscrutable in their content, a mystery that, in fact, renders Barrymore perpetually relevant and intriguingly mysterious to any new generation who views his screen performances.

It is perhaps strange, at first glance, to consider Barrymore as this kind of modern figure, and yet, as many of our authors explore throughout the book, his work could be given to intriguing ironies. Steven Rybin's chapter focuses on Barrymore's performance in the 1933 film adaptation of *Topaze*. In this film, the Barrymore character discovers the power of irony, and uses it as a path to a new kind of expressivity and knowledge, all while the performance itself ironically draws from, and builds upon, previous Barrymore performances and characterizations. And, in Will Scheibel's chapter on *Night Flight* (1933), we find a Barrymore not only thoroughly imbricated in the modernity of "planes, motors, and schedules," but also now a Barrymore working against the romantic screen image of many of his earlier roles onstage and onscreen, including *Grand Hotel* of just the year before. Here in *Night Flight* we see a callous, even cruel, Barrymore figure, whose performance offers us clues to reading this hitherto neglected film. Where these authors explore the self-reflexive qualities in Barrymore's early sound films, Barry Langford's contribution to our volume uncovers the nascent modernity of Barrymore's work in the late silent film *The Beloved Rogue*. In this film, Barrymore gives a self-referential screen performance that anticipates the relatively restrained and more colloquial performances in his later films, but without the turn to self-parody that would characterize his work near the end of his life.

THE MIRROR WORLD

The self-aware rejections of tradition and the various ironies at play in the roles discussed above transition in the second half of the 1930s to John Barrymore's final period as a screen performer. This period in the actor's career is marked by performances that serve as veritable commentaries not only on Barrymore's established reputation and legend up to that point but on the art of screen acting itself. This late period might be considered an extension of the "modern Barrymore" just discussed, and yet there is the prevailing sense, even at the time of the release of these films, that Barrymore the actor was on the decline. Many previous commentators tend to frame the latter half of the 1930s and the first year and a half of the 1940s (the final months of Barrymore's life) as the weakest of his periods on film, with the large exception of 1934's *Twentieth Century* (regarded by many as Barrymore's grandest achievement on film).

Critics tend to devalue, in particular, his roles in late works such as *The Great Profile* (1940) and *Playmates* (1941). These late films may not be the equals of Barrymore's heights of performance in *Dinner at Eight* and *Grand Hotel* but, for his committed viewers, the Barrymore on display in his final works is still capable of startling revelations.

No case need be made at this point for *Twentieth Century*, widely considered one of the finest screwball comedies and a great Howard Hawks film, and perhaps also Barrymore's finest hour on the screen. This film was, famously, the one that introduced the world to the comedic talents of Carole Lombard whose gift for cinematic buffoonery blossomed opposite Barrymore and under the tutelage of Hawks. As William Rothman's new appreciation of *Twentieth Century* reminds us, a great film and a great film performance always give us more opportunity for renewed insight and discovery. As Rothman shows, Barrymore's own discovery in this film is his complete characterization of a man who lives life as if it were a perpetual movie—a script of which he is the star, the director, the producer, and the writer. Barrymore brings Oscar Jaffe to life through his masterful performative relationship to Hawks's camera, and also through his canny self-mockery. If *Twentieth Century* remains the most deservedly celebrated of Barrymore's late works, *The Great Profile* is perhaps one of his most undeservedly neglected. R. Barton Palmer, in the final chapter of this book, suggests that this neglect is understandable, if not finally justifiable: the actor's offscreen biographical legend (his alcoholic fall from grace and his physical deterioration in comparison to the stunning good looks of his 1920s lover roles) has always overshadowed the film which itself refers to the public's perception of Barrymore in "real life" through the adoption of a highly self-referential title. Nevertheless, even as Barrymore plays a version of himself in this film, he is engaging in an authoritative example of screen art, successfully constructing (and in full control of) a screen version of his own reality. In so doing, he successfully demonstrates what he had in fact shown throughout his entire career: that artistic achievements and "real life," even when they are enmeshed as they are in *The Great Profile*, are always fundamentally distinctive and separate realms. Barrymore's achievement in *The Great Profile* (and his other underappreciated late films) is finally to convince us that he is, indeed, successfully and complexly *playing* himself, rather than simply "being" the "real" Barrymore onscreen.

These chapters, written by fifteen leading scholars of film performance, offer us new ways of looking at John Barrymore, movie star, theatrical genius, actor: an actor whose gift to his viewers is to transport us out of expected realities through his marvelous inhabitation of the movie screen.

CHAPTER I

The Pre-Bard Stage Career of John Barrymore

Philip Carli

Early in the sound film revolution, the major American studios decided to emulate a current Broadway trend by creating revues—films that featured discrete musical and dramatic sequences designed to dazzle all the senses and show off the various talents of their major stars. These often exposed stars' less attractive attributes as well as exploiting what they were good at, *Paramount on Parade* (1930) proving, for example, that Clara Bow's singing voice was not strong. Warner Bros.'s contribution to the genre was one of the earliest and most commercially successful: *Show of Shows*, released in April 1929. It was as variable in entertainment, artistic merit, and technical sophistication as any of its competitors' efforts, and was certainly as long (clocking in at well over two hours in its initial screenings) but among the musical and comic acts was an anomaly: the studio's most celebrated "serious" star, John Barrymore, famous as both a stage and screen actor and personality, making his sound film debut by delivering the Duke of Gloucester's soliloquy from William Shakespeare's *Henry VI, Part One*, on an impressive set featuring a menacing barren mountain, the whole affair introduced and concluded by spare but suitably ominous sound effects. Before his performance, Barrymore, clad in evening dress, steps in front of a stage curtain; the camera cuts to a medium close-up and he delivers the following introduction with an air of charm and almost diffidence. I include his pauses and emphases, particularly in the first part of the address, to convey Barrymore's informality and indeed intimacy with the audience:

> Ladies and gentlemen: The, uh, soliloquy you are about to hear is from the, uh, First Part of Henry the Sixth, when Richard the Third was, uh, Duke of Gloucester and before he became King. In it, he, uh, not only discloses his own . . . *piquant* psychology, but he also infers that he

THE PRE-BARD STAGE CAREER OF JOHN BARRYMORE

Figure 1.1 John Barrymore with Constance Collier in *Peter Ibbetson* (Theatre Republic, New York, April 17, 1917). Courtesy New York Public Library.

will never be king—unless he destroys his elder relations, one by one. Although it is not clearly indicated in this particular soliloquy whether he does so or not . . . permit me to assure you that he eliminates them *all* . . . with the, uh . . . graceful impartiality . . . of Al Capone [which Barrymore pronounces in the correct Italian manner "Caponeh"].

From his first words, John Barrymore demonstrates what made him so compelling—an ease, wit, and grace that invited audiences to invest themselves in his personality and thoughtfulness as an actor. These qualities brought him a considerable fame and respect which eventually changed to notoriety as, through his career, vicissitudes and the decline in his personal circumstances, he gradually descended in the public's mind to being the epitome of a "ham actor," overemphatically declaiming without comprehension of his own ridiculousness or the public's contempt. Yet this same public forgot that it was his inner intelligence, passion, and communicative ability that had originally allowed them to relish his extraordinary qualities as a romantic actor, the last, perhaps, of a line extending back to Edmund Kean. Edmund Kean (1787–1883) was the leading Shakesperean tragedian in the early nineteenth century. Coleridge famously said, "To see him act, is like reading Shakespeare by flashes of lightning." And, ironically, both Kean and Barrymore's dedication to their art, coupled with fighting their personal demons, made them both self-destructive personalities—they gave their all in every respect, especially when young. But the cost to themselves was devastating. In looking at John Barrymore's overall acting career, however, it is strange to note that he actually spent a very limited time on the boards in New York and, in that time, he mostly played roles that completely go against the commonly held belief that he took on only the personas and parts associated with Great Actors. Why was this? What parts did he mostly play and in what kind of plays? Are these plays, in which he appeared most often, to be dismissed, not being "great literature" but "mere" theatrical pieces of their time? What special qualities could and did Barrymore bring to these works?

Like his siblings Lionel and Ethel, John Barrymore did not intend to follow in the acting profession—and, indeed, tradition—established both by his mother's family, the Drews, and by his father Maurice, born a scion of an upper-class Anglo-Indian family and become one of the late nineteenth century's most celebrated romantic stage personalities. John's legal name was Blyth—John Sidney Blyth—and, retaining Maurice's original family name, rather than his stage name, separated the offspring of his parents' union from the celebrity and notoriety of the actors (for such was the mixed regard Americans and the British held for acting and actors, not without reason). It offered them a chance to be who they wanted to be, at least in theory. But, for all three children, the family heritage (like the stage name) proved ineluctable, and for John not only in the matter of profession. The disreputable influence of Maurice showed itself in an incident at John's interview for admission to Georgetown Preparatory School where, at age twelve, in front of his father and the headmaster, a pair of brass knuckles, a packet of cigarettes, and a half pint of whiskey tumbled out of his pockets when he did a handstand on the gym's horizontal bars (Kobler 39). Four years later, his father's second wife, Mamie Floyd, seduced John, leaving him permanently scarred emotionally and psychologically. For good and ill, family molded John's personality as well as his acting career.

John made his stage debut, quite unwillingly, in a walk-on part alongside his father in the late spring of 1896. Maurice Barrymore, though celebrated, was practical in that, when work was scarce, he took what was available and so, when Oscar Hammerstein I, offered to mount a short play of his choice as part of the bill at his Olympia Music Hall, Maurice readily accepted. Though his friends told him that appearing in vaudeville was degrading, the Music Hall was no ordinary vaudeville house: it was a gigantic, rambling, extravagantly decorated entertainment complex for which one fifty-cent ticket admitted you to two main auditoriums (the Lyric, for extended plays, and the Music Hall for top-flight internationally renowned variety acts), two small theaters (a Concert Hall for singers and solo performers, and the Roof Garden summertime open-air dining and variety venue), an oriental cafe, bowling, and billiards. It stood at what was fast becoming the new heart of New York's uptown theatrical district in Longacre Square at Broadway and 44th Street and had opened to great acclaim in October 1895.

In keeping with both the celebrity of the venue and his own substantial reputation, Maurice selected *A Man of the World*, a one-act "comedietta" by the highly regarded playwright Augustus Thomas (1857–1934) which Maurice had introduced to New York viewers in 1889, playing the title character of a sophisticated gray-haired soldier who has learned many of life's lessons from his own past mistakes. It is a slight piece, but naturalistically written, and very much a star vehicle; an ideal display piece in a variety program. John, then fourteen, was enlisted for the premiere performance in a non-speaking part. Not being given any directions as to makeup, he put on a handlebar mustache to appear older than his years. Maurice paid no attention to his son and, in accordance with his own established makeup for his part, donned what turned out to be an identical handlebar mustache. When Maurice Barrymore made his entrance onstage, followed by what appeared to be a younger, smaller doppelgänger, the house broke into uproarious laughter. Maurice's later remarks to John are not known but the incident drove John away from the stage and into art studies and books. He remained away from the theater for the next seven years.

His son's retreat into apparently more intellectual pursuits gave Maurice the idea to send him to England where John's older sister Ethel was acting. There John acquired a fragmentary but ultimately broad-based education, including studies at King's College, Wimbledon, the University of London, and the Slade School of Art. All of these experiences fed into John's voracious but undisciplined desire for knowledge and ultimately, in various ways, informed his approach to acting. His English academic wandering ended with a return to New York in 1900 where he studied with painter George Bridgman (1865–1943), a man he came to admire immensely. He also began to sell his artwork, including a drawing to Andrew Carnegie (for $10) and a series of macabre pen-and-ink works to *Cosmopolitan* magazine where they attracted favorable notice. The *Cosmopolitan* sketches point up John's lifelong interest in grotesquerie and a sense of his own Jekyll-and-Hyde personality—great warmth and wit coupled to manic depression and occasional cruelty—tendencies that he later deployed onstage in his portrayal of the Duke of Gloucester and Richard III, and onscreen in *Dr. Jekyll and Mr. Hyde* (1920). Scrabbling in the journalistic world, John got a series of evanescent sketching engagements, the longest being eighteen months on William Randolph Hearst's *New York Evening Journal*, which gave him confidence, marginal stability, and rough newsmen for company, until his dismissal for a botched illustration (not entirely his fault) in 1902.

In fact, it was in October 1901, while he was working for Hearst, that family duty called and John made his debut as a speaking actor. This was at Ethel's request as a one-performance replacement for an indisposed actor in her return engagement in *Captain Jinks of the Horse Marines,* a comedy by the then highly successful Clyde Fitch (1865–1909) at Philadelphia's Garrick Theatre. For most of the latter part of the twentieth century, plays written for the American stage in this period have been consistently dismissed as unworthy of scholarly or literary attention, an attitude brutally summed up by John Kobler, John Barrymore's principal biographer, who pronounced, "The American theater during the first decade of the twentieth century had a simplism verging on idiocy" (89). Whether these plays were successful or failures mattered little or nothing to critics and historians, and their social significance as indicating audiences' taste and intellect, not to mention the effort and craft expended in staging them, meant little as well. It is only within the last twenty years that a change in attitude has arisen and some (by no means the majority) of these stage works are attracting reevaluation and appreciation of their workmanship and entertainment value—the elements that accounted for their existence in the first place. Barrymore himself inherited and accepted a realistic view of what he was doing, and he rarely, if ever, disdained his audiences, though his turbulent intellect and personality chafed at the consistent discipline demanded of an actor faced with a lengthy run.

He did not act again until he took a very low-billed part in Fitch's *Glad of It* in December 1903 which turned out to be one of the playwright's rare flops. Contemporary newspapers took more notice that John was actually going into acting with this play than they did reviewing his performance, as he was billed ninth and had only a few lines. His next endeavor, however, in the supporting role of a witty and frequently inebriated telegrapher in *The Dictator* by Richard Harding Davis (1864–1916) in two runs in 1904,[1] was favorably received, especially as he was playing up to the seasoned veteran actors William Collier Sr. (1864–1944) and Edward Abeles (1869–1919). The play itself drew upon Davis's experiences as a reporter in Cuba and Central America, and, though billed as a farce, included some sharp social commentary on North and Central American relations. Barrymore, billed fourth, made a striking appearance in the opening scene as Hyne, described in the stage directions as:

> a young man of rather dissipated appearance. He wears soiled duck trousers supported by a belt, a striped linen shirt with pink garters round the sleeves, a handkerchief tucked inside the collar, and a duck yachting cap bearing the insignia of a ship's officer. His appearance is of a man who has been up all night. (Davis 4–5)

The lines Davis gave him as Hyne allowed John to establish rather quickly certain traits that would influence many of his characters throughout his career: Hyne's response to his captain retelling a weak joke that the first officer also found funny was a morosely sardonic "Yes—*he* would. Sort of a joke that first officer would laugh at—if the Captain made it." Shortly afterwards, cautioned by the captain against further drinking but joined by another person and a steward passing by with a tray holding a cocktail and a cup of coffee, Hyne offers the man a drink. "No, thanks, it's too early." Hyne blithely responds, "It's never too *early* for a drink. It may be too *late*." Then, drinking the cocktail, Hyne adds, "You're too late for that one." In reality, John often played the part truly inebriated, as he tired quickly of repetition, and drink proved a substitute for fulfillment in his work. By some standards there wasn't that much repetition of *The Dictator*. Although it was accounted a success, Broadway runs at that time were quite short and the two combined 1904 runs of the play amounted to only eighty-nine performances.

John's first real success as a lead was creating the role of Nat Duncan in *The Fortune Hunter*, a social comedy by Winchell Smith (187–1933). A failed roving businessman, Duncan is goaded by his financier friend Henry Kellogg into trying to find a rich wife in a rural community by exercising his personal charm and wit but eventually falls in love with the local druggist's daughter. John was able to use his own gregarious and inventive personality to enliven a part that, in truth, Smith derived from models reaching as far back as Restoration comedy but updated to the gilded, superficial, and often fraudulent social world of upper-class 1910 Manhattan and its cultural clashes with the vast wilderness "north of Yonkers." As with many of the American plays staged in this period, this comedy is one of ease rather than emotional depth, at least as read from the page. Reviews indicate that John carried much more than ease to the part: a febrile energy and genuine romanticism.

John's success as a light comedian brought him to the attention of Adolph Zukor, the head of the Famous Players Feature Film Company, for whom he appeared in ten films between 1913 and 1916. In appearing for Zukor's company he had celebrated stage colleagues making films around him: Minnie Maddern Fiske, Marguerite Clark, Mary Pickford, and William H. Crane, among others. John's early film career, which may be seen as tangential to the subject at hand, did have an impact on his stage work as it gave him a different arena in which to develop his personal expressiveness, even in the farces and comedies he made. Notably, his first director, J. Searle Dawley (1877–1949) had had an extensive stage career before entering motion pictures as a director for the Edison Company in 1909, and it was he who urged Zukor to put John under long-term contract, saying he was the best actor he had ever seen (see Kobler 105).

The person who started moving John from light comedy into serious roles on the stage was the playwright and producer Edward Brewster "Ned" Sheldon (1886–1946), who became a lifelong friend. Sheldon sensed John's untapped potential, and gave him some parts to consider that would stretch his abilities. Sheldon also knew that John would have to work on his voice; he could project but the vocal quality was that of a coarse comedian, brash and unrefined. It may surprise some that John Barrymore considered his voice to be the weakest part of his acting technique. His own stringent self-criticism, as well as the ease with which he acquired lighter parts, may have unconsciously kept him in farcical and comedic rather than serious parts. At first, John worked on his voice himself but later he took lessons with Robert Hosea and Margaret Carrington. His study shows the care with which he at least *approached* each part yet, as with many mercurially brilliant personalities, he found difficulty in refining his playing once he was in a run and rapidly becoming bored, so that invariably he was viewed as acting his best in early performances. As to his voice, which he himself described as a "croak," his seriousness and assiduity paid off and made his vocal flexibility and control legendary onstage and onscreen.

John Galsworthy's *Justice*, always referred to as John Barrymore's breakthrough serious play appearance, is rarely staged today although it is a powerful, plain-spoken, and still relevant drama. A generous, kindly intentioned young clerk, attempting to help an abused wife and her children escape with him to South America, is discovered and arrested for forgery in his office. There follows the ordeal of a trial where mercy for him is deemed socially incompatible with "justice," and he is sentenced to a cruel imprisonment. Kobler's biography devotes a scant four pages to the play and gives an incomplete picture of its effectiveness or of John's suitability for the role. Kobler does mention that John's part, the central figure of convicted forger William Falder, has relatively few lines. "He conveyed emotion for the most part silently, through gesture, facial expression and stance" (119). In fact, in Act 3, Scene iii, which all contemporary critics found to be the strongest in the play, Falder's mental disintegration within a solitary confinement cell is entirely wordless. In this, John's previous experience in melodrama and motion pictures allowed him to be at his most cerebral and inventive, using his body to convey emotional torment and intellectual turmoil. Such dramatic creativity—and ironically, its *wordlessness*—allowed John for the first time to drop some of his cynicism concerning his profession and also alleviated his chronic problem of becoming bored with repeating lines night after night, instead requiring him to go to the most creative part of his imagination, linking his sense for visual artistry and his intellect with his hard-acquired acting ability. It is worth citing this scene in its entirety:

Scene iii
FALDER's cell, a whitewashed space thirteen feet broad by seven deep, and nine feet high, with a rounded ceiling. The floor is of shiny blackened bricks. The barred window of opaque glass, with a ventilator, is high up

in the middle of the end wall. In the middle of the opposite end wall is the narrow door. In a corner are the mattress and bedding rolled up *[two blankets, two sheets, and a coverlet]*

Above them is a quarter-circular wooden shelf, on which is a Bible and several little devotional books, piled in a symmetrical pyramid; there are also a black hairbrush, toothbrush, and a bit of soap. In another corner is the wooden frame of a bed, standing on end. There is a dark ventilator under the window, and another over the door. FALDER's work *[a shirt to which he is putting buttonholes]* is hung to a nail on the wall over a small wooden table, on which the novel "Lorna Doone" lies open. Low down in the corner by the door is a thick glass screen, about a foot square, covering the gas-jet let into the wall. There is also a wooden stool, and a pair of shoes beneath it. Three bright round tins are set under the window.

In fast-failing daylight, FALDER, in his stockings, is seen standing motionless, with his head inclined towards the door, listening. He moves a little closer to the door, his stockinged feet making no noise. He stops at the door. He is trying harder and harder to hear something, any little thing that is going on outside. He springs suddenly upright—as if at a sound—and remains perfectly motionless. Then, with a heavy sigh, he moves to his work, and stands looking at it, with his head down; he does a stitch or two, having the air of a man so lost in sadness that each stitch is, as it were, a coming to life. Then turning abruptly, he begins pacing the cell, moving his head, like an animal pacing its cage. He stops again at the door, listens, and, placing the palms of his hands against it with his fingers spread out, leans his forehead against the iron. Turning from it, presently, he moves slowly back towards the window, tracing his way with his finger along the top line of the distemper that runs round the wall. He stops under the window, and, picking up the lid of one of the tins, peers into it. It has grown very nearly dark. Suddenly the lid falls out of his hand with a clatter—the only sound that has broken the silence—and he stands staring intently at the wall where the stuff of the shirt is hanging rather white in the darkness—he seems to be seeing somebody or something there. There is a sharp tap and click; the cell light behind the glass screen has been turned up. The cell is brightly lighted. FALDER is seen gasping for breath.

A sound from far away, as of distant, dull beating on thick metal, is suddenly audible. FALDER shrinks back, not able to bear this sudden clamour. But the sound grows, as though some great tumbril were rolling towards the cell. And gradually it seems to hypnotise him. He begins creeping inch by inch nearer to the door. The banging sound, travelling from cell to cell, draws closer and closer; FALDER's hands are seen moving as if his spirit had already joined in this beating, and the sound swells till it seems to have entered the very cell. He suddenly raises his clenched fists. Panting violently, he flings himself at his door, and beats on it.

[The curtain falls]

Neither *Justice* nor John Galsworthy is generally known today, and both should be, as vital parts of twentieth-century language drama (in which context there is very often mention of George Bernard Shaw and no one else). Of this crucial scene all contemporary reviews glowed, showing John in a hitherto unseen light. A central importance is that his tragic part is outlined in words *while onstage being conveyed wordlessly*. John was in some senses as much or more a *physical* actor as a vocal one, and his voice, later an instrument of the greatest power, was still wanting at this date. Perhaps the physicality of the performance was possible because of his extensive motion-picture experience by that date.

John was an overnight sensation in *Justice*. The acerbic critic Alexander Woollcott devoted several *New York Times* pieces focusing on his performance. His success was largely confined to New York because, when the play was taken on the road, it was found too gloomy by most audiences and box-office takings were comparatively meager. It did change John's thinking about his profession, however, and he started looking at more diverse pieces than he had previously, to the point that, when he brought *Peter Ibbetson* (an adaptation of George du Maurier's romantic psychological novel) to Sheldon in 1917 and said he wanted to do it, Sheldon accepted it without demur even though the play had been rejected by several other producers. It was a bit of a departure, and a surprisingly uncomfortable one, for John as the title character is wholly and impassionedly romantic; Constance Collier, who was also in the play and directed much of it, noted John's wrestling with the role[2] but having brother Lionel on hand to play a complementarily harsh and vicious villain against him no doubt aided John in refining his portrayal. In the end, as Du Maurier's hero, who can be with his beloved only in dreams, he again received strong critical acclaim, and the play did well on tour as well though some criticism was raised against what was perceived as his occasional vocal monotony. Additionally, the constant repetition of the part strained him mentally to breaking point (Morrison 57) because what was once just a careless dislike of repetition had turned, with his new conscientiousness, to an abhorrence.

Barrymore followed up *Ibbetson* with a play that combined romanticism and a troubled soul, Sheldon's adaptation of Leo Tolstoy's *The Living Corpse*, retitled *Redemption* for the American stage. This also brought the influential theater figure Arthur M. Hopkins (1878–1950) into John's life as the play's backer and guiding force, and also, quite as importantly, the redoubtable director Robert Edmond Jones (1887–1954). The play was fashioned into its

English version by Hopkins and the poet Blanche Oelrichs (1890–1950), who wrote under the name "Michael Strange" and later became John Barrymore's second wife. *Redemption*'s fatalistic nature, and John's searing portrayal of the dissolute hero Fyodor, ran into much the same mix of triumph and rejection that had greeted *Justice* but with greater questioning among the critical accolades about the play's dourness, though John was universally praised for his intellectual capturing of his role. Solid New York business did not translate into success on the road where audiences generally rejected the play's innate Russian gloom. Still, it was another move toward broadening John's range to combine disparate, conflicting emotions and character traits into compelling and, indeed, sympathetic characters of a type hitherto unseen on the American stage—a figure of passionate, intellectual bleakness.

The culmination of John's pre-Shakespeare career came in *The Jest*, Ned Sheldon's 1919 translation of the 1909 Italian play *La cena delle beffe (The Jesters' Supper)* by Sem Benelli (1877–1949). *The Jest* concerns Giannetto Malespini, a frail young Florentine painter in the time of Lorenzo the Magnificent, who is tormented for years by two brutish Pisan mercenaries, the brothers Neri and Gabriello Chiaramantesi. "When they steal Ginevra, his beloved, the painter plots an elaborate revenge. He effects a quarrel between the brothers and ultimately uses his cunning to trick Neri into fratricide and madness" (Morrison 62). This brief synopsis does insufficient justice to Benelli and Sheldon's work which, from the fragmentary sources now available, played onstage with electric force, especially in the confrontation scenes featuring John and Lionel. I say "fragmentary" because Sheldon's version was never published but a detailed synopsis containing considerable passages of dialogue was included in Burns Mantle's *The Best Plays of 1919–1920* from which I take my references. *La cena delle beffe* had an interesting transgender performance history prior to its New York appearance; the leading man collapsed before a 1913 staging and actress Paola Pezzaglia (1889–1925) took his place as Giannetto. She continued to play the part for the rest of her career and apparently even Sarah Bernhardt appeared in the role. That this part could encompass both the masculine and feminine sides of a psyche in its interpretation was just the kind of intellectual stimulus that brought out the most creative interpretive power in John, and the Renaissance setting and sensibilities embodied in Benelli's drama no doubt struck a chord within the depth of his reading, preparing him to move toward true Renaissance drama in Shakespeare. For *The Jest* John prepared especially carefully, stepping up his voice lessons and rehearsing with a dedication that surprised even those who knew how hard he could work when his interest was engaged.

Benelli/Sheldon gave some robust dialogue to Giannetto early in the play to show his sensitivity as a boy, his strength emerging as he reaches manhood, and the hatred he feels for Neri, as he expounds to his friend Tornaquinci:

GIANNETTO. And yet, ferocious, savage though I be, I am a coward. That's why the Chiaramentesi chose me for their victim. I'm seventeen. Five years ago I was twelve. Then's when I met them first. In May it was and I was going to school. They had just come to Florence and were wrestling before the barracks in the Via Fossi. I stopped to watch them. They were strong as lions. And as I stood there, wondering in my childish way if Ajax and Achilles had been half so glorious, they spied me out and as they looked at me my heart stood still. "Hi, Tickle-my-chin," the tallest one cried, "what are you, cock or hen?" I was so frightened I began to weep and then they spat on me and made me catch twelve big blue flies and eat them, one by one. *[Pause]* What could I do? I was so weak and small.

But by Act 3, John's soft youth has hardened. In his confrontation with Lionel's Neri, where Neri is apparently about to be executed after having already suffered considerable torture, the audience must have been spellbound:

GIANNETTO. At last! *[with exquisite tenderness]* Poor Neri, are you very tired? Too tired to lift that handsome head of yours? *[Neri stiffens and glares at him silently]* How pale you are! Dear friend, I fear that you have suffered much! But do not mope, for all will yet be well. Come, come! Remember that we only seek to cure you. We do what we must do for your own good . . . Poor thing, I wonder if he understands? Perhaps. For he is smiling. How I love that radiant, happy, sunny smile of his!

NERI. Wait till my brother hears of this in Pisa! He'll tear the windpipe from that silky throat of yours.

GIANNETTO *[easily]* Tush! How you fret! Yet I can guess the secret of your petulance. It is Ginevra!

NERI *[interrupting]* No!

GIANNETTO. You chafe because the dear child may be weeping for you— eh? How like a lover! Well, I bring good news! Dawn found our young friend raised upon one elbow, teasing my nostril with a lock of hair.

NERI. You lie, you lie.

GIANNETTO *[continuing]* I dreamed it was a rose. She scents her hair with roses, you remember . . . And then I woke and drew the baggage to me. That velvet bosom, those slim ivory flanks . . .

NERI *[gasping]* Enough! Be still! *[Turns away]*

GIANNETTO . . . And as we lay and laughed in one another's arms, she put her rosy mouth close to my ear—like this—and whispered . . .

[Giannetto is leaning against Neri and whispering in his ear]

NERI *[with a sudden howl]* The bawd! The harlot!

The Jest finally brought about the full flowering of John's intellectual bravura, tempered with humanity but a strong sense of darkness that had evidenced itself throughout all his previous creative work back to newspaper sketching. Critics were enthusiastic and generous though few in number even at this date. Dorothy Parker rarely wrote rave reviews but of *The Jest* she said, "It is more difficult to write about the production and acting of *The Jest*—superlatives are tiresome reading," and

> They say—they've been saying it for years—that it is impossible to hold an audience after eleven o'clock. The final curtain fall on *The Jest* at a quarter to twelve; until that time not a coat is struggled into, not a hat is groped for, not a suburbanite wedges himself out of his mid-row seat and rushes into the night to catch the 11.26—There can be no greater tribute. (*Vanity Fair* [June 19, 1919])

In writing on John Barrymore's "working up" to playing Shakespeare, I have hoped to show that *all* of his experiences enriched and filled—perhaps overfilled—the imagination and aptitude that emerged in *Richard III* (as well as in the passage from *Henry VI* with Richard in his pre-kingly role of the Duke of Gloucester cited at the beginning of this chapter). His stage career encapsulated the commercial theater of his time and often enlivened it with grace and wit. When necessary, he found the professional courage to trust that he had the *gravitas* to bring depth and introspection to a wide variety—and sometimes entirely new varieties—of plays for the American public. Circumstances and character may have made the trajectory of his career somewhat erratic but, in his passing, he opened the minds of many theatergoers, regardless of their later knowledge of him as the screen's Great Profile. Even in film he was always inventive and, ultimately, it should be acknowledged that he was one of American acting's most thoughtful, creative, and inspired proponents but that his talents were not native; he worked very hard in many different directions to bring them to full fruition.[3]

NOTES

1. In spring and fall; the play went on hiatus during the summer months in New York, when unventilated theaters frequently shut down owing to heat, and actors went on the road.
2. Constance Collier remembered that, at times, Barrymore was "hard to handle because he was ashamed of himself playing love scenes" (quoted in Morrison 56).
3. I am heavily indebted to John Kobler's seminal biography of John Barrymore, *Damned in Paradise*, and the first part of Michael Morrison's insightful *John Barrymore, Shakespearean Actor*, as well as the invaluable assistance of Anthony Labbatte and Alice Carli in bringing this piece to completion.

CHAPTER 2

Dangerously Modern: Shakespeare, Voice, and the "New Psychology" in John Barrymore's "Unstable" Characters

Michael Hammond

On October 27, 1963, a late-night discussion of *Hamlet* with Peter O'Toole and Orson Welles was chaired by Huw Weldon for the BBC television program *Monitor* (online at wwwyoutube.com/watch?v=x2jWx4IqgEM). Weldon asks Welles who was the best Hamlet he had ever seen, "Is there such a thing?" Without hesitation, Welles replies, "Yes, Barrymore." Barrymore, Welles insists, played Hamlet as "a man of genius ... who happened to be a prince." In a slow cadence that emphasizes each adjective, he goes on to say that Barrymore's Hamlet was "*tender* ... and *virile* ... and *witty* ... and ... [even more emphasis] ... *dangerous*." In proclaiming Barrymore's Hamlet as dangerous, Welles implies that this quality was distinct, that the actor had brought something out of the Danish prince that in previous incarnations lay dormant. Michael Morrison, in his detailed study of Barrymore's Shakespeare roles, demonstrates that Barrymore had, indeed, been distinct from the Victorian Hamlets of Johnston Forbes-Robertson and Henry Irving in that he brought a naturalism in his cadence of speech and an emphasis on Hamlet's psychological motivation that rendered Shakespeare accessible and "modern" (Morrison 253–4). Morrison points to Barrymore's influences on John Gielgud and Lawrence Olivier. Having seen Barrymore's Hamlet in the 1925 London performances, Gielgud praised his range: "He had tremendous drive and power, and a romantic sensibility which was very rare" (253). Olivier commented that the Victorian Hamlets of the likes of Irving had "descended into arias and false inflections ... castrated. Barrymore put back the balls." While it may be that, along with Welles, each actor's comment says as much about his own approach to the role, they all underscore a masculinism as one of the distinctive modern forces in Barrymore's performance: danger, power, and balls.[1] This quality in his work was put into service to convey Richard III's

Figure 2.1 Barrymore as Richard III in John G. Adolfi's *The Show of Shows* (Warner Bros., 1929). Digital frame enlargement.

rage against his twisted body and to render Hamlet's uncertainty devastating, which became the basis for the monstrous and/or aberrant masculinity that Barrymore carried into his sound film work at Warner's in the early 1930s.

This dangerous quality is evident in the only filmed recording of his soliloquy as Richard III, that featured in the Warner Bros. 1929 variety film *Show of Shows*. Barrymore employs his power and range as he works through the twisted logic of Richard's descent into villainy. The segment begins with the sounds of battle and men shouting and screaming over a black screen. Slowly the image emerges, a mountain of dead bodies juts into the frame cast against a streaked sky. The Duke of York and his sons Edward and George clamber up to the top of the mound. As his sons show him the blood of his enemies on their swords behind them, his son Richard scrambles over the corpses holding the severed head of the Duke of Somerset. In close-up and to the head he says: "Speak thou for me, and tell them what I did." Richard's father praises him and announces he will soon have King Henry's head. He tells Richard he loves him and departs, followed by Edward and George. Barrymore, his almost shoulder-length black hair lank and splayed closely to his head and neck, follows them with his eyes and begins the soliloquy with a derisive hiss, "Would they were wasted, marrow, bones and all." Richard here states upfront that, since he has been "foresworn" in his mother's womb and is deformed and undesirable, he will instead "dream upon the crown." Denied by nature any earthly pleasures, he states, "And from this torment I will free myself / or hew my way out with a bloody axe." In his introduction to the scene, Barrymore, as himself in modern dress, points out that Richard does, indeed, dispatch his "elder relations" who stand between him and the crown, "with the graceful impartiality of Al Capone."

Barrymore towers in the frame, and his voice ranges in register from low, whispered tones to a high muscular mania. This short segment demonstrates three areas of Barrymore's acting style as it developed in the 1920s and early 1930s. Firstly, in featuring his voice, it shows Barrymore's full talent through Warner Bros.'s new Vitaphone sound system. In turn, it lent Warner's the prestige that Barrymore carried as a celebrated Shakespearean. His vocal quality added a depth of acting virtuosity that had been hinted at in the physicality of his performance in the silent *Dr. Jekyll and Mr. Hyde* (1920) and *The Sea Beast* (1926). It became an important part of a turn toward playing roles of aberrant masculinity such as *Svengali* (1931) and *The Mad Genius* (1931). Secondly, in his introduction, Barrymore says the soliloquy "discloses [Richard's] own piquant psychology." He is referring to the wider cultural context of a popularization of Freud's theories at the time. This "new psychology" was not only carried through in the creation of Barrymore's Richard III and Hamlet but was an important element in making Barrymore's interpretations of the Bard "modern." Finally, the "danger" that Barrymore carried from his Shakespearean roles became a central element in the unstable characters he chose to play in his Warner's sound films. That instability was predicated on a conception of psychic wounding in the motivations of Ahab in *Moby Dick* (1930), the more fantastic characters of *Svengali* (1931) and Tsarakov in *The Mad Genius* (1931), and in his later portrayal of war veteran Hilary Fairfield in *A Bill of Divorcement* (1932).

FROM MATINÉE IDOL TO MODERN SHAKESPEAREAN

Barrymore's early career, and status as a "matinée idol," stood on his work as a light comedian in romantic comedy fare such as *The Fortune Hunter* (1909) and *A Slice of Life* (1912). Throughout the 1910s, however, he took on more dramatic roles through his association with playwright Edward Sheldon. By 1916 he had successful roles first as the doomed bank clerk William Falder in John Galsworthy's stark drama *Justice* and, in 1917, as a troubled youth in George du Maurier's *Peter Ibbetson*, both of which Sheldon had adapted for him in 1916. *Peter Ibbetson* was a highly sentimental story of a "dreamy" youth who, as a young man, reunites with his childhood sweetheart. He accidentally kills his evil uncle Colonel Ibbetson and is imprisoned. He visits his sweetheart by "dreaming true" each night, and the play ends as they die within a day of each other to spend eternity in heaven. Despite the sentimentality of *Ibbetson*, both of these plays offered a deeper kind of role than his romantic comedies of the early to mid 1910s. Barrymore's acting had an added dimension of danger and pathos that drew the critics' attention. Alexander Wolcott in his column "Second Thoughts on First Nights" praised Barrymore's range: "He subtly combines the English shyness with the Gallic spirit that burned unquenchably in this lonely chap . . . The fine black rage is here in telling force— . . ." (3). Woolcott's praise was a premonition of Barrymore's success in the Shakespeare roles.

With Sheldon, Barrymore was positioned to take a leading part in the emergent modern trends in American theater. In the next three years they added to their team the director Arthur Hopkins and the set designer Robert Edmond Jones. Together with voice coach Margaret Carrington, these artists would contribute to more than just the development of Barrymore's career and image as a Shakespearean. Woolcott noted,

> There was an ambitious plan not only to put the enormous Barrymore potentialities to work, but also to bring lasting prestige to the American stage. It was not an amateurish venture like a church social. Everyone concerned in this labour of love was a successful person in their own professional right. (quoted in Fowler 163)

Before the war, Hopkins and Jones had attended Max Rheinhardt's experimental Deutches Theatre in Berlin. Jones had briefly worked in the Shakespeare productions. Rheinhardt's approach derived from the English theorist Gordon Craig whose work *The Art of Theatre* (1905) had "espoused simple, permanent or semipermanent settings and subtle lighting effects that symbolically 'suggested' the essence of the play" (Morrison 16). Barrymore's team, at the crest of an emergent modern American theater, was employing these combinations of realism and symbolism at the same time that Eugene O'Neill's *Beyond the Horizon* premiered in April 1919. The seismic shifts in taste and aesthetics in American theater were also part of the longer effects of the impact of the 1913 Armory Show on American modern art as well as being concurrent with changes in literary taste that had been taking place throughout the 1910s, led by critics such as H. L. Mencken in his articles in *Smart Set* and a canon of American literature that featured Mark Twain, Theodor Dreiser, Willa Cather, and later Ernest Hemingway and F. Scott Fitzgerald.

These developments were, in turn, having an impact on the Hollywood film industry. Lea Jacobs's recent study of Hollywood in the 1920s outlines the specific problem studios had in incorporating "sophisticated material." Stretching the rules of middlebrow taste brought the risk of alienating rural and neighborhood cinemas while such "modern" stories and themes were appealing to audiences in the urban areas. "Film producers thus had to steer a course between the minority whose tastes might be epitomized by the hip and irreverent *Smart Set* and the vast majority who remained loyal to Norman Rockwell and *The Saturday Evening Post*" (Jacobs 22). Jacobs argues that the shifts in taste which took place in the 1920s resulted in a decline of sentiment as the preferred, though not wholly dominant, aesthetic that shaped the Hollywood film style of the 1920s and 1930s.

THE "NEW PSYCHOLOGY"

In the last three months of 1919 Barrymore worked exhaustively on his 1920 production of Richard III while playing in the Sheldon/Hopkins/Jones success *The Jest*. At the same time, each morning he was filming scenes for the Artcraft/Paramount feature adaptation of *Dr. Jekyll and Mr. Hyde*. The result of this effort was that the matinée-idol persona was beginning to shift. By April 1920, his critical success as Richard III had conjoined with his film role in *Dr. Jekyll and Mr. Hyde* to add weight to the perceptions of his talent in both forms. *Variety*'s review noted that the "picturesque actor" had a "natural beauty of form and feature [which] stood him in good stead and he offers a marvelous depiction of bestiality in the transformed personality of Mr. Hyde" (April 3, 1920, 93). The combined effect of the critical accolades afforded Richard III and Barrymore's performance in *Jekyll/Hyde* cemented his main appeal as that of a theatrical virtuoso, and it was this reputation that characterized the way his film work was promoted.

There was a synergy between the work on *Jekyll/Hyde* and the transformative success of Richard III, with elements of the film finding their way into the play. Barrymore had been working on the characterization of Hyde and his dissolution into a hideous spider-like creature who walked in crab-like movements. The extreme makeup for that role guided the makeup and bodily contortions he employed in his portrayal of Richard. The transformation from Jekyll to Hyde and the gradual overtaking of Jekyll's personality by Hyde throughout the film had their parallel in the Barrymore teams' characterization of Richard and his psychological motivations. Edward Sheldon had added Richard's soliloquy from *Henry VI*, the same that Barrymore used in *The Show of Shows* segment, to set out a psychological motivation drawn in part from Freud's analysis in his 1916 *Some Character Types Met with in Psychoanalytic Work*. As Michael Morrison has shown, Hopkins had explicitly seen Freud's work as central to a modern approach to acting (72). Freud's analysis used Richard's motivations to demonstrate a common childhood experience:

> Richard is an enormous magnification of something we find in ourselves as well. We all think we have reason to reproach Nature and our destiny for congenital and infantile disadvantages; we all demand reparation for early wounds to our narcissism, our self-love. (Freud 314)

Freud noted that such experience, not accommodated within the balance between libidinal drives and the ego, would likely result in neuroses or aberrant behavior, just such as Richard's. He leaves to the artistry of Shakespeare the ability to "hint at these feelings" in order to bring the audience to a recognition of similar impulses they have repressed, which makes the villainy of Richard more complete.

The topography of a double-sided self, where the darker impulses are repressed as in the good Jekyll/evil Hyde, was itself part of a number of late nineteenth-century texts alongside George du Maurier's *Trilby* (1894) and Oscar Wilde's *The Picture of Dorian Gray* (1890), that made use of "doublings." These texts, as well as the stories of E. T. A. Hoffmann, had been subjects, or been used as metaphors, in the published work of Freud and his acolytes by the early 1920s. It is of little surprise that, in May 1920, noted theosopher Albert E. S. Smythe introduced a private screening of Barrymore's film to "leading members of the medical profession in Toronto Canada with a talk on the problems of psychoanalysis" ("Doctors View Privately 'Dr. Jekyll and Mr. Hyde,'" *Examiner Herald* [May 29, 1920], 44). The association with the "new psychology" in Barrymore's case added to his persona not only a counter to the effeminate matinée idol with a monstrous and aberrant masculinity but also a dimension of "the modern." The Hyde/Richard combination was not the first time that the "new psychology" had been applied to Barrymore's roles. Along with Louise Brinke, Smyth Ely Jelliffe, American psychologist and early acolyte of Freud, wrote psychoanalytic critiques of Barrymore's versions of *The Jest, Redemption*, and *Peter Ibbetson* for the *New York Medical Journal*. Of *The Jest* they highlight the psychology of the characters that drive the events.

"The author conceives a certain situation or continuity of events which is utilized to develop the psychological thought for which the drama internally stands." They emphasized the play as

> coming as it does out of the fifteenth century . . . a section through the development of human civilisation at a period remote enough from the present to reveal . . . an openness of impulsive action according to the freedom of individual desire . . . which culture does not so directly permit today. (573)

The emphasis on the repression of desire was a tenet of psychoanalysis emphasized in the popular press. This tendency was at play when Freud, or the "new psychology," was invoked in the reception of Barrymore's *Richard III* and *Dr. Jekyll and Mr. Hyde*. *Wid's Daily*, the film exhibitor's journal, while not explicitly referring to psychoanalysis, focused on the good/evil dichotomy of the story, calling the film's story "A triumph of a man's evil self over his good self" and Barrymore's performance "a thing of fine shadings and violent emotions . . . His entire body from top to toe is an ugly picture of restrained passions" ("John Barrymore's Performance a Tremendous Drama in Itself Alone," *Wid's Daily* [April 4, 1920], 4).

"ONLY THE SOUND OF THOUGHT . . ."

It was not simply the Freudian emphasis that set out Barrymore's performances as modern. His recasting of vocal delivery revolutionized twentieth-century Shakespearean acting. In spite of the *tour de force* performance of aberrant masculinity as Mr. Hyde, Barrymore's image in the silent period remained primarily within the realms of the costume drama. His theatrical reputation, consistently a part of his films' promotions, was not fully realized until the coming of sound. Ironically, it is not until the soliloquy as Richard III in *The Show of Shows* that his abilities as a stage actor are fully revealed for cinema audiences. His voice had been central in developing a more "natural" technique for the Shakespeare stage productions. The singular influence on Barrymore's vocal development was Margaret Carrington who had coached him for Richard III as well as for the New York and London productions of *Hamlet*. Carrington had had an early career as a singer/recitalist known for her interpretations of Debussy and Hugo Wolf, particularly their *avant-garde* work (Morrison 130). Carrington's approach with Barrymore was to "naturalize" the rhythms of the Shakespearean verse through breath control and a more colloquial range of intonations. Morrison has characterized her approach as an effort to eliminate "tragic elevation" characteristic of the

Victorian and Edwardian periods, while her "intolerance for pomposity and vocal affectation" offered a "modern alternative" that set the standard for Shakespearean acting in the following decades (154). Carrington was committed to finding the meaning in each sentence and letting that meaning guide the interpretation. For Richard they found "the complete key" for the character in the same opening lines that Freud had used in his example four years earlier. But, more crucially, it was the type of vocal inflection that Carrington and Barrymore developed for the soliloquy, a means of making the lines seem to "have only the sound of thought" and to let the audience in on it (139). His performance in the soliloquy in *The Show of Shows* demonstrates the extent to which Barrymore's work on the Shakespeare plays prepared him for movie acting. The technology of sound afforded the means of achieving on film the intimacy Carrington and Barrymore strove for in the theater.

UNSTABLE CHARACTERS

Having developed Richard III and Hamlet via modern notions of character psychology and by employing vocal techniques that strove for intimacy, it is not surprising that Barrymore so easily accommodated himself to film acting and to the new sound technology. Apart from his innate abilities as an actor, the strategies of his team in the Shakespeare plays, in their reach for a new, modern, "natural" Bard, incorporated elements that employed a cinematic aesthetic. Robert Edmond Jones's use of stark sets and tactic of lighting specific spaces to highlight characters and settings in the play combined with Arthur Hopkins's staging which kept the supporting players still while the speaking player moved and spoke his lines. These techniques functioned much as editing and camera placement do in focusing spectatorial attention on significant moments in the narrative. This is immediately evident in the Richard soliloquy in *The Show of Shows* in contrast with the rest of the acts in the film, many of which are shot in proscenium arch and with cut-ins to medium shots. The close-ups of Barrymore work in tandem with his voice control and inflection. The medium close-ups bring the spectator into an intimacy with Richard as he wends his way through a logic of murder. *Variety* described it as a "thrill moment," as the soliloquy was "close-uped to the audience with Richard in shiny black armor against a menacing flame background . . . his sickly pallor and those glinting Barrymore eyes are simply grand" (Ruth Morris, "Uncommon Chatter," *Variety* [November 27, 1929], 53). The set, with its ghastly pile of dead soldiers under an expressionistic "menacing flame" sky, cast in high relief the figure of Richard leering like a satiated predator over the corpses, recalls Jones's style for the Shakespeare productions. The overall effect was an entertaining villainy and a calling card for Barrymore's acting prowess.

Adding Barrymore's voice to his performances had been an important part of Warners' strategy of introducing sound. They had added a music soundtrack to his silent *Don Juan* in 1926 as a means of attracting interest and investors in their Vitaphone system (Crafton 11). Barrymore's voice, heard for the first time in *The Show of Shows*, was highlighted in the publicity for his next Warner Bros. feature, *General Crack*: "John Barrymore—Yesterday a speechless shadow—Today a vivid living person—thanks to Vitaphone!" (Warner Bros. advertisement, *Motion Picture* [March 1930], 7). Fully "embodied," as this suggests, in the next three years Barrymore under his Warner Bros. contract played a range of characters: a tipsy upper-class English gentlemen in *The Man from Blankley's* (1930), an embittered and vengeful Captain Ahab in *Moby Dick* (1930), the sinister hypnotist and lead role in *Svengali* (1930), and Tsarakov the club-footed and sinister puppet master in *The Mad Genius* (1931), an adaptation of Martin Brown's play *The Idol* (1929). These four films are unusual in that Barrymore's contract with the studio allowed him to select his own material and gave him more creative control than he would be allowed in his subsequent films elsewhere. His selection of Ahab and Tsarakov as characters, each with an impediment that prompts and connotes instability if not outright villainy, are versions of Barrymore's dangerously modern style. Tsarakov's clubbed foot prompts Richard III's "I that am curtailed of this fair proportion," that motivates his bitterness and creates the empathy central to his villainy. The impediment is the motivation for the puppeteer's descent into the manipulating ballet impresario he becomes. Early in the film he recounts a dream he had as a boy: "A great shining figure, white and beautiful would come to me with wings shimmering, and put them on my back . . . and when I start to fly . . . a great claw would grasp my foot and pull me down, down into the swamp, black, bubbling and I'd scream and wake."

Tsarakov puts all of his energy into developing a talented boy whom he rescues from an abusive father and manipulates all those around him to ensure the boy's success, and for his own pleasure and fortune. When the boy Fedor grows up and falls in love with Nana, a dancer in the troop, Tsarakov fires her, forcing her into a relationship with his patron Count Renaud. By keeping Bankieff addicted to cocaine, he keeps control over his choreographer who ultimately murders him with an axe on the stage at the foot of a stylized Aztec god, and this leaves the couple free to marry.

Anton Grot, the influential art designer at Warner Bros., teamed with Michael Curtiz on *The Mad Genius* and was central to providing that film and *Svengali* with their affective eerie mise-en-scènes. Grot had worked on *Little Caesar* that same year and was the noted designer for *The Thief of Bagdad* (1924). His designs for the Barrymore films were in line with Jones's sets for *Hamlet* and *Richard III* in offering stylized objects and settings that reinforced the nature of the stories. In the case of *The Mad Genius*, the "moderne"-style

Figure 2.2 Barrymore as the sinister Tsarakov in Michael Curtiz's *The Mad Genius* (Warner Bros., 1931). Digital frame enlargement.

ballet settings combined with classical Louis Quatorze backings and exaggerated objects, such as the puppeteers' wagon, to visualize the conflicts between Tsarakov's twisted Old-World classicism and the modern young couple Fedor and Nana.

The Mad Genius was a follow-up to the success of *Svengali*, which *Film Daily* called "a John Barrymore field day all the way through." It praised the film as "artistic and splendidly acted" and singled out the sets and the cinematography in the "painstaking production" ("Review," May 3, 1931, 30). Svengali, a mysterious Jewish musician, adept at mesmerism, finds the perfect subject in Trilby O'Farrell, a young artist's model in Paris. Through hypnosis he steals her from the young English art student Little Billee and transforms her into a world-renowned singer. Billee pursues them and finally manages to break Svengali's spell over her but they both die, interconnected with each other to the end (see also Diane Carson's chapter in this volume, eds). Svengali's character psychology emanated from the anti-Semitic tradition in theatrical representation of Jewishness dating from at least the nineteenth century, one in which Barrymore had been steeped as a young actor and theatergoer. In a detailed study of the Svengali character in Western culture Daniel Pick has noted that Jews in these theatrical incarnations were often represented:

> ... through a mixture of fawning and arrogance [playing] upon gentiles, asserting mastery ... Svengali provided the case *par excellence* ... If the grotesque egoism of the display were [*sic*] clear enough, so was the demonic ability. Both aspects of the character were taken as exemplary,

> symbolizing far more than an individual part. Svengali was viewed . . . as an illustration of a complex character type. (160)

The psychic wound here is the man's ethnicity, his Jewishness, brought in fully formed, in the way Pick has described, and posited as motivation in the same way as the physical deformities of Richard and Tsarakov. Barrymore's approach to the performance to some degree repeats the combinations of setting and staging that the Hopkins/Jones team had done with the Shakespeare plays. He used the same scenarist he had used for *Moby Dick*, J. Grubb Alexander, and would employ again for *The Mad Genius*. Crucially, Anton Grot again devised a stylized expressionistic version of the bohemian world of Paris for the film.

Svengali's power of mesmerism was relayed through Barrymore's own device of using glass covers over his eyes for his close-ups in the hypnosis scenes. Like the play and the novel, the film is redolent with the sexual implications of a Trilby entranced by Svengali. At the opening of the film, Svengali has another young woman to whom he has been giving lessons but the implication is that there is more to the relationship.

> "What did we do last?" he asks her as they are about to begin the lesson.
> "Don't you remember?"
> SVENGALI. "I am talking about music!"

The most virile character in the play is Svengali, and his villainy lay in the dichotomy between his abilities as a musician and his diabolical use of his power as a mesmerist to fashion Trilby as a Galatea to his Pygmalion.

Having left his Warner Bros. contract, Barrymore played a character the following year which had specific reference to the "new psychology" as an implied explanation for mental instability, albeit with a subdued sense of malevolence. This was the shell-shocked veteran Hilary Fairfield in a film adaptation at RKO of Clemence Dane's 1921 play *A Bill of Divorcement*. The apparent motivation for Hilary's behavior was explicitly modern and psychological. The story tells of Hilary's return, after fifteen years in an asylum, to his wife Margaret (Billie Burke) and their daughter Sidney (Katharine Hepburn) just as Margaret is about to remarry. Hilary cannot understand that he fought for a "law-making machine that I've called my country" and now finds himself divorced. He seesaws back and forth between reason and rage and is finally convinced that Margaret would be happier with her fiancé Gray Meredith. His side of the family holds the deeper secret of insanity, however, which has emerged because of his shell shock. Because of the threat of passing on insanity to her own children, Sidney breaks her engagement with Kit and chooses to spend her life taking care of her father.

David O. Selznick had long wanted to make a film of the play but claimed he "could never sell it to my bosses, because of the insanity angle which was supposed to be taboo for pictures" (45). In his new role in charge of production at RKO, Selznick devised the film as a highbrow effort with Barrymore and Burke, another leading light of Broadway, introducing stage ingénue Hepburn and choosing theater director George Cukor to helm. The film depends upon Hilary's veteran status and Barrymore's performance of his mental instability which is the threat of madness about to erupt. Barrymore's performance ranges between exuberance and anger, between intensity and repression. When he first returns this expresses itself in his body and costume, a trench-coat bound around him to suggest simultaneously the uniform of an officer and the straitjacket of the asylum. He holds his shoulders somewhere between a childish slouch and world-weary slump. When Sidney, who has been watching him unseen, asks, "What are you looking for?," he turns around and his expression is bright again as he thinks she is his wife, Margaret, or 'Meg' as he calls her. She says she is not Meg and he slightly recoils, his expression one of catching himself. She asks, "Where have you come from?" His face darkens into a depth not yet shown, his eyes dart, caught up in a dark memory. "That place," he responds in a deep voice, a combination of fear and menace.

Through his gesture and expression Barrymore conveys the conflict within his character and provides a sense of warning, in tandem with Sidney's expression of fascination bordering on horror and, later, Margaret's genuine fear that he could go much further. His rendering of Hilary demonstrates his range, in Welles's words "danger." His voice modulates between anger and tenderness, his body between youthful hope and dark despair, sometimes exuberant, sometimes pleading, sometimes explosive.

Barrymore's performance offered an additional means of modernizing the social issues the film was attempting to address while, at the same time, gaining the approval of the Hayes Office. "The portrayal of a man believing himself sane when as a matter of fact he is semi-sane is so delicately handled by such an excellent cast to stamp it as one of the finest pictures of the year" (Hart to Joy). The motivations for Hilary's psychological instability were "modern" in their reference to shell shock but it ultimately becomes clear that his insanity is inherited, a deep family secret. The eugenic solution is for his daughter to break off her marriage and not pass on the "damaged genes." Barrymore brought to the role the prestige Selznick had hoped for.

From *Dr. Jekyll and Mr. Hyde*, Barrymore's performances of unstable characters in film were interpretable through the "new psychology." The theme of an all-consuming dark unconscious appeared in *Jekyll/Hyde* where a title proclaims, "... outraged nature took her hideous revenge ... and out of the black abyss of torment sent him the creeping horror that was his other self." The quality of menacing remove had been developed in the

Barrymore team's modernization of Shakespearean performance through Jones's set design, Hopkins's staging, Sheldon's adaptation, and, importantly, through Carrington's and Barrymore's development of the actor's vocal range. Barrymore's short-lived creative control at Warner's demonstrates the influence his work on Richard III and Hamlet had on those films. Coming as these roles did at the moment of the transition to sound, his powerful voice fully "embodied" his image and became as iconic to the sound revolution as that of Al Jolson. The new technology afforded the wide circulation of his abilities as an actor and the roles he chose were deliberately dark, troubled, and at times villainous. Richard's twisted desire for the crown, "I'll pluck it down!" and his invocation of the abyss and the exasperation of being dragged down by afflictions into it became a consistent theme in Barrymore's sound films of the early 1930s. His characters verbalized these qualities through his powerful voice: Tsarakov's fear of the "great claw" pulling him down "into the black bubbling liquid" or Hilary's fear of the "black hand reaching up through the floor." He delivered them with the powerful force of his voice recorded by the new technology and motivated through the "new psychology" lending a truth to Welles's claim that his Hamlet was "dangerous" and his acting "dangerously modern," ensuring his influence on both film and theater acting in the first half of the twentieth century.

NOTE

1. I am grateful to Michael Morrison for his advice on this chapter and his thoughts on whether Welles had ever actually seen the Barrymore Shakespeare performances. It is certainly unlikely, in that he would have been seven years old during the Richard III performances and ten when *Hamlet* ran in London. He was living in Chicago at the time and Barrymore's *Hamlet* did not play there. He did work with him at least once on radio and it is more likely that Welles is referring to later recitations of the soliloquys.

CHAPTER 3

The Curious Case of *Sherlock Holmes*

Colin Williamson

> He was, I take it, the most perfect reasoning and observing machine
> that the world has seen.
> Arthur Conan Doyle, *A Scandal in Bohemia*

If, in this line from Conan Doyle's 1891 short story, Watson's description of Sherlock Holmes resembles a camera, it is because both the fictional detective and that other "observing machine" share an affinity as emblems of a distinctly modern way of seeing. Holmes is "perfect" because nothing escapes his gaze. His eyes constantly detect and collect visual evidence that others do not and in ways that others cannot. His visual acuity is matched by the speed of his reasoning which allows him to decipher a person at a glance and, in turn, masterfully to navigate a world of deceptive appearances.

The photographic apparatus is not a "reasoning machine" but, in the latter half of the nineteenth century, its powers of detection were preeminent. At the time that Conan Doyle was writing, the mechanical "eyes" of cameras employed for still and motion photography were radically transforming visuality and the experience of modern life. With innovations in chronophotography and early cinematic uses of techniques such as time lapse and slow motion, the camera developed an identity as a detective that could reveal secret realities in the hitherto undisclosed zone beneath the appearances of things, that which Walter Benjamin called the domain of the "optical unconscious" (510–12). The *avant-garde* filmmaker and theorist Germaine Dulac described the cinema along these lines as "an eye wide open on life, an eye more powerful than our own and which sees things we cannot see" (39).

In the early twentieth century the resemblance between Holmes and the camera evolved considerably into a cinematic phenomenon. Throughout the silent era Conan Doyle's detective stories were adapted into short and feature-length films by a wide range of studios, including Biograph, Vitagraph, Universal, Essanay, Goldwyn Pictures, Éclair, and several smaller companies in Britain and Germany. The international popularity and pervasiveness of Holmes are quite remarkable. Between 1908 and 1911, Nordisk Film in Denmark produced a series of at least twelve short films featuring Holmes; Éclair in France produced eight in 1912 alone; and, from 1921 to 1923, Stoll Pictures in England produced a total of forty-five shorts and two feature-length films. The vogue, which included Buster Keaton's celebrated *Sherlock, Jr.* (1924), survived the transition to sound, persisted throughout the twentieth century, and is alive and well today.

Holmes's proliferation in early cinema culture is no doubt attributable to the widespread popularity of Conan Doyle's stories but it also stemmed from the cinema's immediate and enduring resonance with detective fiction. Like the closely related popular-science film and trick-film genres, the detective genre harbored a unique affinity with the cinema that Holmes seemed to embody and reflect as an "observing machine" (for more on the connection between the detective genre and popular science and trick films see Gaycken). (Coincidentally, Biograph's *Sherlock Holmes Baffled* from 1900 is a trick film about a thief who eludes Holmes's grasp by appearing and disappearing in a series of quick changes made possible by the use of special effects.) Tom Gunning explains that "the early success of the detective genre in film is due in part to a match between a pre-existing literary genre which centers on interrogating visual evidence and the devices available to early cinema to convey visual scrutiny" ("Those Drawn" 60). The "match" is expressed in the resemblance between Holmes and the photographic apparatus noted above. For example, the detective's penetrating gaze and iconic use of the magnifying glass found an ally in the cinema's way of seeing through the technique of the close-up. What this suggests is that there might be something deeply cinematic about Holmes that helped to make him a mainstay of the silent period.

With so many affinities, it would be an understatement to say that Conan Doyle's literary detective was not only well known but also well established as a screen persona when John Barrymore performed the titular role in Albert Parker's feature film *Sherlock Holmes* (1922). The film is an amalgamation of several stories, including "A Scandal in Bohemia" and "The Final Problem" (1893). It follows Holmes and Watson (Roland Young) in London as the detective tries to locate a collection of secret letters before his nemesis, Professor Moriarty (Gustav von Seyffertitz), can steal them and use them to blackmail the British royal family. While *Sherlock Holmes* was in dialogue with the many films about Holmes that came before it, it was most directly based on two earlier and very successful works: a 1916 Essanay film and an 1899 stage play on which that film was based, both with the same title as Parker's film. The play and the Essanay film starred the American actor and playwright William Gillette whose stage and screen interpretations of Holmes created an image of Conan Doyle's detective that dominated popular visual culture throughout much of the early twentieth century.

As an adaptation of other adaptations, a great deal can be said about the fidelity of *Sherlock Holmes* to the stories in Conan Doyle's *oeuvre*. For example, a significant point of contention in the reception of Parker's film was the inclusion of a romantic subplot.[1] In the film, as in Gillette's play, Holmes falls in love with a woman named Alice Faulkner (Carol Dempster) who possesses letters written between her sister Rose (Peggy Bayfield) and Prince Alexis (Reginald Denny). When Rose commits suicide after Alexis breaks off their engagement, with plans to wed someone else, Alice seeks revenge for her sister and threatens to ruin the prince's new marriage arrangement by making the letters public. Holmes prevents her from following through on this plan and the film ends with Sherlock and Alice embracing before departing on their honeymoon. The romance was viewed by many as being frustratingly out of character for Conan Doyle's "observing machine." One critic saw it as "a romantical heresy as sad as Oscar Wilde's love scenes between Salome and John the Baptist" (P. W. Wilson, "Elucidating Conan Doyle," *New York Times Book Review and Magazine* [June 18, 1922], 1).

While analyzing *Sherlock Holmes* as an adaptation is undeniably important, in what follows I focus less on the story and more on a curious dimension of the film's reception. By the time Barrymore assumed the role, Holmes was already a celebrity in his own right, holding a status that Barrymore was still cultivating as an actor while appearing (like Holmes) on both the stage and the screen. As we shall see, because Holmes had such a strong visible presence in the early twentieth century, his identity as a star in 1922 centered largely on his recognizable image. Film spectators, in turn, expected Holmes not only to behave in a certain way, based on Conan Doyle's characterization, but also to look a certain way, based on how the character circulated in film and visual culture. Barrymore's star image was similarly taking shape around the actor's look which resembled that of the Holmes with whom people were already familiar. Because of these resemblances, the encounter between Barrymore and the famous detective in *Sherlock Holmes* unfolded in such a way that the actor and the character were caught up in a curious and quite fitting game of identities and appearances.

THE FACE OF SHERLOCK HOLMES

The production of *Sherlock Holmes* coincided with a significant transitional period in Barrymore's acting career. By 1922 he had moved away from the comedic roles he often played on the stage and the screen in the 1910s and was growing into his identity as a serious artist. In the early 1920s he was performing dramatic roles, such as title characters in a 1920 theatrical production of Shakespeare's *Richard III* and John Robertson's Famous Players-Lasky film *Dr. Jekyll and Mr. Hyde* (1920). Immediately following *Sherlock Holmes*, Barrymore also starred in a very successful theatrical run of *Hamlet*. Playing Conan Doyle's detective was an opportunity to explore a character that fitted naturally with this evolution. Holmes is a virtuoso forensic scientist and a calculating rationalist but he is also emotionally complex and eccentric, morally and ethically precarious, and prone to the use of drugs such as cocaine. Playing Holmes in a silent film challenged Barrymore to capture this complexity, not with the voice that the actor used so eloquently in the theater but with one of the most salient emblems of acting in the silent era: his face.

In Conan Doyle's stories, much of Holmes's characterization as an "observing machine" comes through in the vivid details the detective describes catching when he explains to other characters how he solved, or plans to solve, a particular crime. In *Sherlock Holmes*, this process of observing and reasoning is visualized partly with the aid of intertitles but mostly by focusing on Barrymore's facial expressions. For example, Holmes is first introduced in the film sitting beneath a tree contemplating the nature of love while watching a family of birds and a happy couple. As Holmes records his observations in a notebook, a series of medium close-ups with black vignettes focuses our attention on Barrymore's pensive looks that allow us to "see" the character puzzling over the scene. Throughout the film Barrymore's face is framed predominantly with a range of medium and close-up shots that similarly highlight the actor's ability to convey, in a look, Holmes's investigative gaze and what one reviewer called "lightning deductions" at work (Fletcher 67).

While *Sherlock Holmes* received mixed reviews, audiences remarked frequently on the suitability of Barrymore's countenance for acting on the silent screen. In a glowing review of the film from *Motion Picture Magazine*, one critic observed:

> If we nurtured a belief in witchcraft we would believe that Barrymore transmitted the psychology of his characters to his audience by supernatural means. He sways his audience as the winds sway slender reeds . . . But his magic is that of the artist and of the craftsman. His technique is colored by the great imagination with which he endows his work. By a hundred and one *subtleties* he portrays that which others fail to capture

even after going to great lengths in their desire to achieve it. (Fletcher 67; my italics)

"Subtleties" is a reference to the expressiveness of Barrymore's face which played a prominent role in the positive reception of *Sherlock Holmes*. For example, the *Los Angeles Times* explained that, in the film,

> Barrymore is so clever that he could go even Sarah Bernhardt one better. Mme. Bernhardt is said to have once recited the alphabet in a manner to wring tears from her hearers' eyes. Barrymore could do that before the camera where he couldn't even be heard, and still get results. (Grace Kingsley, "Flashes: He's Sherlocking" [October 16, 1922], 8)

Many reviews contain similar reflections on how much of the film's value stemmed from the fact that Barrymore was "an expressive pantomimist" ("The Screen," *New York Times* (May 8, 1922), 14) who was exceptional at "getting a mental process on the screen" (Frederick James Smith, "Griffith On Way to Goal," *Los Angeles Times* [May 14, 1922], 31).

The value that audiences placed on being moved by such expressive looks in *Sherlock Holmes* was, of course, not unique to Barrymore's performance. The first few decades of the cinema were characterized by a deep fascination with faces represented in close framings. The close-up in particular afforded spectators a level of access to actors' expressions that was unavailable in the theater where proximity to the actors on the stage is relatively fixed and can be limiting. Writing in the 1940s, Béla Balázs explained,

> In the silent film facial expression, isolated from its surroundings, seemed to penetrate to a strange new dimension of the soul. It revealed to us a new world—the world of micro-physiognomy which could not otherwise be seen with the naked eye or in everyday life. (65)

The close-up's capacity to select and magnify the nuances of an actor's gaze or the movement of a mouth foregrounded the power of such details to provide spectators with subtle visual evidence of a character's thoughts, feelings, and even motivations. In other words, the cinema turned spectators into detectives of the human face (for more on the face and physiognomy in the early and silent cinema periods see Gunning, "In Your Face"; Moore; and Turvey 21–48).

For many silent-film viewers, Barrymore's face was not only powerfully communicative and moving, it functioned as something of an attraction in its own right. When the actor performed in *Sherlock Holmes*, he was already quite well known for having a handsome face. Of great interest to spectators was Barrymore's distinctive profile, namely the shape of his brow and nose which is highlighted frequently in his films—including *Sherlock Holmes*—through shots that feature the actor looking to one side, most often to showcase the left side of his face. Barrymore's profile became a defining feature of his star identity—he would eventually acquire the moniker "The Great Profile"—and seemed to hold a curiously strong grip on the popular imagination, one that the actor actively engaged. Writing about Barrymore's performance in the early sound film *When a Man Loves* (1927), Mordaunt Hall observed, "Throughout this production one has ample opportunity to study Mr. Barrymore's perfect profile. It is rare, in fact, that he presents his full face to the screen" ("The Screen," *New York Times* [February 4, 1927], 16). Indeed, such opportunities were fairly common in his films.

The idea that Barrymore's face was viewed as a thing to be "studied" is interesting when we consider that *Sherlock Holmes* is part of a very rich history of reading faces. The detective film revolves significantly around questions of identity and appearances that the cinema inherited directly from institutional uses of photography by police in Europe and America to study criminals and their physiognomies in the late nineteenth and early twentieth centuries. Like the silent film face in Balázs's description of the close-up, the face of the criminal was treated as a source of evidence that, upon being photographed, could be scrutinized in a broader effort to identify and understand criminality. It is striking from this perspective how much Barrymore's tendency to showcase his profile in performing Holmes resembles a mug shot which was standardized in the late nineteenth century by the Bertillon card, the full-face and profile photographs used to document and catalog criminals (for more on which, see Gunning, "Tracing"). It is almost as if, by playing to the popular fascination with the actor's face, the film invited viewers (intentionally or not) to scrutinize Barrymore's physiognomy in the same way that Holmes might study the face of a criminal.

And scrutinize they did. Spectators of *Sherlock Holmes* were markedly preoccupied with the question of whether Barrymore's look, like a good disguise, made for a convincing Holmes. In a lengthy piece in *Strand Magazine*, published in 1922, for example, Hayden Church explained,

> Barrymore, with his long, narrow, aquiline face, deep-sunk, magnetic, penetrating eyes, and somewhat brooding expression, is already Holmes in the flesh so far as countenance is concerned. He has the lithe, loose-limbed figure that one associates with the great detective, too. All that he needs to be an ideal Sherlock is a few more inches, but the illusion of commanding height will be obtained . . . by having players of inconsiderable stature in the subsidiary parts. (356)

While noting the popularity of the fictional detective, Alison Smith of *Picture Play Magazine* remarked similarly, "Here was John Barrymore to play it [the part of Holmes], looking as if he were the original model from which Conan Doyle drew his famous pussy-footed hero" ("The Screen in Review," *Picture Play* 16: [August 6, 1922], 63). *Variety* was slightly less convinced: "Mr. Barrymore plays the detective-hero with plenty of dash, and while in stature he does not quite typify the popular conception of Holmes, he does endow the role with sufficient artistry to make it stand out" ("Fred.," "Sherlock Holmes" [May 12, 1922], 33). Such claims have to do less with the presence in *Sherlock Holmes* of iconic markers of Conan Doyle's character—for example, the famous deerstalker hat and bent pipe made popular by Gillette years earlier—although these were important, and more with the nature of Barrymore's physical resemblance—in "stature" and "countenance"—to an image of Holmes that was already established in popular visual culture.

By 1922 Holmes's physiognomy, like Barrymore's, circulated so widely that it was immediately recognizable. In her review of *Sherlock Holmes* in *Picture Play Magazine*, Smith speaks to this when she argues that, despite the richness of Holmes's character, the film "doesn't permit him [Barrymore] to do anything except pose in a series of pictures strikingly like the Frederic Dorr Steele illustrations for the Conan Doyle Series" (64). Steele was an American illustrator who depicted Holmes between 1903 and 1904 in the publication by *Collier's Weekly* of Conan Doyle's short stories known collectively as *The Return of Sherlock Holmes*. (In Britain, *Strand Magazine* simultaneously published the stories with illustrations by Sidney Paget.) Steele modeled his version of Holmes on Gillette who starred in the 1899 stage play on which *Sherlock Holmes* was based. Though Steele's version of Holmes appeared well before "The Great Profile" intersected with the character, Barrymore harbors a striking resemblance to the illustrations in *Collier's*. Steele's Holmes is also depicted frequently—and most notably on the magazine's cover—in poses that emphasize the detective's profile, a fact that might have made recognizing Holmes in Barrymore pleasurable for viewers.

Notwithstanding Barrymore's resemblance to Holmes and the "subtleties" of the actor's face mentioned earlier, audiences generally criticized the story and Holmes's character in *Sherlock Holmes* for not being sufficiently developed in depth. As one reviewer explained,

> John Barrymore is there, and he is interesting, but you do not feel the presence of that peculiar individual, Sherlock Holmes. This, it would seem, is not due to any failure on Mr. Barrymore's part, but rather to the fact that Holmes can be revealed only through the work he does, and in this film he is not given any adequate work to do". ("The Screen," *New York Times* [May 8, 1922], 14)

Such claims are common in the reception of the film and mostly stem from a perceived lack of narrative complexity and characterization relative to Conan Doyle's stories. They also suggest that, more than anything, Barrymore's performance made for a noteworthy game of appearances and resemblances that viewers played, like detectives, by comparing the two physiognomies and profiles.

The significance of this game is thrown into sharp relief when we consider that, in one crucial respect, audiences seem to have misidentified Barrymore in the film.

MISTAKEN IDENTITY: BARRYMORE AND HIS DOUBLE

In *Sherlock Holmes* the great detective's nemesis, Moriarty, is played by the German-born Von Seyffertitz as a grotesque figure of criminality. Unlike Barrymore's handsome and refined Holmes, Von Seyffertitz's villain is aging and decrepit. His face is heavily made up to appear gaunt and weathered, and his brow is constantly furled, giving him a permanent grimace. He has the appearance of a disfigured creature that haunts the shadows, no doubt because, as a leader of the criminal underworld, Moriarty spends his life conducting his business literally in basements and caverns beneath the city. Moreover, like Dr. Caligari and Nosferatu, Moriarty moves in a crooked manner with a slight hunch in his posture that Von Seyffertitz extends to the character's bony, claw-like fingers, a style perhaps influenced by the German expressionist movement in the 1920s. The dramatic differences between Holmes and Moriarty, Barrymore and Von Seyffertitz, make the categories of good and evil, hero and villain, unmistakable but the contrast in their physiognomies also had a strange effect on audiences. According to *Motion Picture Magazine*, "Scores of people thought John Barrymore played a dual role in Sherlock Holmes. They insisted he played not only Sherlock Holmes, but Moriarty also" ("They Thought" 78).

Considering that Barrymore did not, in fact, play both roles, what are we to make of this report of mistaken identity? Perhaps the actor's star status fueled a belief that he *could* convincingly perform as Holmes and Moriarty in the same film. In this case the "mistake" might have been less literal and more a kind of hyperbolic reflection of how audiences perceived Barrymore as a virtuoso. Combined with the actor's ability to move successfully between the stage and the screen, Barrymore's emerging identity as a serious artist would certainly have supported this speculation.

Any actual confusion on the spectators' part would most likely have stemmed from a brief moment at the end of the film in which Holmes's and Moriarty's identities are truly called into question. While pursuing the secret royal letters,

THE CURIOUS CASE OF *SHERLOCK HOLMES* 43

Figure 3.1 Moriarty (Gustav von Seyffertitz, left) meets Holmes (John Barrymore, right) for the first time, in *Sherlock Holmes* (Albert Parker, Goldwyn, 1922). Digital frame enlargement.

Moriarty turns his attention to getting rid of the detective. The villain sends his gang to wait across the street from Watson's residence for Holmes to arrive, at which point Moriarty's men are instructed to shoot the detective on sight. To pass undetected by the criminals, Holmes enters Watson's house disguised as Moriarty and, once safely inside, reveals himself to his friend by removing a wig, false eyebrows and teeth, and a large putty nose. Watson is temporarily deceived, and the disguise is somewhat convincing from the audience's perspective, even when Holmes is shown in a close-up before taking off his mask. Because this brief masquerade comes at the end of the film, it is possible that the deception caused audiences to question whether Barrymore had been playing Moriarty throughout, a possibility particularly interesting in light of the fact that Barrymore and von Seyffertitz periodically appear together in the same shot, as in this medium close-up of their first encounter.

Whether or not audiences really believed Barrymore played a dual role in *Sherlock Holmes* is unclear—and perhaps beside the point—but the question is surprisingly neither anomalous nor unprecedented. In 1920 he had performed as both the good and evil manifestations of the (in)famous scientist in the Famous Players-Lasky film *Dr. Jekyll and Mr. Hyde*. The Jekyll/Hyde performance was made possible with the use of some makeup and prosthetics but the transformation was primarily credited to Barrymore's ability to distort his handsome face as the doctor into a visibly crazed one as Hyde. By gesturing to a similar dual role, *Sherlock Holmes* seemed to invite audiences to recall this earlier doubling of Barrymore's identity which they mistakenly projected on to Moriarty because of the resemblance between his grotesquerie and that of Holmes. As *Motion Picture Magazine* explained, "This was great tribute for the work of Gustav V. [*sic*] Seyffertitz, who actually created the role of Moriarty. And it is true that his Moriarty was not unlike Barrymore's Hyde in *Dr. Jekyll and Mr. Hyde*" ("They Thought" 78).

Whereas in *Dr. Jekyll and Mr. Hyde* Barrymore's doubling is in the service of depicting the duality of Robert Louis Stevenson's famous character, in *Sherlock Holmes* it is firstly a trope of the detective genre. In his analysis of detective fiction's early intersection with visual media such as photography and film, Tom Gunning observes that policing and detecting criminality in the late nineteenth century revolved increasingly around a "play of identification and disguise" involving faces and counterfeit appearances ("Tracing" 21). When Holmes masquerades as Moriarty in *Sherlock Holmes*, he is performing the dynamic of (mis)recognition that characterized the relationship between the modern detective and the criminals who attempt to escape visual detection by concealing their true identities. After Holmes reveals himself to Watson, for example, Moriarty disguises himself as the detective's cab driver to gain access to Watson's house undetected but he is discovered and unmasked before he can kill Holmes.

The whole question of identity in this case speaks to a curious dimension of how spectators saw Barrymore's face in the cinema of the early 1920s. The sequence in which Holmes reveals his true identity by removing his villainous disguise is noticeably structured as an opportunity to study Barrymore's face. Holmes is framed in a medium shot next to Watson who stares in slight astonishment and disbelief as the detective slowly peels the prosthetics off his face and explains the point of the deception. Considerable attention is given to the removal of every piece of the grotesque disguise, especially the putty nose, until Barrymore's handsome face is fully visible. The unmasking resembles an actor removing his makeup after a great performance. Holmes even checks himself briefly in a mirror, as if the film's audience is being granted privileged access in this moment to Barrymore the actor in his dressing room, invited, like Watson, to admire and even fetishize Barrymore's "true" face. Here, Barrymore himself becomes the focus of detective work, his face the "secret" in a larger game of concealment and revelation played by Barrymore and his audience. (Much more can be said about this game, especially given the well-known personal struggle in which Barrymore resented his good looks.)

From this perspective, the "play of identification and disguise" in *Sherlock Holmes* has a metatextual dimension that makes it more than a trope of the detective genre. Consider that, in Conan Doyle's stories, Holmes frequently uses techniques of disguise subversively to conceal his own identity as a detective from the criminals he is investigating. Holmes's ability convincingly to take on other roles as part of his craft gives his detective work a layer of theatricality and it is often substantially this that makes him a virtuoso. In "Scandal in Bohemia," for example, Watson responds to Holmes disguised as a clergyman by invoking the theater:

> It was not merely that Holmes changed his costume. His expression, his manner, his very soul seemed to vary with every fresh part that he assumed. The stage lost a fine actor, even as science lost an acute reasoner, when he became a specialist in crime. (Doyle 20)

Holmes's success as a detective, like Barrymore's success as an actor, was thus largely a matter of his ability to play the part in a game of identities and appearances. In the great detective, we might say, Barrymore found his double.

THE ECLIPSES AND REDISCOVERY OF *SHERLOCK HOLMES*

Beyond this game of appearances and the interesting dimensions that connected Barrymore to the popular image of the famous detective, *Sherlock Holmes* did not make much of an impression in 1922. Audiences frequently noted the film's redeeming "artistic" tendencies, especially the beauty of scenes shot on location in London and the gothic and expressionistic uses of light and shadow in shots of Moriarty's criminal underworld.[2] Looking at the reception of *Sherlock Holmes*, however, it is clear that, although the aesthetic potential was noteworthy at best, Barrymore's celebrated star persona was what audiences valued about a film that many saw as otherwise unremarkable. But even Barrymore's performance as Holmes seems to have been eclipsed by his success in later roles, namely as Hamlet, which followed almost immediately. This eclipse is compounded by the fact that Parker's film was subsequently lost.

The print of *Sherlock Holmes* that we have today exists because of an extensive archival project undertaken by Kevin Brownlow and William K. Everson in the 1970s when surviving footage was discovered in the collections of the George Eastman House. (Essanay's 1916 film, featuring William Gillette as Holmes, was similarly lost and found when reels of negative surfaced in 2014 in the archives of the Cinémathèque française.) Everson explains that the task of reconstructing the 1922 *Sherlock Holmes* was like solving a mystery because all that remained of the original film was a large number of negative fragments and the fading memory of Albert Parker who passed away during the project. The reconstruction—a result of detective work on a detective film—is understandably incomplete and, according to Everson, still unremarkable. Writing in 1976 he claimed, "It's good to have it back at last to fill in some of the gaps in our Barrymore and Holmes chronology, but it must be admitted that if it is a major find, it is also a major disappointment" (109).

Bracketing the question of merit—Everson echoes earlier criticisms of the film's lack of depth as an adaptation—the rediscovery of *Sherlock Holmes* is more than an occasion to fill in gaps, however important that may be to the task of writing history. The film has tremendous value as an object lesson in how spectators saw Barrymore's emergence as a dramatic face of the silent screen. That the actor's encounter with the great detective unfolded as a game of identity—of doubling and mirroring—compels us to see Holmes not simply as a role that Barrymore played but rather as a kind of performance of Barrymore's relationship with his viewers and the rich intertextual and intermedial landscape of the silent-cinema period. The performance is doubly significant because, like Holmes, Barrymore holds an enduring grip on the popular imagination. Just as spectators did in the 1920s, we continue to contemplate and question the actor's identity, to scrutinize his artistry, to search his performances for insights into his place in history, and to admire if not fetishize his famous face. In that light, rather than being a major disappointment, *Sherlock Holmes* is a major opportunity to rediscover Barrymore.

NOTES

1. Another key objection raised by audiences concerned Holmes's use of cocaine in Conan Doyle's stories. The drug is not referenced in *Sherlock Holmes* because of the censorship regulations that were shaping classical Hollywood filmmaking in the 1920s.
2. Barrymore reportedly contributed to some of the set designs in *Sherlock Holmes*. See Col York, "Plays and Players," *Photoplay* 22, no. 2 (July 1922): 60.

CHAPTER 4

John Barrymore's Introspective Performance in *Beau Brummel*

Martin Shingler

INTRODUCTION

In her essay "The Great Profile: How Do We Know the Actor from the Acting?" Marian Keane analyzes a scene in Harry Beaumont's *Beau Brummel* (1924) in which John Barrymore performs before a full-length mirror, employing a set of gestures to announce "his thought and the fact of his thinking" (187). This is the moment that Barrymore's character George Brummel practices his poses and gestures in order to acquire a more charming and elegant persona which, in turn, marks the beginnings of his public persona: that is, his "Beau" identity.

> Gazing at his reflection, Barrymore realizes he can make anything of his appearance. Part of him is always on display, while part of him, his inner self, remains concealed. He gazes here upon his reflection with eyes of an author or a creator, or an actor, who examines the unmolded stuff of a character. (Keane 193)

Here Keane describes not Brummel's realization that he can make anything of his appearance but rather Barrymore's. This (perhaps unintentional) slippage between character and actor/star suggests that the image of Barrymore and the character of Brummel are fused here (that is, Brummel is Barrymore and Barrymore is Brummel). It suggests further that, in this instance, Barrymore was able to disclose to his audience the processes of image-making central to stardom: namely, the revelation of some parts of his self and the concealment of others, as well as the transformation of a personality into a persona capable of circulating publicly to enhance the value of the actor. It is the way in which

Beau Brummel provided John Barrymore with an opportunity both to reflect upon and disclose to his audience some key aspects of image-making and star construction that I shall pursue here, building chiefly upon Marian Keane's work as well as Gaylyn Studlar's chapter on Barrymore in her book *This Mad Masquerade: Stardom and Masculinity in the Jazz Age*. I shall also consider how *Beau Brummel* functioned as the perfect star vehicle for Barrymore in 1924, capitalizing on his fame and achievements at that time. Furthermore, taking my cue from Keane, I shall explore more precisely what John Barrymore appears to be thinking during a critical moment of introspection.

A STAR VEHICLE

Beau Brummel was originally conceived as a star vehicle for the British thespian Richard Mansfield (1857–1907) who achieved success on Broadway from the early 1880s in plays by, among others, William Shakespeare and George Bernard Shaw, achieving an enormous hit with *Dr. Jekyll and Mr. Hyde*, adapted from Robert Louis Stevenson's novel by T. R. Sullivan in 1887 (Wilson 206–13). A master of impersonation and disguise, Mansfield played a wide range of physical types, though his dominant personality infused all his stage roles, largely on account of his magnificent voice which was rich and powerful with an extensive range (208–9). Having commissioned a play based on the life of the English Regency dandy George Bryan "Beau" Brummell (1778–1840) from the novice twenty-five-year-old playwright Clyde Fitch (1865–1909), Mansfield subsequently toured *Beau Brummel* across the United States for the next seventeen years.[1] Having first performed the play at the Madison Square Theatre in New York City in 1890, Mansfield revived it on Broadway in 1899 and performed it every year between 1904 and 1907, making his last appearance in the role just a few months before his death. *Beau Brummel* proved to be one of Mansfield's most popular, critically acclaimed, and financially successful plays.

John Barrymore made *Beau Brummel* after his triumph on Broadway in *Hamlet* in 1922 and 1923, his previous film, Albert Parker's *Sherlock Holmes*, having been released in the United States in March 1922. Part of the attraction of playing Beau Brummel for the actor was the chance to commit one of Richard Mansfield's most acclaimed and popular stage roles to celluloid. This also enabled him to consolidate his reputation as Mansfield's successor. Gaylyn Studlar notes that the influential *New York Times* drama critic Alexander Woollcott dubbed Barrymore the "legitimate successor to Richard Mansfield" in his review of *The Jest* on September 18, 1919 (97) while Joseph Garton observes that "Barrymore thereupon seemed to choose roles that would confirm and legitimize this succession" (79). In 1920, for instance,

Barrymore appeared in two of Mansfield's most critically acclaimed roles, as the Duke of Gloucester in Shakespeare's *Richard III* at the Plymouth Theatre and in the title role of the Famous Players-Lasky silent photoplay *Dr. Jekyll and Mr. Hyde* (1920). *Beau Brummel* can therefore be seen as part of Barrymore's concerted effort to associate himself with one of the greatest and most successful actors of the late nineteenth- and early twentieth-century American stage. This should not, however, obscure the fact that the screenplay of *Beau Brummel* allowed Barrymore to capitalize on his own stage successes in the late 1910s and early 1920s while projecting a new persona that decisively moved beyond his image as a romantic matinée idol toward something darker, deeper, and more mature.

While Fitch's play focused on a relatively short period in Brummell's life, the screenplay devised by Dorothy Farnum for the silent photoplay extended the narrative to include episodes in his twenties and sixties. Farnum's script also introduced a host of new characters (for instance, Lady Margery, Lord Alvanley, Lord Byron, Lady Hester Stanhope, and her husband), creating a youthful romance that breaks Brummel's heart in the early part of the film and results in his intention to avenge himself upon the aristocracy by becoming a calculating charmer, social climber, and seducer of high-society women and (by implication, at least) homosexual men. Fitch's play, on the other hand, mostly concentrated on Brummell's time as a leader of fashion in London society and as the confidant of the Prince Regent, charting Brummell's fall from grace in the latter half of the play when he is ostracized from polite society after insulting England's future monarch. While the screenplay maintains this same trajectory of declension, its characters and events are different. Notably, the film ends with a sequence some twenty years later in a debtors' prison in France where a demented Brummel is visited by his former valet and, finally, by the ghost of his first true love, Lady Margery, with whom he is reunited and restored to youth upon his death.

A LIFE IN FOUR PARTS

The 1924 photoplay of *Beau Brummel* consists of four main sections. The first depicts George Brummel in his twenties, besotted with an aristocratic woman, Lady Margery (played by a nineteen-year-old Mary Astor). The second features him in his prime as a leading light and arbiter of taste in English society. The third reveals a middle-aged Brummel living in poverty and isolation in Calais after his rift with the Prince Regent. The fourth and final section presents Brummel as a raving old man at the time of his death in a French debtors' prison. These four distinct parts present very different images of John Barrymore.

During the opening scenes of the film, a powdered and bewigged Barrymore recalls the actor's earlier stage career, specifically as the romantic Broadway matinée idol of *Peter Ibbetson* (1917) and *The Jest* (1919), adored by legions of admiring female fans known as "matinee girls" (Studlar 103–11). As Studlar has noted, in the late 1910s Barrymore cut a rather fey and androgynous figure, being physically slight, beautiful in appearance, and graceful in his movements (109–11). During the opening scene when Brummel presents himself to Lady Margery on the eve of her wedding to Lord Alvanley (William Humphrey), a heavily made-up (forty-two-year-old) Barrymore is shot in soft focus to enhance his youthful good looks. In contrast, the actor is notably older in the second and third parts of the film. Also, as George acquires his image as a dandy, he replaces his initial finery—white powdered wigs and makeup—with a more naturalistic image, despite remaining highly fashionable and stylish. It is in this section that the film charts Beau's rise to fame and glory as the man of fashion and the confidant of the Prince Regent (Willard Louis) until his arrogance leads him to insult his "fat friend" and suffer the consequences of social ostracism. Here, the character of Beau bears many Barrymore traits: his decadence, his indolence and congeniality, his love of attractive women, fine food, wine, and clothes.[2] Meanwhile, in the third part, during the Calais scenes, Barrymore appears as the aging and increasingly disheveled Beau who is losing his looks as well as his fine friends and fortune, a middle-aged man noticeably beyond his prime. While this candid exposure of the ageing matinée idol may have shocked and dismayed many of the star's fans, others may have relished a glimpse of his "private person" and the chance to see the real man behind the glamorous persona, discovering what he really looked like in middle age. Here, Barrymore is revealed as an aging film star, not only careworn but also jowly and baggy eyed. This provides an alternative Barrymore image to all those in circulation in the early to mid 1920s, one that appeared much more consistently in the star's films and photographs in the 1930s. Finally, in the short closing sequence, the adored Barrymore is hardly recognizable beneath a theatrical wig and layers of makeup. Bearing little resemblance to reality, or even to the real John Barrymore, his image here is much closer to that of Richard Mansfield on stage in the late nineteenth and early twentieth centuries.

These different presentations of John Barrymore across the narrative of *Beau Brummel* not only depict distinct versions of the actor/star but also require different types of acting. After adopting a series of stylized poses reminiscent of classical statuary in the opening scenes of the film, Barrymore ends with highly animated and exaggerated gestures, movements, and facial expressions that distort his face and body, transforming him into a caricature and bearing a strong resemblance to the expressionistic performance of Alexander Granach as Reinfeld in F. W. Murnau's *Nosferatu: Eine Symphonie des*

Grauens (1922). By moving from classicism to expressionism from the beginning to the end of the film, *Beau Brummel* proved to be the perfect vehicle to showcase Barrymore's versatility as an actor, especially his command of both nineteenth- and twentieth-century styles of performance.

Barrymore's versatility as a performer was born out of an acting education that was as eclectic as it was informal. This consisted of the following: 1. seeing many of America's leading actors performing at the Arch Street Theatre in Philadelphia, owned and managed by his grandmother Louisa Lane-Drew (1820–97) (Peters 23–4); 2. performing small roles in stage plays starring his father Maurice Barrymore, his uncle John Drew Jr. (1853–1927) and his sister Ethel Barrymore (1879–1959) in the early 1900s (62 and 91); 3. a four-year apprenticeship with one of America's leading farceurs, William Collier Sr. (1864–1944), who taught him the rudiments of stage comedy between 1904 and 1908 (Garton 19); 4. silent film acting, mostly at Famous Players-Lasky between 1913 and 1920, appearing initially in comedies based on stage farces made famous by William Collier Sr., such as *The Man from Mexico* (1914) and *The Dictator* (1915), and subsequently in more serious photoplays such as *Raffles, the Amateur Cracksman* (1917) (62–79); 5. an association with one of America's leading naturalist playwrights Edward (Ned) Sheldon between 1911 and 1923, with whom Barrymore formed a close personal and professional relationship, Sheldon playing a major role in Barrymore's transition from comedy to serious drama (Peters 151–5); 6. extensive vocal coaching and script analysis with Margaret Carrington in preparation for his roles in *Richard III* (1920) and *Hamlet* (1922) (Morrison 75–9); 7. exposure to the work of the Moscow Art Theatre on tour in the United States in 1923 and a private meeting with the company's director Konstantin Stanislavsky backstage after a matinée performance of *Hamlet* (Garton 40; Power-Waters 70).

By 1924, Barrymore had acquired an acting technique that involved studying a script as a blueprint for his character, then developing a detailed understanding of the character, and subsequently focusing on thinking and feeling the character's thoughts and emotions when performing. This approach corresponded in many ways to the method developed by Stanislavsky at Moscow, one that inspired generations of actors in the United States after the company's tours of 1923 and 1924.[3] Barrymore's propensity to "think the thought" while performing his character Beau Brummel required his director Harry Beaumont to let the camera linger on the actor's face during moments of contemplation and introspection so that spectators could speculate on these thoughts as they occurred to the actor.

FURTHER REFLECTIONS ON BARRYMORE'S PERFORMANCE IN *BEAU BRUMMEL*

Marian Keane's essay on Barrymore reveals the extent to which the actor can be seen thinking his character's thoughts during moments of *Beau Brummel*, most notably during the mirror scene that follows the opening sequence in which Brummel loses Lady Margery, the love of his life, to Lord Alvanley. Here, the actor uses a sequence of gestures to convey the thoughts of his character as he stands before the mirror perfecting his poses and gestures (Keane 186). Later in the film, Barrymore once again articulates his character's thoughts before a mirror although, in this case, his reaction is markedly different. After Brummel has fallen from grace by offending the Prince Regent (now King George IV) and suffered the consequences of becoming *persona non grata*, a scene involving a dusty mirror both reinvokes and contrasts with the earlier one analyzed by Keane. Here, Barrymore articulates his character's thoughts with some idiosyncratic gestures, expressions, and looks, as can be observed in the description below.

Barrymore's reflection appears in a dusty and slanted mirror that makes him seem both ethereal and unsteady. As he steps closer, his head, shoulders, and chest appear more clearly in the glass while the left side of his face is out of focus in the upper right-hand side of the shot. After leaning in further to peer at his face, he drops his eyes to stare blankly at his chest, taking in his shabby attire, his finery as worn and weathered as his face, before tilting his head up again. His forehead furrows as his eyes stare into space, seemingly lost in thought. While his thoughts might be undecipherable here, his furrowed brow and blankly staring eyes clearly indicate that he is thinking.

At this point the camera cuts to Brummel's valet Mortimer (Alec B. Francis), looking on anxiously from his position behind his master. When the camera returns to Barrymore at the mirror, he is wearing a rather mad expression, tight lipped and furrowed of brow, his eyes glaring malevolently and failing to connect with his image in the glass. After blinking, he shuts his eyes tightly, grimacing, raising his right hand up towards the mirror to obscure his offending face. With open and outstretched fingers, he almost touches the hand reflected in the glass. Wavering just before making contact, the hand moves off to the right side of the mirror's frame. The fingers almost touch the wall but waver again as Barrymore looks down, biting his lips together as though shutting himself off from his own image. Raising his head, Barrymore's eyes nearly connect with those in the mirror but they waver uncertainly before doing so and, instead, he glares at his chest in the glass while grimacing again. Here, the tension in his brow releases very slightly to suggest more wonder than pain or anger, despite the glare in his eyes, so that he appears to be thinking either "What have I become?" or "How could this happen?"

Figure 4.1 John Barrymore thinking his character's thoughts, "What have I become and how could this have happened?" in *Beau Brummel* (Harry Beaumont, Warner Bros., 1924). Digital frame enlargement.

After suddenly lifting his head and turning away to the left, Barrymore raises his eyebrows to signal a new thought: resignation perhaps. "Oh well, what of it? It can't be helped? Is anyone to blame for this?" might be any of Brummel's thoughts here. This seems to be aimed at Mortimer, Brummel showing him that he doesn't really care, that he's resigned to the situation. Yet this is more the secret George than the public Beau, feigning indifference by utilizing his much-studied nonchalance. With another jerk of his head, Barrymore appears to speak, directing his brief words over his left shoulder toward Mortimer. No intertitles inform us of what he is saying but his frown tells us that these words are harsh. Catching sight of his own eyes in the glass, Barrymore flinches, quickly looking away to the side. This time it is George flinching, not Beau. Again, he appears to utter a word or two with quiet authority. Then, with sadness, he slowly turns his head back toward his own image in the glass, seeming to be lost in his private thoughts once more. A fearful look at his own eyes precedes another grimace, this one suggesting a shock of physical pain. Closing his eyes and baring his teeth, he raises his right hand to obscure his face in the mirror. This time he makes contact with the glass and, as his hand falls limply, his fingers leave tracks in the dust on the surface of the mirror. As he drops his head in defeat, his face contorts into a more terrible grimace and he closes his eyes even tighter than before. Slowly his mouth relaxes while his head remains down for some time until suddenly it springs up with some force as Brummel turns to address Mortimer again, initiating a cut to the manservant appearing to answer his master, though without intertitles still, their conversation is left to the spectator's imagination. The absence of intertitles throughout this scene indicates that the significance of this moment lies in what Brummel thinks rather than what he says.

This is a key moment of the film, one in which Brummel is confronted by the loss of his cultural capital, the only capital he ever possessed, having neither rank nor fortune. It occurs during a dramatic scene in which Brummel dismisses his faithful valet Mortimer and, in so doing, loses his last remaining ally. Just before he instructs his servant to leave his service, Brummel takes a moment to gaze (hesitantly) in the mirror and literally reflect on what he has become and what the future holds for him, penniless and friendless, alone in a foreign land. It is not only mortality that stares him in the face but an empty and impoverished existence. Here, the visual details provide the key information. The dusty mirror, for instance, is less an indictment of Mortimer's negligent housekeeping than of the fact that Brummel has given up looking at his reflection or taking a pride in his appearance. Now aging and disheveled, with shabby clothes and unkempt hair, Brummel is almost a stranger to himself, a grotesque version of his former dandified being. What is notably absent here is the charming, attractive, and elegant Beau who had once enabled Brummel to enter high society and become the confidant of royalty. When Brummel gazes at himself in the dusty, slanted wall mirror he sees an image in tatters. If the earlier mirror scene marked the emergence of Brummel's public persona (his Beau), the second one marks his disintegration. While the former heralded a successful future, the latter heralds tragic demise. Consequently, each of these mirror scenes marks a transformation in Brummel's fortune and identity.

In the case of the second mirror scene, this profound moment requires the actor intelligently to convey his character's thoughts and feelings as they ebb, flow, and change from one moment to another. Dispensing with any conventional or codified physical signs that might enable his viewers more readily to interpret his character's thoughts here, Barrymore uses a range of gestures, expressions, and looks that seem more individuated and naturalistic, placing realism over intelligibility and requiring spectators to use their imagination and intelligence to interpret these. For such an intimate scene, the striking of elaborate poses associated with classical acting or the robust and emotionally charged gestures of neoromanticism must have seemed inappropriate in 1924. In contrast, a more psychologically inflected set of gestures, expressions, and looks, such as wavering and hesitation, unformed movements and uneasy half-completed gestures, may have been selected by Barrymore to suggest his modernity as an actor. When contemplating his image in the dusty mirror, he avoids poetic or stylized actions that might indicate self-possession and confidence, replacing these with inconclusive gestures, expressions, and looks that convey his character's lack of resolve or purpose, suggesting confusion, ambivalence, and uncertainty.

Departing from more ostensive and codified actions, however, increased the risks of spectator confusion, as a review in the *New York Times* on 6 April indicated. Here, it was suggested that "the silence makes the portrayal of the character infinitely more difficult than it was before the footlights" ("Barrymore's Fine Work," [April 6, 1924], X5). Elaborating, the reviewer added that, "although Barrymore undoubtedly benefited to some extent by the lines and situations, it was no easy task to vie with the stage production which carried the actors along." This suggests that Barrymore's introspective performance failed to be interpreted by spectators at key moments of the drama. In contrast, Barrymore was considered to have produced some "truly wonderful work in the scenes of the impoverished and mad Beau's last days": that is, when the actor was at his most expressionistic in the film.

Interestingly, Barrymore's performance in the final section of *Beau Brummel* received particularly harsh criticism many decades later. In 1990, Margot Peters wrote that "Barrymore over-does the mad Brummel with gaping mouth and glaring eyes that would have thrilled a theatre audience but are too exaggerated for the screen" (251). This suggests that sixty-six years after the original release of *Beau Brummel* there was significantly less appreciation for bravura, expressionistic, or histrionic screen performances, with a much greater appreciation of subtlety, nuance, and underplaying. The same criteria for judging good acting can also be found in Joseph Garton's *The Film Acting of John Barrymore* in which *Beau Brummel* is declared to be a dull picture with the exception of a single moment when, "forced to dismiss his faithful manservant, a three second close-up catches his first hint of emotion":

> Through a slight twitching of his mouth and flickering of his eyes it is evident that Brummel has finally been touched and moved. And so, finally, is the audience. It is a startling moment very unlike anything in Barrymore's earlier films. For it is not a grand or theatrical display of emotion as was the norm in stage acting and the glory of *Dr. Jekyll and Mr. Hyde*. It is but a suggestion, an understatement. (91)

Garton adds that "[t]oday underplaying is hardly unusual but in 1924 few actors dared to risk throwing away an emotional scene" (92). For the *New York Times* reviewer of 1924, however, Barrymore had, indeed, thrown away emotional scenes in *Beau Brummel* by failing to clarifying his character's thoughts and feelings at key moments with gestures, expressions, and looks that were easily readable by spectators at the time. In other words, for this critic at least, Barrymore had underplayed too often throughout the earlier and middle sections of the photoplay. Of course, when silent pictures are generally looked at with eyes more attuned to the acting of Hollywood sound films of the 1930s or postwar screen performances indebted to the Method, then Barrymore's acting may well seem to hark back to more classical and romantic performance styles that predate the twentieth century. His grimacing and hand wavering would be read as "melodramatic" overacting or, even worse, "hammy." In the context of 1924, however, and for audiences familiar with silent film acting of the early 1920s, many of *Beau Brummel*'s scenes (for example, the dusty mirror scene) may actually have registered as modern, understated, and realistic, too much so even to be entirely readable, understandable, or pleasurable.

John Barrymore's performance in *Beau Brummel* requires a viewer to attend carefully and closely to get a true sense of what the actor was doing during this late flourishing of silent cinema. He certainly appears to have been combining various styles of performance across the film, moving from classicism at the start to a more realist style, while ending with a grand flourish by evoking both the neoromanticism of Richard Mansfield's stage performance and the fantastic performances of German expressionist film actors of the early 1920s. In so doing, *Beau Brummel* provided Barrymore with the chance not only to deepen his star image but also to preserve the acting styles of his ancestors and idols while appealing to modern spectators across America and the rest of the world. By experimenting with different ways of fusing new and old, modernity and tradition (that is, realism, classicism, neoromanticism and expressionism), Barrymore can be conceived not just as America's leading Shakespearean actor of the early 1920s but also as a highly versatile actor of stage and screen.

CONCLUSION

Having grown up among the traditions of nineteenth-century acting at his grandmother's theater in Philadelphia, John Barrymore encountered the realism of Edward Sheldon's work in the 1910s and formed an important association with him that persisted until 1923 and the production of *Hamlet* on stage. In 1923, Barrymore also discovered the work of the Moscow Art School on tour in America which made a deep impression on him. While the advent of talking pictures in 1927 certainly forced Barrymore to modify his screen acting method, there is sufficient evidence in *Beau Brummel* to suggest that he was already at work in 1924 on finding ways to reinvigorate the acting traditions of his heroes and ancestors by fusing their techniques with those of modern actors. In this way, he was able to preserve elements of nineteenth-century acting on celluloid while simultaneously adapting these into something more suited to modern theater and to the new technologies of the cinema. As such, Barrymore occupies an important position in early twentieth-century acting, situated at the very crossroads between older forms of acting and new methods emerging in America after the First World War.

During the 1920s (and, indeed, thereafter) Barrymore was in danger of being considered old-fashioned, given that he refused to abandon the acting traditions of the past in favor of modernity. It is clear that he had a genuine respect for these older acting traditions and sought a way of using them whenever his roles enabled him to. *Beau Brummel* proved to be the perfect vehicle for this. It is partly Barrymore's attempt to evoke tradition and modernity that makes this film interesting and worthy of academic consideration and analysis. Once, film history acknowledged such films largely to establish what sound cinema dispelled from Hollywood: that is, an antiquated, moribund, and essentially theatrical mode of cinema that needed to be cast off like a chrysalis for cinema proper to emerge glorious and triumphant. The time has come, however, to reengage with such films and recognize them as being more accomplished and versatile, steeped in the traditions of the past but also part of new developments. For, on the one hand, such films recorded and preserved those traditions for posterity, making them accessible to later generations. On the other, these films were also innovative and experimental in their own right, incorporating performance styles associated with Stanislavsky and the Moscow Art Theatre.

Taking a closer look at a film such as *Beau Brummel* and viewing it with an open mind can prove illuminating. For what can be found here is that an actor, often considered to have been old-fashioned, middlebrow, and hammy, was actually modern, experimental, and astute in his judgments, capable of making deft movements between a range of nineteenth- and twentieth-century acting styles. In short, *Beau Brummel* reveals John Barrymore at his most versatile, eclectic, and self-reflexive. In moments of introspection, moreover, he seems not just thoughtful but intelligent, nuanced, and naturalistic. Ironically, while for George Brummell, Beau was a public persona that concealed his true self, in *Beau Brummel* the image of John Barrymore glimpsed in the mirror is perhaps the most sincere and candid exposure of the actor at this point in his career.

NOTES

1. In translating George Brummell's story to the stage, Clyde Fitch removed the final "l" from his surname. Dorothy Farnum did the same when adapting Fitch's play for the screen in 1924. Consequently, throughout this chapter I use "Brummell" to signify the real personage and "Brummel" to refer to the character in the stage play and film.
2. Two years after the release of *Beau Brummel*, the publication of Barrymore's autobiography

Confessions of an Actor revealed him to be charming, feckless, reckless, and proud, not only a spendthrift but also someone who tired quickly and bored easily (Barrymore 17–21).
3. James McTeague has argued in his book *Before Stanislavsky* that many of the methods associated with the Moscow Art Theatre predated the 1923 tour, being deeply embedded in the curriculums of many New York acting schools from the mid 1870s, which accounts in part for the positive reception of Stanislavsky's technique in the United States during the 1920s (243).

CHAPTER 5

"Keep Back your Pity": The Wounded Barrymore of *The Sea Beast* (1926) and *Moby Dick* (1930)

Dominic Lennard

A performer noted for his striking beauty, John Barrymore was nevertheless familiar with contorting his appearance to attract equally the dreadful fascination of his viewers, having done so most remarkably playing the lead in John S. Robertson's *Dr. Jekyll and Mr. Hyde* (1920). A similar transformation also characterizes his starring roles in dual adaptations of *Moby-Dick*: the silent production *The Sea Beast* (1926) and its sound remake *Moby Dick* (1930).[1] Released amid the novel's critical reappraisal, yet prior to its accumulation of unsurpassed prestige in the American literary canon, both films renovate Melville's tale considerably for the screen, focusing on a romantic union thrown into crisis when one of the couple, young harpooner Ahab Ceeley (Barrymore), is wounded by the white whale during the course of the narrative. The metamorphosis of Barrymore's Ahab after his injury is most stunning in *The Sea Beast*: initially a sprightly young sailor, Ahab transforms into a haggard ghoul, with eyes both sunken and penetrating as he pursues his hated prey. The Ahab of Lloyd Bacon's later *Moby Dick*, while not quite the Gothic spectacle presented in *The Sea Beast*, still grimly snarls in marked contrast to the dashing man we see at the start of the film. In both films, the wounding of Ahab effects a deep reconfiguration of both his appearance and his character. The sailor eventually seeks retribution from the whale, yet it is his romantic rejection that lingers most centrally and spurs his vengeful quest. This chapter focuses on both of these roles and on the narratives that articulate and augment them, emphasizing Barrymore's Ahab as the possessor of a confident, desirable masculinity radically compromised by injury. Additionally, I suggest that these narratives of stigma and disability had particular resonance for the postwar period of the films' production and reception in which numerous wounded men, formerly healthy and whole, struggled, with wounds and disfigurements, to be reintegrated into society and the prevailing definitions of masculinity.

"MY DARLING! HOW HORRIBLE, HOW PITIFUL!" THE INJURED AHAB

Both *The Sea Beast* and *Moby Dick* institute any number of changes to gall Melville purists, and a series of modifications further distinguish one adaptation from the other. Nevertheless, both emphasize the stymied (and finally revived) union of sailor Ahab Ceeley and the daughter of a local preacher, in *The Sea Beast* Esther (Dolores Costello), renamed Faith (Joan Bennett) in Bacon's remake. In the earlier film, the voyaging Ahab keenly treasures memories of his beloved fiancée with whom he is in contact through only the occasional but much-cherished letter. In pell-mell pursuit of a white whale, however, Ahab is hoisted overboard by his half-brother Derek (George O'Hara), jealous rival for Esther's hand, incurring his famous bite but remaining oblivious to his brother's complicity in the whale attack until the film's conclusion. In the remake, Derek is innocent of Ahab's wounding but still conspires against him in its aftermath by assuring Ahab of his lover's disappointment at the injury, thereby driving Ahab back to a life at sea. Albeit via different narrative turns, in both films the slimy Derek's treachery is outed, the whale killed and—most importantly—after many years Ahab's fiancée reaffirms her devotion, soothing her lover's epic angst.

Prior to the sailor's disfigurement, both films centralize Ahab's attractiveness and its attendant social and sexual prestige, a focus crucial to maximizing the distressing collapse of that power and his bitter transformation (which overwhelms focus on the whale itself). Early in the film, preparing to go ashore, the crew assiduously attend to their presentation, ensuring themselves adequately prettified for female attention. As one of the admired class of harpooners in *The Sea Beast*, Ahab wears miniature harpoon pins in his hat to signal his special status. His positioning as a desirable (and desiring) man is perhaps most breathlessly evoked in his interaction with Esther the evening prior to his fateful departure. At the dinner table, under the stifling supervision of her father (James O. Barrows), neither of the lovers manages to eat a meal, each anxious to be alone with the other. Overloaded with romantic tension at this moment, the couple inhabits only bodies of desire (banal digestive functions are unthinkable). With the father fortuitously called away, the lovers retire to the moonlight outside before Ahab pulls Esther toward him and kisses her long, longingly, and with striking eroticism. He dips her low, curving his body against hers, and, with her mouth pressed against his, she runs one tensed hand over her own breast. With a more weathered

Barrymore reprising his role, Bacon's 1930 version differs in that Ahab, rather than being a romantic in thrall to a waiting sweetheart, is a drunken rogue reformed by his new lover (Joan Bennett). Without the romantic fever described above, Bacon's Ahab is still marked clearly (even excessively) by his sexual self-confidence and potency. After meeting Faith (and outside her hearing), he phrases his awe at her beauty—"The prettiest son of a gun I've ever seen"—while remarking jovially on his desire for women generally: "Oh I like 'em black, I like 'em white . . ." Early in the film, greeting a bevy of female admirers on the dock, Ahab appraises the backside of a larger candidate with a slap, joking, "If they cut into you, they sure would get a lot of blubber!" The wisecrack (while callous to modern viewers) indicates his sexual confidence through his willingness to enforce normative standards of body image according to which he is privileged. In a later encounter with Faith, he even teasingly shows her his tattoos in tribute to other women. Yet, when he falls for Faith, while outwardly retaining his desirably exotic allure, Ahab is swiftly domesticated by the romance and his womanizing ways abate. Thus, in both versions his proficiency with, and desirability to, women is clearly signaled, his sexual mobility underscored while any threat that power might present is comfortably regulated.

Upon his return, and before he reveals himself to Esther, the sexually confident Ahab is thoroughly dashed and demoralized. The conniving Derek evokes Esther's love of Ahab's body, feeding his insecurity: "Esther was always crazy about your bein' so strong and perfect," he remarks in *The Sea Beast*. This time, as the men sing merrily about going ashore, hopeful of sexual adventure—that "the lassies will be sweet"—the once-bounding Ahab painfully secures his new prosthesis. In both films, far from the assured and princely wayfarer of old, Ahab now struggles to make himself viable. In *The Sea Beast* the sailor meets his beloved for the first time outside a grand ball held by the governor, a scene in which men (and couples) demonstrate their charming and leisured mobility. Ahab first angles his body in the darkness to conceal his ailment; when he reveals it, Esther is aghast. She raises her hand to her mouth indicating her shock but also intimating oral disgust (her mouth previously so receptive to her lover's grand kiss). It is her sympathy, however—"My darling! How horrible! How pitiful!"—that most distresses Ahab, and he turns temporarily from the fullness of her embrace. Later, she warns her father of the same mistake: "Don't let him feel that you are shocked! Keep back your pity." The Ahab of Bacon's *Moby Dick* is similarly self-conscious in his woundedness, and attempts an inconspicuous exit from the ship only to be humiliatingly "caught" by his lover who gives a horrified shriek and flees from him without further word. These upsetting encounters underscore both films' fascination with the mutilation of the male body and the rejection it might precipitate, elevating to the level of tragedy the loss of the romantic confidence and currency inherent in Ahab's earlier depiction. While the quest for the white whale is of course retained in both adaptations, this is certainly secondary to—indeed, spurred by—the harpooner's ruined romance.

FALL FROM GAZE

Both films considerably underscore bodily reconfiguration, forcefully evoking its emotional toll. The presentation of Ahab Ceeley as a spectacle in accordance with Barrymore's star status is crucial to these depictions, and it is worth sharpening focus on the sailor's visual valuing prior to his disfigurement. The Ahab of *The Sea Beast* is framed as an object of sublime visual desire from the character's introduction onward. The intertitle informs us of the wild nature of the whalemen before we see this coarse and briny crew holler shanties that fixate with bravado on peril, death, hanging, and matricide. They revel in the danger of their livelihoods and in their indifference to sentiment, especially as it applies to women. Yet this depiction works to foreground the loner, Ahab: the shot tilts curiously upward on a man tapping his feet to the rhythm of the shanties sung below but dreamily separate from his rowdy cohorts. A medium shot of the star fades in. He is captured in profile, eyes cast to the distance and away from the lens. A small monkey perches in the crook of one arm. An intertitle introduces this splendid gent as a young harpooner instructed to look out for the ship's game but also indicates that his attention is fixed less on whales than on his lover back home, this reinforcing his distance from the shipmates who eagerly eschew all things feminine. After this glamorous profile resumes, a bird's-eye shot of the hard-laboring crew below is posed against another medium shot of this elevated and insular sailor gazing contemplatively down at the tattoo on his inner forearm, a design in romantic tribute to his beloved, "Esther." He rubs his skin as if seeking her touch and gazes longingly toward the camera, as if acknowledging her via acknowledgment of a similarly adoring female audience.

Indeed, at the time of production, Barrymore was especially associated with the infatuated desire of female cinemagoers. Gaylyn Studlar positions him as exemplary among those 1920s male movie stars whose popularity was attributed to female fans (91). In fact, these discourses of female fan desire were strong enough to provoke social concern that they would challenge accepted models of masculinity: "By the 1920s, women were being blamed for promoting a 'womanly ideal of man'" (92). Such concerns sprang from a rise in consumer culture more generally, with women seen to be both central and powerful, a power especially pronounced at the box office through the consumption of cinematic images of men. Studlar points out that "This debate appeared to be reaching a climax in the 1920s, as women were accused of

Figure 5.1 Barrymore on romantic display as Ahab Ceeley in *The Sea Beast* (Millard Webb, Warner Bros., 1926). Digital frame enlargement.

destroying traditional sexual and domestic relations and creating a new type of man, the 'woman-made man'" (93). Studlar argues persuasively that, as Barrymore's career developed and transitioned into cinema, he was increasingly (and for many male commentators disconcertingly) associated with a masculinity constructed by women, highlighting Warner Bros.'s technical investment in his star vehicle *Don Juan* (1926) as indicative of the studio's faith in his power with female spectators (100). Similarly framed by female adoration, Barrymore's Ahab is initially positioned in *The Sea Beast* physically and morally "above" the "manly" devotees (even fanatics) of a violently traditional masculinity, instead leaning in dreamy devotion to the feminine.

Ahab's accompaniment by a monkey complements his foregrounding as a spectacle of exotic visual pleasure. The agile and playful monkey here reflects its master's own physical agility, especially as Ahab slides spiritedly down to the deck, jesting with his shipmates. The tiny primate perched atop his shoulders emblematizes a fabulous mobility that will be later lost. Moreover, the creature is charming and cute but essentially non-functional on a ship like this (indeed, a ship dedicated to transforming animal life into mere commodity). Given Ahab's sublime disconnection from the intense labor below him, both man and beast here are essentially objects of visual play and delight. Yet after his disfigurement, this preoccupation with the spectacular body is tragically inverted. Upon landing in Port Louis, where Esther awaits, Ahab hides far below deck, watching his confused fiancée through a narrow porthole, the frame of which conceals his body from female view. The metafilmic presentation of Barrymore for those female fans is even more pronounced in the opening of Bacon's later *Moby Dick*, including a fuller gesture to a constructed audience (including a consternated male crowd). As the ship sails into port, it is predominantly female onlookers who await it. In the crow's nest high above, Ahab waves extravagantly before nimbly arranging his body in a series of acrobatic poses, including completely upside-down, his legs waggling ostentatiously. A cut to three waiting women on the shore indicates the appreciation of his female admirers—indeed, a grouping of "fans" who share a pair of binoculars that allows them closer visual absorption of their idol. As Ahab executes another maneuver, leaning backward and waving as if in a stage chorus line, a different cluster of women delight in his antics. Faith, his soon-to-be lover, is as captivated as the others while the jealous Derek (Lloyd Hughes) cuts in, "He's showing off for the girls." Faith hardly minds: "He *is* thrilling," she adoringly affirms. "Why, anyone can do that with practice," gripes Derek insecurely. In this moment, Barrymore's Ahab performs conspicuously as a theater or film star, to the rapt praise of one demographic and the envious critique of another.

Accordingly, Ahab's disfigurement should be understood as amplified by his prior performance as a "woman-made man," aimed at a heterosexual female gaze that fetishizes his strong, mobile, and energetic body. Throughout *The Sea Beast*, after her lover's disfigurement, Esther refers longingly to a photograph of Ahab in a posture that shows him standing beautifully upright (and that recalls the film's opening shots of its star: indeed, the cherished image invokes Barrymore's status as an object of fan desire by recalling glamorous studio promotional glossies). Meanwhile, during Ahab's stagy acrobatics in *Moby Dick*, Derek stands in for the jealous male spectator, threatened by the exotic cinema idol's capacity to woo these women and challenge his own drably domestic bourgeois masculinity. In light of this framing, the compromise to Barrymore's spectacular body in *The Sea Beast* is so powerful that it descends into the monstrous, accompanied by the star's newly ghoulish visage. The fall from female regard is dramatic enough to plunge the sailor into a sort of deviancy: as he plots below deck with the foreign Fedallah (Sôjin Kamiyama), a grotesque orientalist caricature, how best to intercept the whale, there is even a sense of occult scheming to his vengeance. His association with this sinister and unsightly character, who paws and whispers at him with a kind of perverse eroticism, cements his ejection from the female gaze, inverting it into a spectatorship of horrified fascination.

Barrymore's ejection from a female gaze in both films is resolved not by any recuperation of his body but, instead, by assurance of the unconditional devotion of the female admirer. While Barrymore's performances and persona around this period were strongly positioned around his female fan crowd, I believe *The Sea Beast* and the later *Moby Dick* complicate the theme identified by Studlar in that, despite the rival Derek's villainous role in both films, his complaints over excessive female desire are implicitly affirmed: in both films the "female-made" spectacle is ultimately disavowed. Through his various humiliations, our sympathy for the disfigured Ahab is painfully evoked; the film underscores the terror of one's ejection from a masculinity defined by a heterosexual (and ableist) female gaze. Moreover, after being further disfigured by years of his own mad hatred, the Ahab of *The Sea Beast* is unquestioningly and implausibly accepted by his lover. Both films comfortingly suggest that male insecurity will always be accommodated and allayed by a woman of adequate virtue. Barrymore's initial presentation as a woman-made man in *The Sea Beast* and *Moby Dick* is thus dazzling but ultimately ambivalent, an ambivalence stabilized by a final renunciation of the male body as an erotically invested site of female desire.

"LONG-GONE DAYS OF GLORY": MAKING WAR ON MOBY

Early in *The Sea Beast,* prior to Ahab's maiming, a haggard and peg-legged sailor on the ship forebodingly advises the nimble harpooner that he, too, used to be able to perform tricks until his disfigurement at the jaws of Moby Dick. While catastrophic rope injuries on whalers were not uncommon during the nineteenth-century whaling trade, Ahab's whale-bite injury in Melville's novel is barely plausible. The notion in this adaptation, however, that the same whale has previously maimed another sailor aboard the same ship, defies literal interpretation and evokes instead a more regular harm to men's bodies recognizable at the time of both films' production. A subtext of war—not only between man and beast but also between nations—is variously evoked in both *The Sea Beast* and Bacon's *Moby Dick*; the opening intertitles of the former refer to "long-gone days of glory," suggesting the thrill and triumph of battle, whereas the Bacon film opens with a wholly different text but still heralds the soldier-like heroism of the whalers—"There never was, nor ever will be, a braver life"—and juxtaposes this with a memorial of sailors killed in conflict with the whale. The communal scenes of the men on the ship recall the jovial rough-and-tumble soldier communities depicted in films such as *What Price Glory?* (1926). Similarly, the evocation of women waiting for their lovers on voyages that lasted years, with only a letter or two to sustain them,

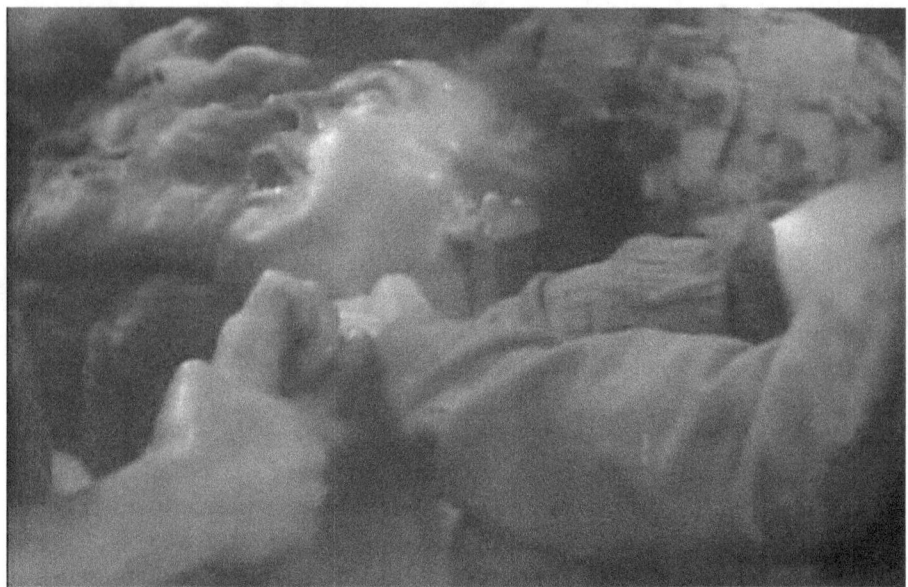

Figure 5.2 Ahab (John Barrymore) is restrained by shipmates as his limb is torturously cauterized in Lloyd Bacon's *Moby Dick* (Warner Bros., 1930). Digital frame enlargement.

strongly suggests wartime absence (invoking the Great War of 1914–18). And, of course, in both films the violence of battle is absorbed and transformed into the nevertheless vigorously martial violence of the hunt for the white whale.

Early on, the intertitular reference to "long-gone days of glory" in *The Sea Beast* invests its evocation of war with ambivalence. On the one hand, it rings of heroism and Victorian masculinity, yet it also evokes their passing. While, in the remake, this redundancy is not suggested through words, the narrative of heroism and adventure is still radically destabilized by violence and tragic rejection. In both films, the most serious rupture in this heroism comes in the scenes in which Ahab's mutilated limb is cauterized. Here we must witness violence to the male body. In *The Sea Beast*, with the harpooner still wincing and heaving from the pain of his initial injury, we see the coals being stoked seemingly outside of his awareness. One of his shipmates advises him of the further torment to come before the wounded man's eyes dart and bulge in terror and his body strains as the hot iron is applied. The spectacle is more mournful and macabre in Bacon's sound remake if only for the chilling complement of Barrymore's audible shrieks; Martin F. Norden described cinemagoers as "chilled to the marrow by Ahab's screams of agony" during the scene (112). "You're going to be all right, my boy," one of the attending men informs the patient just prior to the iron's application, his affected nonchalance amplifying the terror of the incident. At first, the star's face is obscured as he screams, a respectful concealment of his vulnerability even as it is vocally announced. A medium shot eventually amplifies the tension, however, by capturing his straining, sweating, open-mouthed torment as his shipmates hold him down, and steam from the grim meeting of hot metal and flesh rises through the shot.

In this powerful depiction we see a redirected fascination with the trauma of war injury and the limits of a historically sanitized heroic ideology that is applied similarly to soldiers and sailors. In a contemporary review of *The Sea Beast*, the *New York Times*'s Mordaunt Hall drew attention to Barrymore's idealized image in early scenes of the film, noting that he was "classical and pale, his forehead is high and his nose as straight as a die. His hair is wavy. He does not seem to belong to the sea, as there is not the least suspicion of the mark of sun or wind on his cheeks" ([January 16, 1926], 8). After Ahab slides down to the deck from his lookout above, he engages in no actual work but plays the prankster with his shipmates (as befits his simian sidekick); Barrymore's Ahab is essentially an entertainer, a very stylized seaman. The violence of cauterization, however, reinscribes him as punishingly real: the body as a spirited and mobile spectacle becomes the body as a burden and an engine of affliction. The Ahab of Bacon's *Moby Dick* is rougher and more roguish than his earlier counterpart, yet he still conspicuously performs for a delighted female gaze that values his exotic and mobile sexuality (which the "right" woman can quickly and comfortably domesticate). Too soon, however, that assertiveness gives way to excruciating passivity and helplessness. Rather than its thrilling capacity for action and the pleasure of spectacle, Barrymore's body becomes an object of pity and fascination for the traumatic damage it absorbs (and from which it is never restored).

As indicated, however, by the *Sea Beast* scene in which Ahab is too self-conscious to enter the governor's ball, these films bring to the fore experiences of social as well as physical violence. In Bacon's *Moby Dick*, Ahab's fellow sailors ridicule his fall from female attention with boundless cruelty, entwining it with ridicule of his masculinity more generally: "Now I'll be stealin' his women!" one jokes, before his buddy confirms, "Ahab ain't the man he used to be." One sailor even hurls a shoe in his direction: "What's this, the boot you don't need any more? You'd better keep it to throw at your wedding if you think she'll marry a peg-leg!" This focus on exclusion and inadequacy in social and gender terms had particular resonance in an interwar period struggling with conceptualization of disabled servicemen. Ana Carden-Coyne stresses America's new experience of receiving veterans from a foreign war, the reintegration of whom presented a challenge to the unified normalcy of the society at large (545). Much of this social discussion centered on work which, as Carden-Coyne points out, "is widely recognized [as] the signifier of independent adulthood, especially for men": injured veterans unable to work were "configured as physically passive and yet challenging to the norms of masculine independence" (544). In this sense, Ahab's desire to throw himself again into whaling ("with a vengeance") comes as a hysterical expression of his continued industrial competency but one mediated by a broader sense of his invalidity as both worker and man.

The new visibility of disabled veterans around the period of *The Sea Beast* and *Moby Dick*'s production was accompanied by more direct political pressure; Carden-Coyne explains that "Following a number of well-publicized protests and public action campaigns, some political analysts felt the government was being held to ransom by the undue influence of 'highly organized minority lobbies'" (545). This pressure, focused ostensibly around securing increased benefits, was also concerned with defending masculine credentials. In 1921, a poster advertising the first "Forget-Me-Not Day" positioned a man with one leg missing as emblematic of the disabled veteran; this exact injury is echoed by Barrymore's Ahab. The poster's slogan forcefully rebuffed the implication that public assistance to veterans constituted "charity," as opposed to an obligation: "Did you call it charity when they gave their *legs—arms and eyes?*" (cited in Kinder 164). As this poster indicates, disability for men was wrapped up in disparaging implications of "welfare" generally and "charity" specifically which challenged dominant narratives of masculine autonomy and was "associated with children, the elderly, and dependent women" (Kinder 164; see also Carden-Coyne 546). This fear of charity and its emasculating implications are much at issue in both of these early adaptations of the Melville novel. In the silent *The Sea Beast*, Ahab winces at his lover's pity, annoyed to see her lusty momentum transformed into an objectifying sympathy. Still more explicitly, in Bacon's *Moby Dick*, when Derek tells his brother that Faith will keep her promise to marry him despite his injury, Ahab responds with bitter disappointment: "I see: changing her name, from *Faith* to *Charity*. What does that make me?" Barrymore's screen persona powerfully emphasizes the transition between two very different modes of female care: from the thrill of action and beauty that must be reined in to one of pity that underscores dependence. And through this emphasis, both *The Sea Beast* and *Moby Dick* reflect the psychological, socioeconomic, and political tension around newly disabled ex-servicemen.

In the interwar period disability was also intertwined with growing antiwar sentiment. Kinder references the ambiguous ending of the First World War which did little to suggest long-term safety; antiwar activists drew on the wounded to "debunk romantic myths about the grandeur of war and showcase the lingering traumas of military conflict" (170). Accordingly, war cinema was also evolving in this era, and *The Sea Beast* and later *Moby Dick* coincide with the gradual emergence of what would eventually be called the "anti-war movie." Guy Westwell highlights less enthusiastic treatments of the war in this period, including *Tell It To The Marines* (1926) and *At What Price Glory?*

Perhaps most strikingly, however, and released the year before *The Sea Beast*, King Vidor's enormously successful *The Big Parade* (1925) emphasized the cost of warfare by depicting a soldier (John Gilbert) who, after receiving a gunshot wound to the leg, has the limb amputated at the film's conclusion. Influencing numerous films that followed, *The Big Parade* provided an important early treatment of antiwar themes in cinema, and one focused around irreparable damage to young men's bodies.

Nevertheless, Westwell hastens to note that an increasing realism, which swung against the romanticizing of earlier films, did not serve to oust chivalrous depictions entirely. He cites Michael Isenberg's assertion that there was, rather, a "co-existence" of "revisionist verisimilitude" with a traditional emphasis on "valour, honour and duty" (18–19). While early 1930s sympathy for downtrodden ex-servicemen was reflected in a number of films such as *I Am a Fugitive from a Chain Gang* (1932), *Heroes for Sale* (1933), and *Gold Diggers of 1933* (see Doherty 98), by 1930 Hollywood was still "not willing to commit to such a bleak interpretation of the war in any of its features showing American units in battle" and there remained "avoidance of divisive war themes in Hollywood movies of the 1930s" (Westwell 24, 27). Accordingly, both *The Sea Beast* and *Moby Dick* can be understood as transitional texts that engage deeply with some critical currents in war cinema while deflecting or sanitizing others. The historical whaling context means the film can still outwardly maintain a familiar spirit of adventure. For instance, the enemy of the film is conservatively resolved into a "faceless" and "subhuman" one whose moral consideration may be disregarded. The process of transforming the beast into a commodity depicted at the beginning of *The Sea Beast* further "depersonalizes" the opposition; the animal becomes what Carol J. Adams calls the "absent-referent" (66–7). War violence more generally is reprocessed from a destructive labor into a labor of industrial progress and benefit, focused on men who source, in the film's words, "the precious oil." Yet the allegory of these adaptations allows a more powerful and confronting depiction of the social and psychological impact of combat disability than was permissible in the war genre at the time of production. Even Vidor's progressive *The Big Parade* concluded with the soldier's reunion with his beloved and the revelation of his injury, thus omitting depiction of his later social, romantic, and financial life. Yet, in both *The Sea Beast* and *Moby Dick* acute focus is placed on the injured individual's emotional struggle for social reintegration, even if the historical frame itself allows the films to excuse pressing questions of the state's responsibility to provide for injured men. In this narrowed focus, which dispenses with national interests, Barrymore's performance of the sailor/soldier can absorb our interest more completely, the idealized star's physical and social degradation commanding an attention both startling and sympathetic.

With their focus on the high adventure of whaling, both *The Sea Beast* and *Moby Dick* traffic in the kind of historical adventure cinema popular before the war. Both, however, fixate on Ahab's wounded body with a potency that certainly exceeds these sanitary historical confines, powerfully tapping the social and political currency of wartime disability. Perhaps most remarkable is both films' emphasis on the fragility of male identity—on how powerfully Barrymore's Ahab is transformed by his wounding and rejection, and on his deep reliance on his lover's perception to define his identity and self-worth. The star's articulation of a glamorously mobile and female-focused masculinity amplifies the troubling of manhood effected by wartime disability. A consciously romantic, idealized, and "cinematic" male body is transformed into a body that is all too real. Through this process, both films manage to highlight the male body's entanglement in socially constructed yet powerful hierarchies of masculine value.

NOTE

1. A note on spellings. I have preserved accurately the various spellings of "Moby Dick." The novel's title is hyphenated (*Moby-Dick*) but, when the whale is referred to within the novel, its name is not hyphenated. Regarding Lloyd Bacon's 1930 film, Moby Dick is hyphenated neither in the title nor in the film itself.

CHAPTER 6

From Rome to Berlin: Barrymore as Romantic Lover

Douglas McFarland

After his final performance of *Hamlet* in London in 1925, John Barrymore abruptly left the stage for films. His portrayal of the Danish prince had proven to be a huge success in New York as well as in London. But, upon returning from England to New York in 1925, Barrymore immediately left for Hollywood, enticed by money and what must have seemed to him the less strenuous demands of film acting. After all, Barrymore had given over a hundred performances of *Hamlet*, first in New York and then the following year in London. He might very well have been both physically and mentally exhausted. He had earlier starred in several silent films, one of which, *Beau Brummel* (1924), cast him as a dandy with a proclivity for seducing women. The film ends with the aged lover on his deathbed, visited by the one woman he had loved. With a romantically melodramatic flourish, the two die together in each others' arms. The persona of the great onscreen romantic lover will carry over into four films he made from 1926 to 1932: *Don Juan* (1926), *Eternal Love* (1929), *Arsène Lupin* (1932), and *Grand Hotel* (1932). In these films Barrymore proved himself adept at playing a host of onscreen lovers: a psychologically damaged lothario; an overly passionate outsider; a stylish thief; and an insolvent aristocrat reduced to gambling and burglary. Ostensibly, these roles and their contexts differ from one another but they are linked not only by Barrymore the actor but by a set of thematic approaches to romantic love.

DON JUAN

Barrymore's first film upon his return to Hollywood was an adaptation of Melville's *Moby-Dick* (*The Sea Beast*, 1925). Because of audience demand or

Figure 6.1 Don Juan de Marana (John Barrymore) attempts to seduce the virginal Adriana (Mary Astor) in *Don Juan* (Alan Crosland, Warner Bros., 1926). Digital frame enlargement.

perhaps because of Barrymore's own persona, a romantic subplot was added to the script. In his second film, Alan Crosland's *Don Juan*, Barrymore established himself more fully as a great onscreen lover. An attractive physique and acrobatic skills served him well in a film genre that had been established by the dashing Douglas Fairbanks in a series of costume dramas that included such successful projects as *The Mark of Zorro* (1920), *Robin Hood* (1922), and, in the same year *Don Juan* was released, *The Black Pirate* (1926). Barrymore's Don Juan jumps from balconies, swings on vines, escapes a dungeon, duels with a villain, and defeats a host of armed enemies on horseback before, literally, riding off into the sunset with the chaste Adriana (Mary Astor). He is equally skilled at juggling women in and out of his apartment under the suspecting eyes of fathers, husbands, and other lovers. The narrative arc of the film, however, rests on his conversion from a promiscuous lover of many women to a faithful lover of just one.

Barrymore's performance in *Don Juan* may have been influenced by his stage Hamlet. His interpretation of the Dane expressed a deeper psychological disturbance than the Hamlets of the nineteenth (Edwin Booth; Sarah Bernhardt) and early twentieth centuries (Johnston Forbes-Robertson; E. H. Sothern; Robert Mantell). He might well have been influenced by a broad interest at that time in the theories of Freud. In his meticulously researched reconstruction of Barrymore's Hamlet, Michael Morrison has pointed out that

> a bold and conscious effort was made to view Hamlet in terms of modern psychological ideas and more open sexuality that had emerged in the previous two decades, and it is likely that the decision to reinterpret parts of the play in this light was jointly agreed upon by Barrymore, [producer Arthur] Hopkins and [production designer Robert Edmond] Jones. (132)

That Barrymore, in fact, saw a modernist psychosexual element in Shakespeare's play is strikingly substantiated by his extraordinary comments on his state of mind about Claudius during the "O, what a rogue and peasant slave" soliloquy: "That dirty, red-whiskered son-of-a-bitch! That bastard puts his prick in my mother's cunt every night" (Morrison 131). In another interview Barrymore spoke of the "voluptuous atmosphere of the Danish court" (159). Though a Freudian reading of the play did not dictate Barrymore's interpretation, a modern understanding of psychology most certainly influenced the production.

Barrymore's version of the Don Juan legend goes even further in establishing a psychological basis for the behavior of the iconic lover. In a prologue to his adult philandering, the film shows Don Juan as a toddler scarred by a traumatizing event. He witnesses the unmasking of his mother's adultery by a foreboding father (also John Barrymore) who then banishes his wife forever from his and his son's sight. All women, he pronounces to his son, are whores, and should be treated that way. In the next segment Don Juan has reached puberty, ready to be initiated into adult sexual relationships. This moment is informed by another deeply traumatic event. At a bacchanalian banquet, presided over by his father, a bevy of lascivious women make over him until one plants a kiss on his adolescent lips. In his father's world, women are little more than a source of pleasure. The danger that women pose to men is next indelibly stamped on to Don Juan's psyche. A jealous courtesan furtively approaches his father and suddenly stabs him in the heart. With his dying words, the elder Don Juan repeats the lesson he had uttered many years earlier: women are to be consumed, not trusted.

Don Juan heeds his father's advice, using women and then discarding them with careless ease. In his first appearance onscreen as an adult, he juggles four lovers in his apartment, apparently ready to take any woman to whom he is physically attracted. And, though his balancing act is comic in this scene, there is a punishing edge to his behavior. His addictive fixation on women undergoes a dramatic change as the narrative progresses. Don Juan has seen a young, virginal woman, Adriana (Mary Astor), with a beauty that is intensely innocent and enticing to male eyes. This tension between the chaste and the erotic is caught a few scenes later in her bedchamber. She has loosened her tightly bound hair so that it falls luxuriantly down upon the shoulders of her dressing gown. A shrine to the Madonna is prominent in the background. Don Juan suddenly appears on her window ledge, filled with desire. He shocks her by touching her arm, admiring her flesh, and then pulling her to him. Forcing kisses upon her lips, Barrymore adopts conventional silent-screen mannerisms, lasciviously rolling his eyes and smirking at the virgin's fear with an upturned corner of his mouth. In Don Juan's erotic imagination, virgin and whore have collapsed into one woman. Or, to put it differently, Barrymore's Don Juan has the chance to turn a virgin into a whore.

But when Adriana faints, Barrymore changes his acting style to convey a complex emotional and psychological response. He seems at first to be dumbfounded that she has fainted, dumbfounded that, beneath her virginity, she did not desire to be ravished. He then moves closer to peruse her face. With a slight and subtle turn of his head he conveys his confusion over a woman who does not conform to his father's view that all women are faithless. He pulls his head back slowly, still staring at her; then, with a subtle and quick turn of his eye, he shows his disorientation and shame. This shame morphs into an abrupt, seemingly angry movement of his body toward the window through which he came. His anger is not that of a rake who has failed to ravish a virgin but that of a man who has recognized, in a still confused way, his own pathological behavior. It is an anger emanating from his own frustration at being the person that he is. Through deft movements of his body and face, Barrymore expresses this complex psychological moment that initiates his conversion to a monogamist relationship. Barrymore brings his skills as an actor, perhaps honed in his performances of Hamlet, to a sophisticated portrayal of a screen lover entrapped and then freed from a pathologically repetitive behavior.

ETERNAL LOVE

In two films that followed *Don Juan*, Barrymore made full use of his masculine screen presence. In *The Beloved Rogue* (1927) he plays the French poet François Villon whose acrobatics rival those of Fairbanks. But even more striking is the use he makes of his body. If in *Don Juan* Barrymore had been costumed in tights that boldly emphasized the dimensions of his lower body, in *The Beloved Rogue* almost his entire body is uncovered in a dramatic torture scene. In the film that followed, *Tempest* (1928)—not a version of the Shakespeare play— Barrymore plays a Russian officer on the eve of the Communist revolution. Discredited because of his love for the General's daughter, he is thrown into prison. When his beloved visits him there, he stands with the upper half of his body fully exposed in a visceral display of virility. But in 1929 for his final

Figure 6.2 A shameful Marcus (John Barrymore) realizes he is about to lose the woman he most desires (Camilla Horn) in *Eternal Love* (Ernst Lubitsch, Joseph M. Schenck Productions, 1929). Digital frame enlargement.

silent feature, Barrymore's onscreen presence and his role as a romantic lover undergo a decided change. A great deal of this shift can be attributed to the director of *Eternal Love*, Ernst Lubitsch.

What became known as the Lubitsch touch is often understood rather narrowly as a light, sophisticated, witty, decadent, and risqué European style. Films such as *Love Parade* (1929), *Trouble in Paradise* (1932), and *Design for Living* (1933) do much to suggest this. But in *Eternal Love* Lubitsch displays a fuller and richer aspect of the "touch." In her book on Lubitsch's work in Hollywood, Kristin Thompson cites William Noble's assessment of the director: "Lubitsch is noted as a great film producer. He is uncannily deft, stripping the drama till its very life essence is unfolded and the unnecessary eliminated. His master hand deftly weaves the delicate skein of the involved relationship of the characters into an intricate web" (131). This "web" is often achieved by the subtle use of details: a facial expression, an object with symbolic significance, or a suggestive physical gesture. In *Eternal Love*, it is this style that Lubitsch brings to his direction of Barrymore, a screen lover who remains fully clothed, without a "great profile," and, with one small exception, not prone to acrobatic exhibitionism.

In the film Barrymore plays an unrefined and marginalized figure, Marcus, who hunts in the rugged Alps in the early nineteenth century. When the Napoleonic army arrives and demands that all the villagers give up their arms, Marcus refuses, thereby putting the entire village at risk. The first example of Lubitsch's subtle direction occurs early on. Barrymore, despite, his roughness, is in love with Ciglia (Camilla Horn), the niece of the village parson. But even her pleading will not convince him to relinquish his rifle. It has become a sign of his freedom and independence. But then, offscreen, he has a change of heart. His beloved is alone with her other suitor, a respectable and upright villager, who now thinks he will be the chosen one. But the camera cuts from the couple to a vibrating doorbell on a clapper. The door partially opens and the maid silently places a rifle against the doorjamb, then leaves without entering the room, shutting the door behind her. Much is conveyed in this seemingly simple moment: Marcus's willingness to sacrifice an object that signifies his identity; his likely knowledge that the competitor for his beloved is in the room and that his gesture might be strategic and timely; and the possibility that he has come in order to address Ciglia directly and explain that his decision to comply with the demands of the village has been done in her honor. His unwillingness to enter the room fully may be a response to the presence of the suitor, in which case his act is a subtle one, putting forward the rifle as a gift to her, signifying his willingness not simply to give in to the communal will but to demonstrate a change in his character in a direction she would prefer. Previously, he would have charged in and physically confronted his rival. The very absence of Barrymore's physical appearance in this scene, so compelling in *Tempest*, conveys a rich and deep meaning.

Later in the film, however, after the parson's niece has agreed to marry him, the old physical style of acting returns and leads to the loss of his beloved. At a village festival in which he and Ciglia are celebrating their upcoming nuptials, Marcus gets drunk, climbs up on to the balcony, leaps down and generally displays the physical style of acting of *Don Juan* and *The Beloved Rogue*. Barrymore's physical energy dominates the scene and destroys his romantic bond because this type of man, emotional and daring, is not the sort she wants.

In a later scene, Barrymore and Horn display an even finer example of the physical acting style I have been describing. After he is rejected, and now very drunk, angry, and resentful, Marcus returns to his cabin on the outskirts of the village where he is met by a wilder, sexually audacious young woman who is infatuated with him. They spend the night together. On the morning after, she leaves but shortly afterward returns with her mother demanding that Marcus marry her. He has no choice. Aware that he has spent the night with the other woman, Ciglia comes to his cabin to confront him. Alone in his bedroom, she lets her left hand delicately glance against the blanket on his bed as she moves past—the blanket that had covered him and his lover, and the bed in which they had made love. In this one gesture all that goes through Ciglia's mind is deftly represented onscreen: her sense of loss; her sense of the bed as a polluted site; her sense of shame for being involved; her recognition of Marcus's irreparable licentiousness. She then comes out of the bedroom and begins to move past him. Her hand touches his in a gesture of endearment but also of finality. This marks an extremely moving moment between the two, rendered in subtle movements. The film now cuts to a close-up of their faces as Barrymore pulls her to him. The expression on his face is one of shame, his need for forgiveness, his recognition that he has lost what he wanted most in life; and the fact that, in short, forgiveness will not be granted.

This is new territory for Barrymore's silent film acting. Thanks in large measure to Lubitsch's direction, and supported by the nuanced acting of Horn, Barrymore achieves a gravity and depth of expression greater than he had in any previous onscreen romance.

In the final scene of *Don Juan*, the lovers literally ride off into the sunset after Barrymore has gallantly hacked his way through a host of pursuers. The ending of *Eternal Love* erases the necessity of this aggressive masculinity. Marcus has shot and killed the suitor who married Ciglia. The townspeople pursue him up into the Alps. Ciglia comes to warn him, and the couple seeks some final escape. But when they reach the point where the mountainous terrain allows them no further progress, rather than ride off across the horizon in a romantic haze they step together into the obliterating force of an avalanche. The whiteness of the snow does not represent the innocence of the lovers but rather an apocalyptic burial, an erasure of the body as a locus of love and desire. I imagine that the Christian vision of eternity attached to the final minutes of the film might have amused the sophisticated Lubitsch and the worldly Barrymore but is surely out of place in a film that depicts the trials of love through deft direction and finely drawn acting.

ARSÈNE LUPIN

In *Arsène Lupin*, lovers meet on the field of language. The advent of sound opened up new possibilities for Barrymore as a screen romancer. Playful banter now becomes a medium for flirtation and seduction. Directed by Jack Conway, a dependable and able MGM director, *Arsène Lupin* is informed by sophisticated and risqué pre-code repartee between lovers. Unlike some performers, Barrymore made the transition to sound pictures almost seamlessly, relying on a suave and urbane manner, along with good looks, a dapper style, and a richly melodious voice. The intonations of that voice in harmony with the adroit movements of his body replace the acrobatics of earlier films. Though this change to vocalization instead of choreography is partially necessitated by

Figure 6.3 In *Arsène Lupin*, the clever and sophisticated Lupin (the Duke of Charmerace) (John Barrymore) discovers a naked woman (Karen Morley) in his bed (Jack Conway, MGM, 1932). Digital frame enlargement.

time and the excessive habits that wore on his body, it does allow him to utilize a voice trained for the stage.

Barrymore plays a clever upper-class jewel and art thief who has unfortunately fallen into debt. He is debonair, at home in the world, alternately—and playfully—condescending, aristocratic, witty, dapper, and delightful. In his first appearance onscreen he sports a top hat, white gloves, and tuxedo, his persona immediately juxtaposed against the police detective Guerchard (played by his brother Lionel) who is obsessed with catching and sending him to prison. The detective limps, wants to retire, dresses in rumpled suits, wears hobnailed shoes, and is continuously frustrated by Lupin's upper-class identity. The cat-and-mouse game they play sets the stage for similar romantic game playing. The relationship between Barrymore and the girl of the picture, the beautiful and alluring Sonia (Karen Morley), is linked to his relationship to the detective because she is in the employ of his pursuer. In the two previous films under discussion, the male lead was required to undergo a conversion in order to win the girl but in this film the girl must be converted so that the lovers might be together. She must change from agent of the law to partner in crime.

The first scene in which we encounter Barrymore at work as a lover—and I do mean at work—takes place fittingly in his bedroom. Walking in, he discovers a naked woman in his bed. This is Karen Morley who, having played a spy in *Mata Hari* (1931) the previous year, brings a seductive duplicity to her role in this film. Barrymore immediately senses something suspicious. Perhaps he has gone through this process before. But then again, how often does one unexpectedly discover a sassy half-covered beautiful blonde in one's bed? Sonia's nakedness immediately becomes the subject of a game of wits, culminating in her getting up in the dark and slipping into her dress with the clear suggestion that Barrymore is facilitating the rerobing. "I thought Russia was a cold climate," he suggestively muses in the dark. Earlier he had fluidly maneuvered to her side, placing his mouth a few inches from her ear, a technique he would use again in *Grand Hotel*. Herein begins a back and forth that Barrymore seems to be winning: "How do you like my bed? . . . Stay for breakfast . . . I haven't anything on . . . a Russian custom . . . a naughty dress . . . poor Sonia!" He dangles her dress at arm's length and then with playful earnestness threatens to toss it out of the window (perhaps a knowing bow to Cyril Ritchard's ploys with Anny Ondra in Hitchcock's *Blackmail* [1929]). It is not simply the smoothly ironic intonation of his voice that informs Barrymore's presence but also the fluid movement of his body, the charm of his posturing, his upper-class grooming with hair combed back not in a dashing but in a suave and self-assured manner. More than anything else, one senses that life with Lupin as a partner would be fun. More importantly, the assurance with which Barrymore conducts himself, the absence of arrogance and aggressiveness, the invitation to play that he effortlessly extends to those around him suggest that there is no need for him to be converted in order to become worthy of love. Also, the acrobatics of earlier films have been abandoned, with a single exception: at the end, in homage to his earlier career, what is surely a stand-in for the fifty-two-year-old Barrymore gracefully dives 50 feet from a bridge into a river in a daring final escape from the law. But mastery over his physical environment has been in every other circumstance abandoned for mastery in the field of wit and charm.

Though Barrymore's Lupin is a thief operating outside the law, he requires no rehabilitation. Don Juan needs to go beyond—indeed escape—a childhood trauma, and Marcus in *Eternal Love* must lose his crude and passionate style and learn to control his emotions. But the Barrymore of *Arsène Lupin* acts as the agent of change. Seduction is liberating for those around him. Sonia soon changes sides and becomes his partner in crime. She succumbs finally not simply to his suave manners and good looks but to the pleasure in outwitting authority and his delight in ironic play. This reversal of gender roles marks what is perhaps the salient ingredient in Barrymore's newfound persona of the romantic lead. But Lupin's allure is so intoxicating that it extends also to the detective who pursues him. Once having caught his fugitive, Guerchard himself become duplicitous. In the backseat of a police car in which the thief is being taken to prison he tells Lupin that, by the way, he once had a prisoner in very similar circumstances who escaped by jumping out of the door of the car and then leaping off a bridge to safety. Lupin takes the hint, leaps out, and does a perfect swan dive into the river below. The detective fires his gun harmlessly into the air and explains to his supervisor that he had done all he could have done. The allure of Lupin is infectious.

But it is also true that in the final scene of the film one has a sense of some change having taken place in Lupin. Some months and an ocean voyage later, he meets Sonia in a jewelry store to purchase, of all things, a wedding ring. Marriage, we are led to believe, will rid Lupin of his need to violate boundaries and outwit authority. Well no . . . not really. There will be other games to play, other jewels to snatch, other authorities to tease. But for Lupin there will be no other women. James Harvey has pointed out that in the screwball comedies of the 1930s, in which he includes the *Thin Man* series, there is between the couples a "sardonic appreciation of one another" (124). The performances of Barrymore and Horn as romantic lovers, I would argue, set the stage for Nick and Nora Charles who are most at home and most in love when they occupy the space of playful opposition.

GRAND HOTEL

Released just six months after *Arsène Lupin*, Edmund Goulding's *Grand Hotel* (1932) features Barrymore in the role of a jewel thief again. The tone, cultural context, and narrative arc differ greatly from the earlier film, however. While *Arsène Lupin* is essentially a romantic comedy in the context of a clever robbery, *Grand Hotel* is set in a dark mood, the Great War having cast its shadow over the Berlin Hotel in which the film takes place. Though Barrymore will make films for the next decade, one senses here that his days as a dashing leading man are coming to an end. Let me push this further and say that *Grand Hotel* functions as a coda to Barrymore's career as a romantic lover. Unlike his character in *Arsene Lupin*, the Barrymore in *Grand Hotel* is the victim of irony, not its practitioner. He exits the film abruptly and unexpectedly before the film has reached its climax, a climax that is itself informed by irony. His violent death and the final shot of his casket being removed through the hotel's delivery dock violate the bargain the audience has made with the filmmaker and with Barrymore's persona as a romantic figure. But perhaps this should come as no surprise. The demise of Barrymore's character, effected at a shadowy time in history, is forecast by the shadows that hang over many of the other characters. Though MGM provided the film with a patented star treatment, and a fanfare

Figure 6.4 The upper-class Baron (John Barrymore) flirts with the modern working girl (Joan Crawford) in *Grand Hotel* (Edmund Goulding, MGM, 1932). Digital frame enlargement.

of trumpets to announce the opening credits, all the characters those stars play seem continuously perched on the brink of unhappiness.

Lewis Stone, as Otternschlag, the resident physician on call, passes through the Grand Hotel as a spectral presence. His comments at the beginning and end of the film provide a first-person narrative frame. The movie opens with several of the principals speaking on pay telephones in the lobby, each communicating some trouble he or she is in: impending death, financial collapse, artistry that can no longer function, and the immediate need for money. The orchestral motifs from Strauss's Viennese Waltz, "On the Beautiful Blue Danube," that have played in the background lead the audience to expect a just sorting out of these problems. But then Otternschlag, sitting in the lobby and addressing no one in particular, observes in a tired voice: "The Grand Hotel. People coming, going and nothing ever happens." On the one hand, this might provide a wry, ironic commentary because a great deal will happen in the Grand Hotel in the next few days. But, in the weariness of his intonation, Otternschlag also conveys a mood of exhaustion. The viewers see his face in profile and have no reason to expect what comes a few minutes later, as he comes up behind several guests checking in at the front desk and, turning his head, reveals a horrifying scar falling from his scalp all the way down to his neck, essentially covering half his face. He moves from one side of the desk to the other asking the clerk if any messages have arrived for him. Barrymore's character, the Baron, turns and takes a quick and knowing look and then explains to the manager of a ballerina (Greta Garbo) in whom he has criminal interest, in an almost inaudible voice, that Ottenschlag is incessantly asking for, and yet never receiving, messages. Then, as if acknowledging the source of Ottenschlag's scarring, he adds, "Yes, I was in the war." He will not mention the Great War again until a few scenes later when he says to an accomplice who has suggested they use chloroform on their target, "I know all about chloroform. I had it in the War." Moreover, the film takes place in 1932, just one year before Hitler became Chancellor of Germany, when the city was suffering economically and spiritually in the aftermath of its loss in the First World War. It would be difficult to imagine that the audience would not recognize the discrepancy between the economic conditions in Berlin at the time and the ornate interior of the Grand Hotel.

The characterization of Barrymore as a romantic lead comes early in the film. He encounters Flaemmchen, an attractive stenographer (Joan Crawford), on one of the upper terraces of the hotel. She is a new type of woman, one with few cultural ties to the grand illusion that was Europe before 1914. She is a working girl, something of a flapper, and fending for herself in the economic conditions in which she finds herself. I mentioned that the Baron has a furtive interest in Grusinskaya, an émigré Russian ballerina with aristocratic tastes and accomplished artistry. The two women are juxtaposed against one another and offer a variation on the virgin/whore paradigm of *Don Juan* and *Eternal Love*. As the Baron passes Crawford on the landing he turns his head and assesses her figure, looking at her derrière rather than her face. He makes a quick U-turn and begins a flirtatious conversation. She immediately rejects him with the implication that she has been through this before, that since coming of age she had been approached by older men, perhaps even on hotel landings. He gets the hint but then circles back to try again, and she begins to thaw. He moves his face almost into hers, as he had done with Sonia in *Lupin*. Before long she is flirting back and they agree euphemistically to "dance" the following evening. When they are close together and Crawford says she only takes one meal per day—clearly because she cannot afford more—Barrymore asks if she is "reducing." She is taken aback and asks if he sees anything wrong with her figure. His eyes pass up and down before he sighs, "It's perfect." When he escorts her to the room of her employer, he pats the bottom to which he had first been attracted. This moment captures Barrymore as a man experienced in "picking up" young women in hotels. Barrymore has reverted to his role as a Don Juan but in a very realistic modern context.

But the Baron will change. Like Don Juan, he will fall in love with a beautiful and vulnerable woman and this love will ostensibly reform him. It happens in the very act of his profligacy. The Baron is seriously in debt and has planned to steal Grusinskaya's pearls. That evening, after she has left for the theater, he stealthily enters her darkened room and adroitly pockets the pearls. But, when a hotel maid arrives, he is forced to hide in a closet. She is soon followed by Grusinskaya herself who has left the theater without performing. From his vantage point in the closet he watches as she becomes despondent. He suddenly and inexplicably falls completely in love with her, as if a dart had pierced his heart. The scene recalls that of Don Juan when he enters the bedchamber of the chaste Adriana and falls in love. Garbo is shot (as, frequently, by William H. Daniels) in a soft glow. A point-of-view perspective shows her sitting on the floor bemoaning her lack of adulation and the loss of the elegance of pre-Revolutionary Russia. Almost provocatively, at least from the Baron's point of view, she removes her ballet shoes and begins to pull the sleeve of her costume over her shoulder. She begins to rise up, and the film cuts to a profile of Barrymore's head as he watches her. She then returns in a beautiful evening wrap and calls the ballet master to ask how her understudy did after her own abrupt departure from the theater. She listens, then says, "They didn't miss me at all." Her depression derives from little other than the need to be loved. The Baron witnesses her despair and, from out of nowhere, emerges to comfort her. He confesses he came to steal her pearls but, when he genuinely shows his love, almost as quickly she falls in love with him. And they spend the night together. The Baron has been transformed from a thief into a lover.

It is Crawford as the stenographer, however, who proves to be a much more compelling figure than the self-absorbed ballerina. We sense, I would argue, that Barrymore and Crawford belong together, that the Baron would find something genuine in the so-called "bad girl." We sense that they would be a pair of lovers who would also be friends, that flirtation could become the space of romantic play, that the working-class girl would complement, not clash with, the Baron's good taste and patrician manners. The ballerina's problems seem small in comparison to the stenographer's struggle to support herself financially while fending off men. Beneath the surface of the Baron's highly romanticized love affair with Garbo's ballerina lurks the notion that he has made the wrong choice.

To his credit, the Baron refuses Grusinskaya's offer to pay off his debts. But he goes about acquiring the necessary funds through his old ways. He first tries gambling and, when that doesn't work, considers stealing the wallet of his newfound friend Kringelein (Lionel Barrymore). Finally, relying once again on thievery, he sneaks into the room of an industrialist (Wallace Beery) to snatch his wallet. At this point, the narrative makes a radical departure, one that, I think, brings Barrymore's onscreen role as a romantic lead to its final days. Preysing, the industrialist, catches him in the act and, with a violence unanticipated by the audience, yet undoubtedly lurking in the streets of

Weimar Berlin, bludgeons him to death. A few scenes later the Baron's coffin is unceremoniously loaded on to a horse-drawn hearse through the loading doors of the Grand Hotel. The scene offers a brief glimpse of the underside of hotel life, the removal of the Baron's body coinciding with the delivery of meat into the kitchens.

In the final scene of the film, Grusinskaya sweeps confidently through the lobby, unaware of the Baron's death. The irony of the moment strikes very hard. Love is anything but eternal; it is ephemeral, vulnerable, and at times short-lived. Rarely does its path run smoothly. To fall in love is to meet together in a most precarious of worlds. It is a space that belongs to no others but one that is vulnerable to the forces that envelop it. I choose to end my exegesis of Barrymore's career as a screen lover with *Grand Hotel*. Perhaps more can be expressed about love when it fails than when it succeeds. In a film of almost two hours, Barrymore and Garbo are onscreen together for a mere thirteen minutes, thereby suggesting to the audience just how short-lived love can be. The film requires that Barrymore act with a self-awareness that transcends his work in other films. He must, and he does, communicate an impending weariness that is momentarily overcome by love. But he must also show that we bring our histories, our needs, and our traits—both good and ill—into what all lovers want to believe is a self-enclosed space. When violence quickly and unexpectedly shatters love and exposes it as an ephemeral dream, *Grand Hotel* becomes profound.

CHAPTER 7

The Power of Stillness: John Barrymore's Performance in *Svengali*

Diane Carson

Expert actors masterfully control their performances throughout their diverse roles, and John Barrymore proves equal to the multifaceted demands on the title character in *Svengali* (1931). With art direction strongly influenced by German expressionism, set against a backdrop of limited locations, Barrymore effectively guides and anchors the film through a commanding presentation of highly stylized, dramatic choices. With what appears to be minimal effort, Barrymore's restrained physical movements and modulated verbal delivery dominate the flurry of activity and concern swirling around his sinister Svengali. In effect, in director Archie Mayo's version of George du Maurier's novel, throughout Svengali's hypnotic manipulation of the chanteuse Trilby, Barrymore relies on limited verbal and constrained nonverbal choices to wield his devastating power.

Svengali (John Barrymore) tells the story of a supernaturally powerful voice teacher and pianist who hypnotizes women in person and controls them from afar. He carries on an affair with Honori (Carmel Myers) who, leaving her husband and his wealth, is driven to suicide by Svengali. He falls in love with, and dominates, a model, Trilby (Marian Marsh). She and artist Billee (Bramwell Fletcher) plan on marrying but Svengali, exercising hypnotic control over Trilby, whisks her away to tour European concert halls after deceiving Billee into thinking she has killed herself. Billee, discovering that Trilby is alive, pursues them to Cairo. During a concert there, Svengali slumps at the podium, his life force exhausted, praying for Trilby's love. She faints, whispers Svengali's name and, in Billee's arms, dies moments before a happy Svengali also expires.

Critics at the time and in the decades since have appreciated Barrymore's presentation of this devious, destructive character. Praising Barrymore's performance, Mordaunt Hall writes, "This production, which bears the title of *Svengali*, may have lost some of the romantic charm of the author's tale, but it compensates for this by Mr. Barrymore's imaginative and forceful portrayal, and also by Archie Mayo's knowledgeable supervision of the camera work." Hall adds, "Mr. Barrymore's fine performance . . . surpasses anything he has done for the screen, including his masterful acting in the motion pictures of Stevenson's *Dr. Jekyll and Mr. Hyde* and Clyde Fitch's *Beau Brummell*" ("A Lesson in Golf. A Fashionable Rogue," *New York Times* [May 1, 1931], 34, online at nytimes.com). In a later article Hall elaborates, "It is difficult to believe that this bearded and unkempt figure is in real life a handsome man" ("Svengali and Trilby: John Barrymore Gives a Masterful Performance in Hypnotist Role" [May 10, 1931], X5, online at nytimes.com). Biographer John Kobler also applauds Barrymore's acting, writing, "John's performance, aided by makeup and photographic wizardry, belongs among his half-dozen greatest screen characterizations" (266). Contemporary film critics have echoed the acclaim. Leonard Maltin calls it "prime Barrymore" (1339). Scott Ashlin writes, "John Barrymore should have played villains more often. J. Grubb Alexander's script continually peels back layers of Svengali's character, making him seem more and more dangerous each time, and Barrymore plays to that approach very skillfully" ("*Svengali*," online at www.1000misspenthours.com/reviews/reviewsn-z/svengali1931.htm).

In the early 1930s, Barrymore enjoyed a reputation from his extensive theater work and his silent films as one of the most alluring, attractive leading men. As Gaylyn Studlar notes in "'Impassioned Vitality': John Barrymore and America's Matinee Girls," in the first two decades of the twentieth century, Barrymore enjoyed a reputation as "American Theater's preeminent matinee idol" (98). His films in the 1920s, including *Sherlock Holmes* (1922), and *Don Juan* (1926), reinforced his reputation. Significantly in this regard, in *The Beloved Rogue* (1927), Barrymore plays celebrated French poet François Villon in an action-packed melodrama reminiscent of Douglas Fairbanks's vehicles. Barrymore's "glistening, seminude body" (138) and erotic encounters assert his sexual desirability but Barrymore playfully mocks his image. Elected King of the Fools during an early carnival scene, he disguises himself in decidedly unattractive makeup, false nose, and costumes, proving he'd embrace audacious characters onscreen as he had onstage.

Barrymore triumphed as Svengali. In fact, encouraged by *Svengali*'s reception and the contemporary testimonials to Barrymore's performance, Warner Bros. doubled down and banked on a repeat success with a very similar story. The studio released *The Mad Genius* later that same year (1931), again featuring Marian Marsh and Luis Alberni in supporting roles. But the second time was not a charm and Warner Bros. did not renew Barrymore's contract.[1]

Barrymore's physical appearance and affected mannerisms in *Svengali* may strike today's audiences as overly theatrical, histrionic, and melodramatic, all descriptive observations often considered pejorative. As Carole Zucker asserts, however, in "The Concept of 'Excess' in Film Acting: Notes Toward an Understanding of Non-Naturalistic Performance," "The negative sentiments aroused by such performances are born from a lack of awareness of acting traditions, as well as a narrow perception of the possible boundaries of fiction film performance" (54). Analyzing Barrymore's "axis of theatricality" (61)—his exaggerated, ironic self-parody—in a scene from *Twentieth Century* (1934), Zucker notes that "what is theatrical in any historical period develops out of a covenant between the actor and the spectator that is usually culturally determined" (61). Moreover, contextualized within the acting conventions of 1931, we can accept more readily the ways Barrymore effortlessly dominates the screen and commands respect for his portrayal.

To understand more fully how Barrymore achieves this effect, it is instructive to heed Paul McDonald's contention that "any critical study of film acting would benefit from not merely dismissing 'aura' or 'presence' as metaphysical and mystical qualities, but from asking how such effects are constructed from the material elements of the film actor's voice and body" (29). To that end, Laban Movement Analysis (LMA) and Irmgard Bartenieff's effort-shape analysis help in describing and exploring the acting choices by Barrymore and by the supporting cast of Marian Marsh, Carmel Myers, Bramwell Fletcher, Luis Alberni (Gecko), and Paul Porcasi (Bonelli). With LMA, Rudolf Laban (1879–1958) offered "a conceptual framework that facilitates observation and analysis of human movement" (Baron and Carnicke 190). In the 1950s, "through study, Laban and his collaborators located eight basic efforts: pressing, thrusting, wringing, slashing, gliding, dabbing, floating, and flicking" (199), and accounted for variation in performers' movements and energy. LMA originates from "choreographer–philosopher–movement educator Rudolf Laban, who, by 1913, had established an alternative vision of dance . . . in his choreography" (Baron 52). Laban describes movement in several ways: *strong* vs. *light* in reference to the performer's degree of force; *sudden* (quick) or *sustained* regarding the amount of time for the movement; *bound* or *free* in terms of the rigidity or graceful flow of a gesture. In its application to film acting, Laban's rubric enhances examination and interpretation of characters' efforts (also called dynamics), identifying critical performative choices that pinpoint direction and speed of movement, as well as the performers' degree of control. Laban's system of notation was, in fact, a way of inscribing dance choreography on paper, as a kind of "score."

Irmgard Bartenieff's effort-shape analysis (analysis of kinetic energy expended and the sculpting and form of movements) extends LMA by adding a valuable multidisciplinary complement focused primarily on human kinesiology. A student of, and collaborator with, Laban, Bartenieff (1900–81) elaborated on the multiple facets of body movement through her dance choreography and work as a physiotherapist. As Adrienne L. McLean explains in "Feeling and the Filmed Body: Judy Garland and the Kinesics of Suffering," "In describing how anyone moves, effort-shape analysis differentiates *gestural* movement (that which involved a single body part) from *postural* movement (that which spreads throughout the body, visibly affecting all parts of it and usually involving a weight shift)" (5). An attention to LMA and Bartenieff effort-shape analysis yield insight into *Svengali*'s dramatization and the success of Barrymore's acting.

Significantly, as Richard deCordova observes, "Performance is the critical standard by which audiences have judged films, and there is little doubt that the melodrama, in its emphasis on acting as expression, has provided the ideal object for the application of such a standard" (136). In this regard, actors' gestural choices will affect the appeal, or lack thereof, for a narrative, and, deCordova adds, "It is clear that certain melodramatic scenes are written as showcases for performance" (136). Barrymore embraces such a showcase with enthusiasm.

THE BOOK AND THE FILM

George du Maurier wrote the immediately popular *Trilby* in 1894, published it serially in *Harper's Monthly*, then book form in 1895. The material was thereafter adapted multiple times for the stage and screen, with three silent versions preceding Mayo's 1931 film version. For his fourth of five contracted films for Warner Bros., Barrymore wired his manager Henry Hotchener to

> impress the writer with the fact that the male character must be funny and get lots of laughs, particularly in first part of the story. Although a sinister figure, he is a wise, dirty, glutinous Polish Jew, with no conscience and a supreme contempt for all those nice, clean, straight-thinking English Christians. (Fowler 337)

Though no explicit comment denigrates Svengali's Jewish heritage in the film, his clearly coded Jewish identity adds an anti-Semitic dimension to the character, a detail not lost upon Barrymore who reacts to the hostility and animosity between Svengali and the British men with whom he interacts. Moreover, Svengali's appearance borrows from anti-Semitic stereotypes of the period: his beard, nose, and accent, as well as his reputation for not washing properly. This offensive characterization must be acknowledged for, although no categorical insults invoke further vilification within the film, these associations would not be lost upon the audience.

Moving beyond these details and further contemplating his interpretation of the role, Barrymore added in a wire to his manager, "The man's is the better acting part, but if the girl is not perfectly right everything he does is bound to be unbelievable and a little ridiculous" (337). Resisting any temptation to make his character physically appealing, "Barrymore devised a suitably horrible make-up for Svengali, a beard that sprouted in a hellish curl, and glass eyeball covers to bring hypnotic menace to his stare" (Fowler 337). But Barrymore's transformation into the devious Svengali only begins with his external manifestations. Understanding the nefarious character and his mysterious powers, Barrymore translated the psychological and emotional complexity into physical gestures and an unambiguously authoritative presence.

In September 1930, as discussion regarding the *Svengali* project continued via wireless communication, Barrymore was on a cruise with his wife and five-month-old daughter (Kobler 266). During the trip, a gastric hemorrhage and its treatment kept Barrymore weak and in bed until his return to Long Beach on December 2 (Fowler 336). Kobler credits this for Barrymore throwing himself "into the role of Svengali with a gusto unequaled since his Jekyll-and-Hyde" (266). Barrymore certainly welcomed the project and may have been energized with his additional time to reflect on the character. Or, as Patrick McGilligan writes in another context (adopting an approach welcoming emotional experiences), "'Great' actors should laugh, weep, kill, die, suffer desperation and madness. Any screen actor who hasn't done these things should be docked points. Actors should reveal, not withhold. They should invite troubling intimacy. Otherwise they are merely coasting" (38).

Barrymore did not coast through his performance as Svengali, and a "troubling intimacy" commingled with a destructive madness gives his acting an unnerving immediacy. Though the film received Academy Award nominations for Barney "Chick" McGill's cinematography (Floyd Crosby won for *Tabu*) and Anton Grot's art direction (Max Rée won for *Cimarron*), Barrymore did not receive a best actor nomination. Certain to fuel competitive tensions, John's older brother Lionel won Best Actor for *A Free Soul*. With acknowledgment of director Archie Mayo's fine direction and the restrictions imposed by early 1930s sound technology, my emphasis remains on Barrymore's acting, pinpointing his choices during significant moments in the film.

ANALYSIS OF THE ACTING: SVENGALI AND HONORI

Introduced in the first scene after four establishing shots, and viewed from behind in long shot, Svengali animatedly plays a piano in his apartment.

Accompanied by ominous non-diegetic music that segues to the piano music, two cuts within seconds reframe him in a medium shot and then a medium close-up at an angle from slightly above. A knock on a door abruptly interrupts. He turns on his stool to highlight the famous Barrymore profile as he nods three times, raises his eyebrows, and turns more fully toward the camera. Withholding Barrymore's face in the opening shots adds a measure of suspense, and the subsequent revelation of his unattractive makeup establishes a chilling atmosphere reinforced by the relatively bare, expressionistically designed room.

Svengali's movements are constrained as he turns toward the camera, abandoning the agile arm movements of his piano-playing. Now he is stiff and his posture inflexible, representative of his personality as will soon be revealed. Barrymore limits Svengali's direct and bound gestures to a couple of eye blinks, tilting his upper torso a few degrees forward and lifting his eyebrows. These gestures are neither sustained nor flexible. Combined with the stiff postural movements, Barrymore establishes and expresses Svengali's physical rigidity as it also suggests a parallel emotional inflexibility.

Madame Honori enters the apartment's outer room, a study in contrasts with Svengali. She flows through the door in a medium long shot. After a cut to Svengali, who rises from the piano stool by tilting his entire upper body forward and then standing—a postural inelegance—the scene continues with a medium close-up of Honori gesturing directly and lightly with her arm as she asks for him. She coyly smiles, tilts her head, and slowly lowers and opens her eyelids. She is graceful, her energy palpable, and her lovely dress and cloak a further contrast to Svengali's tattered vest, hanging suspenders, and shabby shirt sleeves rolled halfway up his arms. Before any confrontation between Madame Honori and Svengali, their movement and energy establish them as incompatible characters.

This contrasting pattern of postural and gestural movement, the characters' effort-shape differentiation, continue throughout this scene. Svengali walks to the doorway to spy on Honori; then, in long shot, turns, picks up a shabby feather and a piece of sheet music, and, in medium shot, walks into the room where Honori waits. Barrymore uses his eyebrows and eyelids, rapidly fluttering them—a sudden, quick movement—to show a fake surprise as Honori speaks his name. She glides across the room to him, a smooth, sustained, and delicate—in Laban's terminology, "light"—movement. After a cut to a medium close-up two-shot, she and Svengali talk, Honori more relaxed, intently looking at Svengali who looks away from her and then ahead as they walk to the piano in a tracking shot, Svengali remaining stiff in his movements, Honori fluid in hers. As Barrymore's and Myers's choices soundly communicate, no tender intimacy between the two of them is remotely possible.

As Svengali plays the piano for her, the composition frames him straight on from his upper chest to his face. In a medium close-up, Honori suddenly hesitates to sing and Barrymore reacts with one quick, direct, strong head movement left to right. Barrymore again raises his eyebrows and rolls his eyes as Svengali urges Honori to sing: "Come on, come." A pair of matching eyeline reaction shots between Svengali and his assistant Gecko (Luis Alberni) attest to the poor singing while also reinforcing their relationship—in their negative attitude toward Honori as well as in similar qualities of movement. Gecko flees the room in strong, direct action.

Svengali continues to raise his eyebrows and roll his eyes, the gestures strong, sudden, and bound to register his distaste. In the last half of this scene, Honori continues her flexible, free flow of gestures—moving her head, her eyes, and her arms as she lightly shifts her body posture. After Svengali rejects her, Honori's eyes widen and her voice rises, her inflection announcing her distress. Throughout his dismissal of her, Svengali remains stiff, bound, with direct, strong, and sudden gestures. Honori's intense alarm and high emotional energy signal her vulnerable state while Svengali's unemotional rejection of his pupil reveals his heartless, sadistic nature, his immoral intractability.

During the exchanges, Madame Honori sings badly but with enthusiasm as Svengali exchanges disparaging looks with Gecko whose facial reactions and movements are slightly more expressive than his master's but in the same register. Since he's accompanying Honori on the piano, though he faces the camera so that his hands are not visible, Barrymore is limited to upper body movements and facial expressions. Even so, only his eyebrows stretch upward with dramatic emphasis, communicating his discomfort. A quick, sudden, strike of a piano chord leads Svengali to stop his playing: he swivels toward Honori, stands, and, before she can finish, curtails her singing. Honori remains lively, Svengali stiff. As the scene continues, Honori reveals that she has left her husband but has neither claimed nor taken any money with her. Svengali inwardly recoils from her because he is dallying with her only for monetary benefit. Barrymore communicates this with the same inflexible, bound posture and brittle gestures he has already established, reinforcing through his gestures and posture that he and Myers inhabit dichotomous emotional realms.

Kinetic energy is brought to the scene by Carmel Myers. As Madame Honori speaks and listens to Svengali, Myers's body movement, her placement of her arms on her hips, the repeated adjustment of, and tugging at, her dress bodice; the tilt of her head; the lowering of her eyelids with an absence of blinking, showing her teeth as she smiles—all Myers's particulars—convey Honori's malleability contrasted with Svengali's rigidity. As Svengali's disinterest and dismissal dawn on her, as she moves from behind to face him, imploring with her hands and wide-eyed disbelief, Svengali stands immobile, sideways to the camera, his face turned away as Honori retreats in horror pleading, "Take your eyes off me."

I have described this approximately seven-minute scene in some detail in order to highlight the gestural and postural movements that illustrate characters' conflict or cooperation. Good actors eliminate dissonant elements in their verbal and nonverbal choices with, as shown in this scene, a multifaceted array of minutiae. Because introductory scenes also bear the burden of establishing personality and disposition, this early interaction between Svengali and Honori sets the stage for his later behavior appearing motivated and coherent in conveying consistently duplicitous, perverse qualities. As Bartenieff writes, "Every movement in any part of the body reflects something of the mover" (quoted in McLean 5). Values and predispositions, attitudes and emotions speak through effort-shape dimensions. Barrymore establishes Svengali's characteristics and, in his destructive male-female relationships, remains consistently powerful with minimal, understated gestures, relying on his eyes and the artificial lenses that intensify his disturbing look and nefarious power. It is with his concentrated gaze alone that Svengali exercises his supernatural control. Motionless, all but imperceptibly inclining forward, he locks his victim's eyes with his overpowering stare and his domination is secured.

This oppositional pattern of actors inhabiting different emotional registers is unique neither to *Svengali* as a whole nor to this opening sequence. Actors learn to cultivate a spectrum of levels of energy, to evince restraint or activity. In dramatic exchanges of two or more characters, actors quickly learn that matching intensity with one another does not ignite dynamic rapport, whether the scene is quiet or flamboyant, ostentatious or restrained. With the possible exception of scenes of comedic intent, actors realize that mirrored, echoed choices usually lessen the engaging vitality of complementary or contrasting gestures and energy. If one is animated, the other is still. When one uses strong, sustained gestures, the partner relies on light, short ones. Therefore, it is not surprising that, as the central plot takes over, distinctly dissimilar behavioral choices for Trilby O'Farrell and Svengali will define their interaction as well.

ANALYSIS OF THE ACTING: SVENGALI AND TRILBY

Svengali first meets Trilby when she arrives for her modeling commitment. Enamored, he takes control of her through his raw magnetism conveyed with repeated strokes of his beard and an exaggerated widening of his eyes. Barrymore chooses a strong, sustained, direct gesture, reasserting his visual dominance (as he did with Honori, leading to her suicide) and calculated exploitation. As Trilby gradually comes under Svengali's control, she shifts

Figure 7.1 Svengali (John Barrymore) taking control of Trilby (Marian Marsh) in *Svengali* (Archie Mayo, Warner Bros., 1931). Digital frame enlargement.

her gestural and postural movement as well as her spatial and temporal efforts from light, free, and indirect to stronger, bound, and sudden. Initially animated, bright, and flirtatious, Trilby segues to a relatively comatose deportment as Svengali exercises escalating control. Barrymore further increases his stillness and stiffness, relying on direct, strong, sustained gestures and his (in this film) typically rigid posture. Ironically, Svengali's most energetic gesture, a quick jumping and jerking of his arms, comes as Gecko pulls him away from his British friends' apartment with his stolen suit and money, perhaps Barrymore's way of including the humor he believed Svengali must have, at least in the early scenes, as he claimed in his wire correspondence with his manager Henry Hotchener.

Another critical scene occurs twenty-six minutes into the film as Svengali interrupts and then spies on Trilby and Billee declaring their love and intention to marry. Svengali appears absolutely stationary in close-up, intently watching, with shadows across the right side of his face. He is metaphorically and literally dark while Trilby and Billee are bathed in illumination, their love expressed through smiles, relaxed facial expressions, and gentle touching, all light, sustained, flowing movements. But even here, Svengali glowers and Trilby freezes briefly twice before catching her breath to respond to Billee's promise that, after they're married, he'll take her to England and his mother will be proud of her. Marsh's choice of a faltering physical response foreshadows Trilby's weakness to Svengali's power, just as Barrymore's election of a sustained, disapproving reaction reinforces Svengali's malicious intent.

As the scene progresses, Billee describes England as "beautiful: green fields and hedgerows, and hollyhocks, primroses . . ." Billee speaks softly, lightly intoning in pleasant cadence. Svengali interrupts brusquely, in a lower register, sharply mocking with "and fog and pneumonia and shopkeepers and flat feet and boiled beef and cabbage," as he walks stiffly forward in long shot, his arms dangling. He adds, "Trilby in England would be like a butterfly in mutton soup." He cackles as he continues his negative descriptions of England. As they walk across the room, she is relaxed, graceful, and light; he remains characteristically rigid, awkward, and heavy. Enamored of Trilby, Svengali exercises control by guiding the conversation and hypnotizing her, his sclerotic white lenses adding to our unease as he puts her to sleep and then awakens her. Throughout his interaction with her, with Billee, and with Billee's two artist friends who come over to Trilby when they observe Svengali's intrusive presence, Barrymore bends his body stiffly from the waist and his arms from his elbow, keeping them close to his body. His gestures and posture are again shown to be as inflexible as his perverse principles.

Significantly, the contrasting acting choices between Svengali and Billee, Trilby, and the oppositional English friends establish and intensify their conflicting values and behavior, an important feature of melodrama. As Sarah Kozloff notes, one noteworthy characteristic of this genre is "a clear dichotomy between good and evil" (85), an element "which activates our pity and emotional investment" (83). After indulging the specter of the most dire outcomes, including permanent separation and death, this genre of "emotional excess" (97) reinforces traditional values and romantic ideals, especially love. We see, therefore, that, as established in the opening sequence with Honori, the tragic effect of Svengali's cruel indifference is death; in her case, incited suicide.

For Svengali himself, his uncompromising love culminates in his own death, his life force drained by the energy required to control Trilby and block Billee's love. Kozloff observes, "Physical or emotional separation and death constantly threaten various characters within the narrative" (86), and this formula applies to *Svengali*, producing an added layer for performance complexity. Billee suffers the most because of his physical and emotional estrangement from Trilby to whom he remains devoted as he pursues her and Svengali wherever they travel. Fletcher expresses his pain primarily through a sustained, bound stillness. His eyes communicate his longing, his body often shifts slightly forward, and he remains immobile, frozen in his hopelessness. Billee's suffering reminds us that, as Kozloff writes, "Melodramas activate and then assuage viewers' primal separation anxieties, which, say some theorists, underlie the basic emotional responses viewers have to film" (86). Through Billee's sustained constancy and affection, *Svengali* conveys the romantic ideal and indulges its painful corollary: separation from and loss of one's love.

Throughout the film, Svengali consistently exerts his depraved control, enforced even from a physical distance in a noteworthy special-effects scene that occurs after he has become captivated himself by Trilby. In this night scene, the camera pulls back from a close-up of him, retreats through his window, and, after a cut, tracks left to right, swoops over rooftops, and, after another cut, pushes in through Trilby's window to pivot into a close-up of her. She turns restlessly. A cut to a close-up of Svengali follows, with Trilby awakening and, in a trance, walking back and forth, ending up outside his door. Supernaturally, he knows she's there and invites her in. Sitting slouched in an armchair, he casts a shadow of a raven on the wall behind him. A cut from a medium close-up yields to a distorted low-angle shot of Svengali, legs parted, his black coat covering his body and a black cat on his lap. The expressionistic style fittingly visualizes the menace and psychological warp expressed in Trilby now speaking hesitantly and dispassionately, her gestures minimally expressive and much less relaxed, sustained but weak. Trilby flees, Svengali laughs, and a cat hunting a mouse establishes the metaphor for this relationship.

He and Trilby travel through Europe (Berlin, Vienna, Paris) and eventually to Egypt where the film and Svengali's life end. Overseeing their recitals, concert manager Señor Bonelli (Paul Porcasi) contrasts more dramatically with Svengali than does any other character. Fifty minutes into the eighty-one-minute film, on the occasion of a performance in Paris, Bonelli awaits Svengali's and Trilby's arrival to let Svengali know that three men are requesting an interview. Bonelli's effusive arm waving, his strong, sustained, jerking movements of his hands, and his rushed, high-pitched comments offer histrionic contrasts with Svengali's subdued presence and bound gestures, and also offer a dramatic reminder of Svengali's rigidity. Similarly, Svengali's conducting of the orchestra during Trilby's Parisian concert consists of sudden, strong, sharp baton slashes accompanying thrusting body movement. His power waning, Svengali succumbs to increasing pain as he and Trilby leave the concert hall and Trilby momentarily escapes Svengali's power.

The dramatic scene that concludes the film reiterates Barrymore's well-crafted design for conveying Svengali's aberrant behavior despite his solicitous, oppressive care of Trilby. As announced in a newspaper article, Madame and Monsieur Svengali will perform at the Sphinx Café in Cairo, Egypt. Gecko begs Svengali to cancel the concert because "that spell you had tonight, it was the worst you ever had." Svengali's sadistic vitality has waned in the face of Billee's love for Trilby and pursuit of her. Hunched over, moving slowly, Svengali is externally cramped: a metaphor for his emotional constriction and loss of potency. Before the performance, his arms dangle, he directs Trilby to watch him closely, to look only at him, to think only of Svengali, but his energy lags, his movements are constrained, his intonation flat, his delivery slower than ever before. The shot lingers as he kisses and then pats Trilby's hands and walks weakly from the dressing room to the stage. Barrymore thereby signals Svengali's demise, his loss of domineering energy, before Trilby enters for their final performance. In the last two-and-a-half minutes of the film, Barrymore's gestures diminish in strength and length. Accompanied by short bursts of music from the orchestra, Trilby glides to her position on the stage, standing above Svengali, nearly motionless as she begins to sing. Her focus, and ours, is entirely on him.

Without sustained vigor, Svengali flicks the baton but falters mid thrust as he attempts to conduct the orchestra and guide Trilby's singing. He staggers and sits, nods indirectly and briefly at Billee with an exchange of glances between them. Then his head falls forward as Trilby chokes on the notes, her left hand cupped at her throat. A quick cut to Svengali shows him slumping forward, his posture collapsing awkwardly. In a sudden, strong movement, Billee leaps to his feet and we cut back to Svengali with Gecko catching and holding him. Awake, aware, Trilby holds her right hand at her throat now, looks right and left as her head and eyes turn in subtle, indirect movements. She looks down at Svengali still slumped in Gecko's arms, his head arched back. A brief close-up of her is followed immediately by a long shot as she collapses downward and out of view. In another long shot, Billee races in sustained, sudden movements to her, moving more quickly and deliberately than he has in any previous interaction. Kneeling in medium close-up, he lifts Trilby, gently strokes her right cheek in repeated, soft caresses, and calls to her in quickly spoken, direct pleas. Fletcher's sprinting to Trilby, his tender embrace, and his frozen expression testify to Billee's panic over Trilby's collapse and his ardent devotion to her. His soft body contours contrasted with Barrymore's angular physique further highlight their oppositional values, just as Billee's action counters Svengali's fragility in his final moments. In the film's final minute, Fletcher's and Barrymore's movements and gestures communicate Billee's ineffective vigor as opposed to Svengali's still dominant, albeit enervated malevolence.

A close-up finds Svengali, his head arched back, exhaling breath, blinking, his eyes looking up, softly and haltingly imploring God to "grant me in death what you denied me in life . . . the woman I love." In medium close-up Trilby lifts her head lightly, half smiles, and softly intones, "Svengali," as her head slumps to the side. An immediate cut to Svengali finds him opening and closing his eyes and arching his eyebrows in direct, quick movements as he sharply inhales and exhales, begins to sing, stops as suddenly as he began, chokes on his words and freezes, mouth and eyes open. The camera tilts down his right arm. As he softly drops the baton, "The End" appears on the screen, music increases in volume behind the title. In death, Svengali has, indeed, won the love he yearned and plotted to have in life, his pathological, sadomasochistic power absolute and finalized, his sublime narcissism consummated in mortality.

Commenting on his own approach to acting, John Barrymore said, "It's a curious mental state. I never can understand the actors who say they lose themselves completely in a part. I don't know what they are talking about" (Cole 594). In *Svengali* there is no mistaking that this is John Barrymore acting a role. Nevertheless, he commits so fully to it, immerses himself so thoroughly in the character's malicious intent through his gestures and his postural choices, that Svengali comes to life. Even today, Barrymore's magnetism transcends 1930s acting tradition and affectations, so effectively does he perform his captivating deceit.

NOTE

1. In an earlier film for Feature Productions, *The Beloved Rogue* (1927), Barrymore plays François Villon, a dashing Douglas Fairbanks type. Though beyond the scope of this chapter, the striking performance promises a potentially provocative, fruitful exploration of the comparisons and contrasts with *Svengali*.

CHAPTER 8

Prospero Unbound: John Barrymore's Theatrical Transformations of Cinema Reality

George Toles

John Barrymore is the supreme embodiment of theater on film. No matter what roles he plays, the aura of theater inescapably and (so often) magically defines his relation to the camera and to his fellow performers. Theater for him offers the potential to burst the boundaries of an assigned role at any moment, to annul the threat of confinement to a tediously fixed disposition. Barrymore seems always a visitor to the land of film from another country. He carries the burden of exile though in an antic fashion. We feel his true home and deepest commitments lie elsewhere. Like his character the Baron in Edmund Goulding's *Grand Hotel* (1932), he is drawn to shadow spaces on the periphery of the main action. He emerges for brief intervals as a half-spirit, half-charlatan, seeking a kind of connection and fulfillment that are unattainable. One feels he prefers the elusive or impossible goal, and secretly craves to have his aims thwarted.

His roles frequently seem designed to test the distinctions between film's sense of the real and theater's. He is a creature of this borderland, and many of his most famous characterizations highlight division and the necessity of repeated transformation. Film offers the possibility of direct human revelation. The camera desires to discover who the man Barrymore is without the protections of disguise. Barrymore resists exposure of the self behind the theater personage yet so many of his characterizations are precisely about masks gradually torn away and a subjection to merciless social scrutiny. Perhaps the role in which Barrymore is most caught up in theatrical flummery and, at the same time, most painfully probed by the camera is Larry Renault in George Cukor's *Dinner at Eight* (1933), a figure who is lethally entrapped on the illusion-shredding stage of his hotel room. Interestingly, Barrymore's conception of this ham actor stresses that his destruction results in large part from insufficient belief in theatrical transformation and in theatrical means for approaching truth. Renault cannot hide behind a mask and, as a result, he is prey to almost everyone. The elements of Renault's failure to *believe* in theatrical metamorphosis, until the role of a literal dead man presents itself to him as a way out of his difficulties, will be my primary focus in this chapter. But, before examining the Renault performance in detail, I should like to talk briefly about the characters of Oscar Jaffe in Howard Hawks's *Twentieth Century* (1934), and François Villon in Alan Crosland's *The Beloved Rogue* (1927), and examine them as keys to Barrymore's whole conception of acting.

One reason Oscar Jaffe is widely regarded as Barrymore's lodestar film role is because it places no limit on his transforming impulses. Jaffe is free to improvise his attitudes, needs, values, and behavioral language with reckless abandon and no fealty to coherence. Only the chalkmarked space of a rehearsal stage makes sense to Jaffe as a realm where things have a dependable order and intelligibility. Elsewhere he is "transcendentally homeless" and, though often frantic as his masquerades crumble, happy to stay that way—unsettled to the core. Though Jaffe is a creature of farce, there is what Freud beautifully terms a plaintive "afterwardness" to his contract with existence. Whatever might be *real* in his life has happened to him already, in an earlier, irretrievable time. All that is left to him now is a succession of gossamer incarnations, taken up as mood dictates, to deflect the exigencies of a too onerous present tense. He commits himself wholly, but briefly, to the predilections of each mask in turn. They facilitate the retrieval of precious, zestful desires that were once natural and even authentic to him.

In a letter to his second wife, Michael Strange, written during their courtship, Barrymore spoke about his intense identification with the fifteenth-century poet, François Villon, whom he regarded as an extraordinary mental escape artist and incessant wanderer, after his own heart. Villon, in fact, might supply an approach applicable to the creation of any film character:

> He [Villon] was a creative artist, a poet, and everything happened in his *head*. When he is caught by Life in these movie situations, which always demand a rather asinine, heroic activity, he is frightfully up against it. Only by his amazing dexterity and imagination can he elude them, maintain a certain whimsical integrity, and prevent himself from looking like an ass, the audience being the only person he takes into his confidence. I think the picture of Villon skipping, bounding, and crawling on his stomach through a Gothic dimension of a dying chivalry and a brutal and slightly sacerdotal materialism till almost the very end, when he is forced, through the reality of suffering, his mother's death, etc., to a different attitude—always, however, flecked by a sort of pinched gaiety—is

something I can have genuine fun with and accomplish something real. (quoted in Fowler 188)

Barrymore addresses here the vexing dilemma of an actor being "caught by Life" in false situations and their attendant false attitudes. He conceives "heroism" as a behavioral stance foisted on him by those who have no conception of what such an ideal might actually entail by way of sacrifice and suffering, and who make it into something self-servingly "asinine." He invokes the counteragents of tart whimsy, burlesque, buffoonery, and "a sort of pinched gaiety" as the surest means of preserving a degree of integrity in the midst of script- and director-dictated heroic posturing. The film or stage Villon, for example, must contend with the Gothic rigmarole associated with a "dying chivalry." The actor must oppose the convention of languid gestures and a perfumed fatalism by adding exuberant outbreaks of physicality—"skipping, bounding, and crawling on [one's] stomach" through misty poetic territory. He should release brutality in the rendering of wistfulness and a harsh materialism in his quest of the sacred.

To pursue acting on a higher, freer level than current theatrical and film conventions dictate demands a dexterous, spontaneous imagination which allows one to "elude" ready made solutions at every turn. Barrymore sees the crucial channel of communication existing not between himself and the other characters, important as those are, but between himself and the spectator. It is easy for those circling you onstage to impose script-sanctioned demands that drastically hem you in, with a fearful need for predictable limits. The spectator will be the only one Villon takes into his full confidence. Barrymore describes the final destination of the Villon performance—the place where its truth crystallizes—as a "something real" forcibly held back until "almost the very end." He will secure the right to honest sentiment, pathos, nobility, tragedy by strenuously resisting the facile temptations counterfeit versions of these qualities offer him throughout the dramatic narrative. It may require an entire performance to clear a space for a few real, unforeseeable moments of revelation. (I think of Barrymore's brief spasm of weeping near the close of his segment of *Dinner at Eight*, immediately preceding his character's return to delusion.)

When Barrymore is on film, his association with theater is linked with power—power from another realm that is equally tied to make-believe and the spiritual. His apparent access to power is never far removed from his character's manifest weakness and he often deliberately betrays the true nature of that power by using it as a mere protective shield for his weakness. A character such as Svengali, for example, fears that to expose his abject dependency on his seeming puppet Trilby is to ensure destruction. So much of his art-making power, then, is futilely lavished on control and concealment. Barrymore's more contemporary characters—such as the Baron in *Grand Hotel*—seem socially adept and available to others, after a fashion, but the Baron's preferred mode of conduct has to do with stealth. As noted earlier, he moves around the edges of his milieu, almost destitute, alone and in shadow. He performs his relationships with a smiling verve but his exertions—even in his love scenes with Grusinskaya (Greta Garbo)—are suffused with an unshakable melancholy. The theatrical component of his self-presentation cannot be relinquished, and the play-acting fatigues and sequesters him. His brief love affair with the ballerina is possible because they recognize each other as fellow creatures of the stage, equally imprisoned by it.

Barrymore characters often appear ready to be destroyed from the outset. Part of that readiness comes from the theatrical burden they carry. There is a sense that the Barrymore character, wearily stoic after a chain of defeats, almost relishes the prospect of being robbed of his theatrical resources even though he can't conceive of anything to replace them. The gaiety that survives the Barrymore character's stripping down to bare essentials may be "pinched," flecked with gallows humor but what inspires it is a deep relief—akin to rejoicing—from no longer having to keep up appearances. So often Barrymore is allowed to be alone with the camera in his final extremity. The ghostly audience outside the world of the film is all he has left. What he has to show to this audience is his performance failing but its failure is his channel to truth-telling. Barrymore yearns for a tragic conclusion marked by the laughter that comes with the surrender of his theatrical identity.

George Cukor's adaptation of the Edna Ferber–George Kaufman play, *Dinner at Eight*, is a remarkable example of how every aspect of theater and role-playing can be turned against Barrymore. Theater is made into an instrument of relentless humiliation which conspires with other sorts of delusion to drive his character to suicide. Barrymore might, at first, seem to be masochistically cast in this film. At a time when his authority as a film star was still uncompromised, he elected to play Larry Renault, a has-been silent-movie actor who is presently alcoholic, penniless, no longer handsome, prey to massive self-deception, and distastefully autocratic to the few underlings who can still be made to do his bidding. We are even informed that Renault's acting talent, when he was successful, had never been substantial. His reputation depended entirely on his looks and a confident bearing. His agent, Max Kane (Lee Tracy), disdainfully alludes to the "great profile" at one point which was a crucial feature of the Barrymore stage and film persona. The figure of Renault begins as a small man who grows steadily smaller in the eyes of all who have dealings with him. The viewer witnesses a series of repellently deflating defeats in which our judgment of Renault differs little from those who reject him. He is granted no quarter or effective acts of resistance during a many sided onslaught. The Renault scenario is literally a chamber piece.

Barrymore's entire performance is limited to two extended scenes, both of which take place in one room of his hotel suite.

Within this tightly confined space of borrowed opulence, Renault offers a moderately convincing performance of a renowned actor, with plentiful career prospects, to his easily impressed current lover Paula Jordan (Madge Evans). While pontificating tipsily to her, he receives a phone call from Paula's mother, inviting him to a formal dinner party later that same evening, an invitation he reluctantly accepts owing to Paula's surprising insistence. Paula's mother, Millicent (Billie Burke), is ignorant of their affair; Paula hopes that it can soon be revealed to everyone. Renault's change of heart about the dinner during the phone call—with Paula hovering nearby, as coach—is the single act of calculated deception that the actor does not bungle in an ever-accelerating ordeal of unmasking. Yet, even in his handling of the phone call with the foolish society woman, Barrymore emphasizes Renault's lack of ease. He projects an air of dated—almost moth-eaten—gentility, bringing a quality of waxy stiltedness to his assumption of the grand manner. As Renault attempts to charm Millicent, he is revealed facing a framed photograph of himself set by a window. The window's floor-length, cord-tied drape strongly evokes a theater curtain. Behind Renault is a folding screen which suggests intimate concealment. Cukor noted in an interview that Barrymore added the phrase "dear lady" to his talk with Millicent in order to make his courtesy feel old-fashioned rather than a supple display of sophistication (24).

The ensuing dialogue with Paula about the state of their relationship is played as though he can hardly summon the energy to hold on to her, to maintain even the appearance of continued romantic interest. He is clearly in desperate straits but makes no attempt to hide his alcoholism from her. He is equally transparent in his display of emotional enervation and his fatigue with the rigmarole of desire, despite the fact that Paula may be the only person who remains convinced of his value.

Barrymore specializes in playing characters who can feign an affable engagement with the affairs of life but who have, in fact, no continuing stake in the din and strife. Barrymore is stunningly versatile in his ways of embodying remoteness. His unconcern is sometimes joined to the tasks of winsome benefactors. But his "remoteness" can also manifest itself in pitched battles with isolation and the siren song of self-destruction. In Mitchell Leisen's *Midnight* (1939), Barrymore plays Georges Flammarian, a wealthy fairy godfather for the radiantly covetous chorus girl Eve Peabody (Claudette Colbert). Though fully aware of her deceit and her schemes to advance her own financial interests, he nevertheless becomes a secret supporter of her false identity as Baroness and of her plan to procure a wealthy husband. Georges is attempting to break up his wife's affair with a sophisticated, well-off ladies' man, Jacques (Francis Lederer). He imagines that Eve's "Baroness" will provide an even more bewitching romantic prospect for the charming Lothario rival to woo. But the film provides only the flimsiest evidence that Georges remains vitally attached to his wife (Mary Astor). He appears more persuasively entranced by Eve's belief that her world is pure theater. Her gold lamé dress and her similarly lustrous evening bag are her sole surviving possessions but she is confident that they are sufficient to open the right doors and carry her where she wants to go. She is a kindred spirit to Georges, given her view that one can sensibly devote all one's life energy to playacting. Georges has long ago forsworn a grounded, consequential existence, one that contains serious, ache-inducing attachments. He is an untroubled, untroubling Prospero, dwelling on an island of gossamer magic and stratagems. Eve's staged, delectably "made up" self is as close to the melancholy fog of reality as Georges is willing to venture. His efforts on her behalf are carried out with no hint of trepidation or solemnity. He is as outside the game he is playing as if he were already a ghost. Theater is what remains visible to him but it no longer offers a route to something meaningful.

Returning to Larry Renault's impatient love scene with Paula in *Dinner at Eight*, we are shown Barrymore alternating between several different voices in his responses to her, none of which emerges convincingly as the voice that identifies his true position. Each vocal register Renault takes on is steeped in feigning, often unconscious. Renault assumes that he can distinguish between straight talk and posturing but, in fact, the voices available to him have no power to express his actual (desperately moribund) condition. Even when he is profoundly humiliated at a later point in the narrative, he cannot speak from the place where humiliation thrusts him. It is a case of a bad actor having no escape route from spurious theatrical effects.

One of his voices is that of the petulant, intransigent drunk who flaunts his out-in-the-open, massive consumption of alcohol and regards his outbursts at Paula's gentle remonstrances as daredevil valor. He declares the rebel's right to "do as I please." The second voice he employs belongs to the gruff-speaking man of the streets, the sort who can report on life's accumulated hardships with bracing honesty. Renault uses this same harsh vocal pitch to assess the defects of the play he imagines he will soon be signing a contract to star in. He rasps out reassuring reminders of his ability to put over weak material by sheer force of personality. While he is still applauding himself for shrewd, pragmatic accommodation, and describing his skill at "dominating" onstage, his nerve fails him. His hard-headed tone and stance become hollow and his voice crumbles. His third stage voice is wrapped in romantic gauze. It strives for the mellifluous cadence of Dickens's Sydney Carton at the end of *A Tale of Two Cities* as he evaluates his magnanimous sacrifice.

Barrymore shifts rapidly between his petulant and man-of-the-streets voices as he tells Paula of his three failed marriages and of his current numbed state which is beyond the reach of love. He weaves dizzily between a farceur's mockery of his marital misfortune and rueful resignation to his accursed luck. Then he shrilly pours forth his envy at his third wife's massive success as a film star before finally arriving at the promised land of sweet-voiced largess. He encourages Paula to be done with him and return to well-meaning, eligible Ernest, her fiancé. Renault comes nearest to "unstaged" utterance when he declares she knows nothing whatever about him, brushing briefly against the usually suppressed fact that her lack of such knowledge matches his own. He pauses at one point in his recitation of his woeful love history after saying, "And now I'm . . ." but is at a loss for a way to finish. His attempt at a large, meaningful gesture to Paula occurs as he sits on the sofa and admits that he is "burned out," with no loving substance inside him to draw upon. Moments later, however, he is converting his confession to Paula and his relinquishment of any claims upon her into a theatrical event of shimmering grandeur. He views it as a tearful theater patron might, and appraises its value (with tender surprise) as perhaps the only decent thing he has ever done. But Paula is by no means ready to give him up, and he knows it. Her stubborn youthful ardor soon pushes him back into petulant mode and he spoils the mood of heroic sacrifice with a weak, cranky insistence that she submit to his befogged will. And, in fact, she resolves to have her own way. Renault must capitulate as they are interrupted by the arrival of his overtaxed, exasperated agent, Max, who brings with him a lewd knowingness about the tryst and some further word about Renault's still unsigned contract.

Preparing for the challenge of his first major Shakespeare role, the lead in Arthur Hopkins's legendary 1920 production of *Richard III*, Barrymore worked extensively with the great vocal coach Margaret Carrington to expand his limited range. Arthur Row, who played Henry VI in that production, recalls that, by opening night, his intensive, fiercely disciplined vocal study had resulted in "an English as near perfection as any human being can achieve" (89). In *Dinner at Eight*, Barrymore makes the maladroit ham actor, Renault, into someone who flounders vocally. The sounds he makes are awkwardly unfitted to his needs and the sense he hopes to convey. His rapid shifts of vocal character imply a frantic scramble among dwindling, mechanical options. All of his impersonations feel tentative, uncommitted. His vocal skittering deprives him of centeredness and its accompanying weight. He lacks a voice that can serve as home base on which he can stand and hold his ground after his bouts of conscious playacting.

As I noted previously, Barrymore's performances consistently announce his license to use theatrical devices—heightened physical and vocal expressiveness and nimble mask-to-mask transitions. In *Dinner at Eight* it is not Renault's overt theatricality that does him in but rather his poverty of stage resources, his lack of belief in what he acts out, and hence his lack of adaptability. Barrymore endows Renault with minimal panache, charismatic pathos, or self-awareness in his vain strutting and helpless fretting through the demeaning encounters he undergoes in the hour before his suicide. Apart from his time with Paula, Renault has no moments with any of his visitors where he rises above the indignities heaped upon him. The bellhop he sends out for alcohol, the room-service waiter he asks for a meal, his agent, his prospective theatrical producer, the hotel manager and his assistant who serve notice that Renault must promptly vacate his suite—all see through his transparent maneuvers. They treat his disarray and lordly, muddled pronouncements with embarrassed distaste or open scorn. He is an unmasked individual who still mistakenly believes he has command of his audience. He flails clumsily and obtusely, without a trace of ingenuity, through every theatrical gambit, especially the *act* of self-possession. An actor who has no vital artifice to transform himself, Renault stands stricken and rigid in the glare of the hideous real.

Barrymore is deeply drawn to characters who are pushed to a "poor bare forked animal" state of extremity. Renault most fascinates him when he has lost his last pathetic safeguards and defenses and is pinned, writhing, under a collective repudiating social gaze and then, finally, his own gaze. The latter proves so unendurable that Renault fabricates a suicide *role* to perform as his sole means of interrupting it. The prototypical scene of a Barrymore character held captive as all his dishonor and iniquity rush to the surface, for another's burning scrutiny, occurs in *Dr. Jekyll and Mr. Hyde* (1920). Sir George Carewe (Brandon Hurst), the father of Jekyll's fiancée, confronts the doctor in his laboratory, demanding to know the nature of his relationship with "a vile thing like Hyde." Jekyll's answer to Carewe's demand—which is accompanied by a threat to end his daughter's engagement—is an involuntary transformation into Hyde. What Barrymore emphasizes is not the terrible ignominy of Jekyll's exposure but the ebullient triumph of Hyde's release from concealment. Yet there is enough residual fear of discovery imbibed from Jekyll that Hyde pursues Carewe into the street and clubs him to death with his walking stick. Barrymore loves to consider the ugly remnant of an actor who has forfeited his role-playing privileges and must contend with the nullity of an evacuated self.

The Hyde ugliness has its counterpart in *Dinner at Eight* when Max Kane (Lee Tracy), Renault's agent, forces him to examine himself in a mirror. Kane taunts him with the assertion that he was never an actor. "You did have looks, but they're gone now . . . Just look in any mirror. They don't lie." As Kane's diatribe proceeds, Barrymore is framed in what appears to be a haunted mirror reflection. Renault can't quite manage to focus on himself in his drunken stupefaction but the viewer can. The face swims forward from a mirrored darkness. There are intimations of a former nobility in his features but stronger evidence of present decay. Barrymore bravely exhibits a fifty-one-year-old face that seems considerably older, plainly disclosing the effects

Figure 8.1 Barrymore's Larry Renault gazes absently at his ghostly mirror image in *Dinner at Eight* (George Cukor, MGM, 1933). Digital frame enlargement.

of Barrymore's epic intemperance. To paraphrase Max's capping insults: "Your looks are gone, Renault. Without them, you have no acting power, no ability to enchant or persuade, either in film or onstage." If this is the case for Renault, how do we see differently the Barrymore visage here, with its disintegrating aura? Is it a face shorn of secrets, revealed with the shock of a sudden Mr. Hyde eruption, a monstrous laying bare? Or is the face saying that all showing is a complicated intermingling of being and hiddenness? Barrymore allows himself to emerge defenseless in the guise of Renault, a man who cannot rise to the challenge of assessing his own image. Barrymore sees what Renault dares not confront, accepts the image verdict and absorbs the wound of visibility in Renault's place.

Renault's fleeting, second mirror contact transpires just after Max has made his merciless farewell speech and departed. When Renault is alone, he staggers back to the glass Max has forced him to peer into, in order to confirm the agent's verdict for himself. He is too clouded over with the effects of drink to absorb the stranger's image that unsettlingly tries to meet his gaze. The reflection at this point feels more solid to Renault than he does. He spots a crumpled telegram on the floor, that Max left behind, one which describes him as a "bit player," but stumbles and collapses full length on the carpet as he endeavors to retrieve it. The fall would appear to mark the moment when Renault touches bottom. Surely there is nothing more for him to suffer by way of mortification.

It is part of the brilliance of this segment of *Dinner at Eight* that Renault's downfall plays out in such a streamlined manner with the mad tempo of farce. The doorbell sounds and he must deal in short order with the contemptuous bellhop, returning the worthless valuables he has been sent to pawn for drink; and the hotel manager and assistant who politely evict him. When he is by himself once again, he reaches for the fireplace mantel and undergoes another head-bowing collapse. Barrymore grants Renault the release of a few piercing sobs—the only such untrammeled, despairing lament of Barrymore's film career—before he hits upon the idea of suicide. It is striking that the wails arise without any accompanying insight into how this dire predicament has come to pass. It is woe made more terrifying, perhaps, by including an element of blankness. Renault is like an animal thrashing in a trap whose meaning he cannot penetrate. Barrymore places Renault's hideous, piteous outcry at the threshold of a last theatrical recognition. Theater arrives like a ministering angel to light up a clear path to an ending, an ending that makes luminous sense, if he is enough of a performer to believe in it.

The decision to terminate his ghostly life having been made, he approaches the mirror a third time. He is finally able to examine his features closely and dispassionately, as an actor preparing to go onstage. Instead of emptiness, Renault contemplates an image of himself he can live with, fastidiously adjust, and die with. He smoothes back his hair, strokes his mustache like a stage gentleman attending a soiree, and dons his fancy dressing robe once more. Tie, shirtfront, and jacket must perfectly ratify the noble head that crowns them. It is not his suicide that Renault is readying himself for but, rather, a post-death discovery scene that can be properly staged, lit, and felt. If his death pose can be foreseen and controlled by an actor who correctly gauges the theatrical impact of its presentation, then the audience response to his work will also be under his control. Spectators will have no choice but to be moved. Those who dismissed Renault as "being through" will recognize that he now rests serenely above and beyond their degrading touch. Like the manifold hero of a Shakespearean tragedy, he at last breaks free of the petty appraisals and standards of measure applied by lesser men. Deathly stillness offers a powerful reply to the chaotic storms of life.

Before Renault turns on the gas, seats himself, and assumes his striking "great profile" pose for the hereafter, he recalls the photograph of Paula that might be found among his few effects and draw her needlessly into a scandal. He carries the photo to his window, high above the city streets, gazes at Paula's image fondly, then tears it into pieces and watches as they flutter down toward the pavement. The irony of his theatrical deportment is not unduly emphasized here. We may well be moved by his ability to recall the needs of another person as he hastily completes his preparations for quitting the earth. In part we are moved by Barrymore's honesty in his approach to this moment of sentiment. Renault tries to make his act of leave-taking from Paula count for something. Barrymore suggests that it counts for less than Renault thinks it does. Renault's appeal to the theatrical, even here, keeps his awareness blurred. He releases the torn fragments to the night air but they provide little ballast for the moment he strives to build. He is not, of course, the sole observer of this episode. The camera beholds him and Barrymore treats the camera as surrogate for Renault's imagined theater audience. His death scene, Renault is confident, will play to a larger, more real group of spectators. His only concern after his "backstage" mirror check is that the elements of the stage picture for his last appearance are right. He repositions the armchair near the opened fireplace gas jet and makes the standing lamp behind the chair function as a spotlight. He straightens his hair one more time as he seats himself and takes his stage position. Once he has placed his arms on the chair and leaned back, he can relax. As he does so, his arms slip from their resting place. The stage business he executes here removes for him the necessity of taking stock or bringing things mentally to a close in his own right. Instead, he has looked after the requirements of his stage character, ignoring all else. He is fully lost in his role.

George Cukor's camera announces itself at this juncture, dollying in for a close-up of Barrymore/Renault that restores his time-ravaged countenance to a semblance of its former radiant beauty, and acknowledges his classic profile. Renault's delusions are redeemed somehow by the camera's eagerness to partake of them and to declare "saving appearances" as cinema's highest priority. A bell chimes on the soundtrack as death quietly submits to theatrical reconfiguration.

CHAPTER 9

A Star is Dead: Barrymore's Anti-Christian Metaperformance

Kyle Stevens

Silent Hollywood stars who continued to play leading roles in the sound era were often said to have *survived* the industrial transition. Yet, in a way, every silent star died, for audiovisual performance is a different métier. We might more accurately say that those actors who persisted, such as John Barrymore, were resurrected for, and through, sound. In Barrymore's case, the studios could thank the heavens. The voice fitted the famous profile. He would not go the way of some of his peers, such as Douglas Fairbanks, Sr., or that other romantic leading John, John Gilbert (on Barrymore's transition to sound see Fowler 324). This may have seemed predictable at the time, given Barrymore's fame onstage, in a period when actors' voices were highly trained, and because he had even recorded Shakespearean soliloquies for Famous Records and RCA Victor. Nevertheless, there is no face more silent than a profile. Mouths are shut in profiles. We gaze at a profile; we do not expect it to speak. In fact, it is because of his history as respected Shakespearean stage actor, silent screen star, *and* sound movie star that Barrymore presents a unique case for thinking about the relation of stage to screen acting—and of silent acting to audiovisual acting—as Hollywood learned to speak. To do this, I shall focus on Barrymore's work with George Cukor, a director known for his keen interest in the institution of stardom, in such films as *What Price Hollywood?* (1932), *A Double Life* (1947), *The Actress* (1953), and *A Star is Born* (1954) (see Pomerance and Palmer; Phillips). Cukor's work with Barrymore is, I shall show, particular to Barrymore; yet, in that specificity, it critiques the way that foundational myths of Hollywood stardom comport with Christian attitudes toward the births and deaths of celestial beings.

Barrymore's legendary theatrical family was central to the proliferation of what "legitimate" stage actors *ought* to sound like as the New York theater scene developed into what we now think of as "Broadway"—meaning that middle classes began to have access to it in industrialized New York. In the 1920s, Barrymore made the transition from being the most celebrated American Shakespearean actor to the Hollywood screen where he became a household name as a dashing leading man. Then, as the 1930s inhaled and began to yawn, both Barrymore and the country entered a depression. The profile, that ancient emblem on coinage, and the figure for which Barrymore was most famous, no longer carried the same weight.

But even his theatrical pinnacle, his Hamlet, had been a qualified success. In a letter that multiple biographers claim was among Barrymore's most prized possessions, George Bernard Shaw penned a scathing missive, the particularities of which are interesting when thinking about Barrymore's move to sound cinema. Indeed, according to biographer Alma Power-Waters, "It had been said by several people that it was Shaw's adverse criticism of John's *Hamlet* that sent him to Hollywood" (143). Shaw writes:

> You saved, say an hour and a half on Shakespeare by the cutting, and filled it up with an interpolated drama of your own dumb show ... In modern shop plays, without characters or anything but the commonest dialogue, the actor has to supply everything but the mere story, getting in the psychology between the lines, and presenting in his own person the fascinating hero whom the author has been unable to create. He is not substituting something of his own for something of the author's; he is filling up a void and doing the author's work for him. (quoted in Kobler 202–3)

Shaw's objections indicate, first, that contemporary theater, the "modern shop play," foregrounded the storytelling labor of the actor quite as Hollywood did, and that such reliance was traditionally rare in theater. Second, Shaw suggests that Barrymore was already doing something like silent cinema acting—his "dumb show" that told the story beyond the script. Shaw thus advises Barrymore to "concentrate on acting rather than authorship" (142). Shaw's words may have propelled Barrymore to the dream factory but it was silent cinema's lack of dialogue that placed emphasis on his profile and, in turn, resulted in his being repeatedly cast in the role of romantic lead, a role he found tedious. Consequently, "No one welcomed the advent of the talkies more than Jack Barrymore" (Power-Waters 157). Barrymore starred in a quick succession of talkies (including his pet project *The Sea Beast*, an adaptation of *Moby-Dick*) as Hollywood rapidly standardized synchronized sound, with the negotiation of which Cukor was precisely imported to help (Fowler 235–8). And it was Cukor, I shall show, who made movies not just *starring* Barrymore but *about* him.

A BILL OF DIVORCEMENT

Cukor and Barrymore's association began before *A Bill of Divorcement* in 1932. Cukor is known as the quintessential Hollywood actor's director but this reputation was first gained not in Los Angeles but through directorial work in New York. Not only did Cukor worship Barrymore's talented sister Ethel but, as Cukor biographer Patrick McGilligan puts it, "No single person exerted a more subtle or far-reaching influence" on Cukor than director Arthur Hopkins who directed Barrymore in his Shakespearean triumphs (20). Above all, Hopkins was known for "good taste, the well-knit play, the introduction of new talent, and—something revolutionary for the times—a laid-back approach to steering the performers toward truth in acting" (19). Cukor developed this desire to nurture and protect actors and, thus, despite his relative lack of big theatrical hits, screen stars such as Helen Hayes and Dorothy Gish (in her 1928 Broadway debut) insisted upon having Cukor guide them. (His homosexuality may also have appealed to women who wanted to focus on their work.)

Owing to both his attractiveness to actors and the preponderance of dialogue in the plays he had helmed on Broadway, Paramount took note and contracted Cukor. He was named a "dialogue director," a kind of apprentice to, and safety net for, more experienced directors "who might be unsure of dialogue situations or uneasy about the newfangled technology" (McGilligan 60). Dialogue directors' primary task was to facilitate the capture of dialogue that sounded "natural" as well as "to polish the enunciations and calm the quavering voices, while learning the ropes of the business" (60). One of Cukor's first feature films (codirected with Cyril Gardner in 1930) was *The Royal Family of Broadway*, a satire of the Barrymore dynasty penned by Edna Ferber and George S. Kaufman.

The following year, Cukor would make his first film with John Barrymore himself. *A Bill of Divorcement* (1932) was based on a play of the same name—that had been a hit a decade earlier—by Clemence Dane (the nom de plume of Winifred Ashton who also wrote novels, such as *Enter Sir John*, which would be adapted by Alfred Hitchcock into *Murder!* [1930], and the screenplay for Greta Garbo's *Anna Karenina* [1935]). The story is simple but deep. Meg Fairfield (Billie Burke) is about to remarry after divorcing her husband, Hilary (Barrymore), who has been in an insane asylum for years since the First World War. Their daughter, Sidney (Katharine Hepburn), is also getting engaged, to a man with whom she is passionately in love and wants to have many children. Hilary's escape from the asylum and reappearance disrupt these women's plans. After learning that the propensity towards insanity is hereditary, Sidney breaks it off with her beau, and the film concludes with father and daughter isolating themselves, pledging to care for each other in words indisputably marital—till death or insanity will them part (the end fulfills an incestuous undercurrent evident since Hilary initially mistakes Sidney for Meg). Reminiscent of Henrik Ibsen's *Ghosts* (1882), *A Bill of Divorcement*'s narrative thus turns upon Barrymore's return, though now the sins of the father are visited upon a daughter rather than, as with Ibsen, a son.

Critics unanimously heralded the birth of a new star in Hepburn and, looking back, it smarts to see that less than a decade after *Hamlet*, Barrymore was considered over the hill: "By this time in his life, he had a slightly tarnished air, with a slur, a paunch, and a milky complexion" (McGilligan 84). Still, Barrymore fared well: "Many critics agreed that he was given an opportunity for the most magnificent performance of his movie career, and made the most of it" (Power-Waters 181). *Variety* said, "John Barrymore distinguishes himself anew in the role of the unhappy Hilary, a part far from his accustomed range" ("A Bill of Divorcement" [December 31, 1931], online at http://variety.com/1931/film/people-news/a-bill-of-divorcement-1200410643),
and *The New York Times* concurred: "[Hilary] is a character study worthy of Mr. Barrymore's talent and his performance is incisive and telling, and never for an instant is he guilty of extravagant histrionics" (Mordaunt Hall, "John Barrymore, Billie Burke and Katharine Hepburn in a Film of a Clemence Dane Play" [October 3, 1932], 15). Even Ethel admitted, "You're very good in this one—you're not an ass" (Power-Waters 182).

A Bill of Divorcement has since received little attention. Michael DeAngelis reads it as concerned with the idea of family and the doubling that occurs between Sidney and Meg, or between the past and present Hilarys, "as when Hilary protests, 'I wasn't myself then,' emphasizing the sharp contrast between [his] two 'selves'" (96). DeAngelis's reading highlights a crucial aspect of Cukor's signature: scenarios that allow for what James Naremore calls metaperformance, and which are helpful for understanding all of Cukor and Barrymore's work. Not simply a kind of performative reflexivity (where a performance calls attention to itself as a performance), metaperformance occurs when actors "signal that they *act persons who are acting*" (72). This effect is central to Hollywood style for Naremore: "We could say that realist acting amounts to an effort at sustaining opposing attitudes toward the self, on the one hand trying to create the illusion of unified, individualized personality, but on the other suggesting that character is subject to division or dissolution into a variety of social roles" (72).

Sidney metaperforms a change of heart when she breaks off her engagement and Hilary similarly metaperforms madness so that she can remarry in good conscience. That both deploy the same strategy prepares us for their union at the narrative's end. Such moments afford Barrymore the opportunity to create the depth for which he was praised but the meta-level aspect also encourages us to think about Barrymore's performance in a different register. *A Bill of Divorcement* has already drawn attention to Barrymore's persona: the

Figure 9.1 In *A Bill of Divorcement*, viewers meet Hilary through a portrait that showcases the profile for which John Barrymore was famous during his silent-screen days (George Cukor, RKO, 1932). Digital frame enlargement.

film is only seventy minutes long and he is not introduced until almost twelve minutes in—and even then only via a photograph. This image is not of Hilary as we shall soon meet him but of the younger Hilary. Rather, it is precisely an image of the youthful Barrymore as silent cinema audiences knew him: dashing, handsome, with heavy eye shadow, and, most crucially, in profile. When Barrymore finally enters the picture, he does so in emphatic silence. Hilary creeps into Meg's domain and, for almost two minutes, we watch him reorient himself to his former home, wandering, touching things. What makes this moment even more reflexive of Barrymore as a former silent actor entering the world of sound cinema is the fact that Sidney/Hepburn (home alone while the others attend church) watches him. She occupies the position of cinematic spectator—seeing unseen, as Stanley Cavell described it—and therefore Hilary that of the cinematic image.

If this meditation on Barrymore/Hilary's rebirth from silent profile to sonic father suggests Christian iconography, that is an association heightened in context, as Christian faith is heralded as a sticking point for familial happiness in the film's opening scene. The story takes place on Christmas day, the most widely acknowledged Christian holiday, despite Easter being the commemoration of the religion's central event. Sidney has given her aunt Hester (Elizabeth Patterson) a scandalous cigarette case as a rebuke for what she rightly anticipates receiving in exchange: a prayer book. When chided for her insolence, Sidney defends herself: "It's beneath my principles to kneel down and say I'm a sinner. I'm not miserable and I'm not a sinner." It was surely shocking at the time that the character declares this after spending the night with her boyfriend.

This religious discussion builds the context for Hilary's return to be consistently and explicitly construed as a resurrection. When, in the beginning, the devout Hester chastens his now ex-wife and daughter for not appreciating that "Hilary is master of this house," Sidney protests—given that she had never even met him—that it is as though he is dead and has been dead for quite some time. Later, when Hilary describes his time in the asylum as hell, Sidney very clearly states: "My poor father. You died." There is a twist in the allegory, though. The potential savior returns but no one is saved. In fact, the father's miraculous revival brings only tragedy, unhappiness, and the demand for self-sacrifice.

Trying to describe his experience while institutionalized, Hilary protests: "I was always really sane, but the face was turned away." In response to the question of what face, he replies, "The face of God." If Hilary could metaphorically see God's face turned away, we might suppose that he saw it in profile and that this profile caused him to feel abandoned and unhinged. Hilary takes on Christian iconography as both father (of the family) and Jesus, away from whose face God turned at the moment of crucifixion. We might see Barrymore in this doubling light, too: famous both as son (of the Barrymore clan) and as star (a being worthy of worship). And when Sidney, worried about the hereditary nature of his insanity, now a metaphor for original sin, asks, "It's in our blood, isn't it?," we might be reminded of the Barrymore family's apparently obsessive need to perform.

The value attached to the facial schema described by Hilary, whereby healing, or sanity, comes from frontality, from seeing an expressive face, is echoed in the film's form. And if we extend the affiliation between Hilary's and Barrymore's pasts established by the photograph, we might see the film as making a case for Barrymore as a sound actor. When madness threatens to overtake Hilary again, and when he decides to perform madness, Cukor's camera concentrates on Barrymore/Hilary's profile (perhaps reminding us of the kind of histrionic gestures often associated with silent screen acting [for more on the history of this association see Pearson]). The Hilary of the profile must be packed away, contained in the past. It is not the true Hilary. The true Hilary will conclude the film by playing his concerto with Sidney at his side, facing forward. That Hilary is called upon to metaperform in order for the film to reach its conclusion, and that Hilary's and Sidney's actions are offered up as noble, suggest that acting is the way to resolve problems, to introduce truths, however painful, into the world. It is not enough for Hilary simply to appear, even after so many years away. He must perform. Again, following the parallels drawn between Hilary and Barrymore, the film tacitly argues for

Barrymore's resurrection from silent to sound star, which it offers as an ideological shift. While the younger, silent profile may have been sufficient then, it is insufficient now. Now, Barrymore will truly perform. He will be sonic, making virtuosic music with his instrument as Hilary does with his.

DINNER AT EIGHT

Cukor and Barrymore's next collaboration, *Dinner at Eight* (1933), was a high-profile, star-studded ensemble picture also based on a hit Broadway play, this one by George Kaufman and Edna Ferber, and adapted for the screen by Herman J. Mankiewicz and Frances Marion, with additional dialogue by Donald Ogden Stewart. The production—completed in twenty-eight days—was as swift as its dialogue and Cukor was delighted to work at the prestigious MGM studio. (One wonders if the moral turpitude clause installed in Cukor's contract because of his closeted sexuality made the director more sympathetic to the studio's suspicion of Barrymore's alleged bad behavior.) Dinner happens at eight but the story essentially follows four in operatic structure: Billie Burke, whose voice is famously high-pitched, plays Millicent Jordan, something of a soprano planning dinner; her husband Oliver (Lionel Barrymore) provides a kind of bass line; Jean Harlow, an alto even when baby-talking, is Kitty, fabulously parvenu wife to a blustering business thug; and John Barrymore takes up the tenor line as Larry Renault, once-famous actor of stage and screen whose career has dissolved. Unable to mount a comeback, he commits suicide. Sympathizing with Cukor's task of corralling a stellar cast, Mankiewicz reportedly told the director, "Nothing can compare with your problem in getting Jack Barrymore to understand the part of a fading matinee idol" (McGilligan 95). How wrong "Mank" was. Not only was Barrymore "cooperative and good-natured with Cukor, his sister's staunch friend," but he regarded Cukor as a coconspirator. (George Bernard Shaw visited the set and Barrymore convinced Cukor to let him "dumb it up" as a joke on the visitor.)

In the interim between *A Bill of Divorcement* and *Dinner at Eight*, Cukor made *What Price Hollywood?* (1932), a film that explicitly considered the art of acting and how that stood in tension with Hollywood's commercial interests. Though "Larry" is a supporting role in *Dinner at Eight*, it is a vital one—it is he alone who does not make it to dinner—and one that allows Cukor and Barrymore to continue to comment on the difficulty of balancing living and performing, even if the scales are only ever in one's mind. In this way, Larry is central to the film's preoccupation with the theatricality of life, and the relation of theater and film which, at the time, was largely conceptualized as a division of dialogue—of the visual versus the verbal, with gesture as the overlap—and increasingly construed as a difference between pageantry and realism. Going into these concerns in relation to the film would take us too far afield from a focus on Barrymore, but even a glimpse at the film's conclusion, in which the cast/family finally goes into dinner marked by a set designed to resemble a proscenium, meant as an image of contentedness, testifies to its preoccupation with the idea that the stage may be both all the world and all its aspiration.

The reflexivity of Barrymore's character is impossible to miss. He is a previously respected actor struggling to maintain respectability and also an alcoholic with a couple of ex-wives. This is precisely the information that comprised Barrymore's star persona at the time. Indeed, Barrymore reportedly told Cukor that "he was playing [Larry] as a combination of his father-in-law (Broadway matinée idol Maurice Costello), his brother-in-law (Lowell Sherman, married to Helene Costello, sister of one of Barrymore's wives), and himself" (McGilligan 96). Moreover, at one point in his first scene—and not briefly—Barrymore speaks directly to the camera. We experience ourselves encountering him. The gesture recalls his ability to take over works to which Shaw objected but it also makes the moment feel theatrical as well as cinematic (because the convention of parabasis—giving asides to the audience—is endemic to the theater), aiding Cukor in this project of finding common ground between the two art forms.

Even before Larry is introduced, the film encourages us to acknowledge the overlap between him and Barrymore. Millicent has lost a dinner guest, and her friend suggests, "Why don't you get an actor . . . a movie star! Aren't there any movie stars around?" Millicent immediately thinks of Larry, recalling meeting him years before, when women fought over him on the beach while "he was wearing even less than the girls!" Her friend reports that "he isn't so hot since the talkies," but admits she'll "say this for him: in his photographs he has the most heavenly profile." Cukor then cuts to Barrymore on the telephone, Larry in perfect profile.

We begin to learn of Larry's problem. After trying to end his romantic entanglement with the Jordan's daughter Paula (Madge Evans)—"the first decent thing [he's] ever done in [his] life"—his agent, Max Kane (Lee Tracy), enters, asking "How's the great profile today?" before getting around to informing Larry that the offer of a lead role in a play has been rescinded because of a change in producership (but the subtext is clear: Larry's questionable talent and age are to blame). Larry does not want to play a bit part, of course; he wants the lead. Yet, if this seems too insurmountable a problem, more than his vanity prevents him from being happy. He wants to be an actor in the artistic sense, one who can give range to expression and interpret a substantial role, but reconciling ambition and ability is never an easy feat and is perhaps particularly difficult in a profession upon whose tools one relies every day for self-expression.

Barrymore emphasizes the vocal register throughout this scene. Having just been privy to his metaperformance with Paula, we now hear the difference between the sort of verbal irony involved there and the more general irony of performing in an actorly sense: we hear the difference between his pretending to want to break it off with Paula, and playacting. Informed that he's been usurped by an English actor, Larry suddenly puts on a broad English accent to proclaim, "I can be English, English as anybody." And when he discovers the identity of the new producer, Larry sneers, "They tell me he does those high-brow plays—Ibsen." He half closes his eyes and says, "I want the moon, mother," in a euphonious tone and smooth cadence that demonstrate that this is how Larry believes actors in Ibsen plays speak, and that this is the sort of thing they say. Barrymore's character spontaneously produces "a scene which never existed and which he invented all the way. It was all so obvious—he had never heard of Ibsen," Cukor fondly remembered years later, but "he went on, not quite knowing what the hell he was saying. But he did it all with the greatest truth" (Long 24).

Cukor also sings Barrymore's praises in examples that emphasize the actor's vocal acumen and ability to create metaperformative depth, as when Larry speaks "in a rather actorish way" at one moment and then tries to be tough with the bellhop when he says, "I gotta have a drink, see?" in the next. Cukor even recalls Barrymore changing dialogue to shape his characterization:

> If you remember he was in his hotel room talking on the phone. This society woman was asking him to come to dinner and he was saying, "Yes, I'd love to come." Well, Jack asked me if he could put something in and I told him he could do whatever he liked. So he added something to the line and it came out: "Yes, I'd love to come, dear lady." This little addition painted the whole character: a rather cheapish actor, slightly old-fashioned. He created all sorts of wonderful *nuances* that way. (Long 24)

Barrymore's vocal agility is crucial to the pathos of his first scene, again making the case for Barrymore as a sound screen actor. We hear—if we do not see—that Larry does not have to be washed up. We believe his situation is a predicament because we hear—if we do not see—his capability. There is a musical part of Barrymore—a part that was not useful to him as the "great profile"—that does not display the wear of aging. The optimism suggested by the upspeak when Larry role-plays as an actor contrasts with the level melody of his speech when the mask falls, and even more so with the downward inflection when he advises Paula to leave him. One senses the shame Larry feels proffering himself as an advisor when he is himself barely hanging on yet, at the same time, a man who feels compelled to express. Even if his expression is futile, he can try to be a good guy but, in taking on that mantle, he becomes aware of how uncomfortable it is, how he never broke it in. Or, to take one last example of Larry's vocal dexterity, his mocking tone and bland Ibsenian words suggest his attitudes toward highbrow theater, even as he aspires to it. Larry is thus caught between wanting to be an artist and not wanting to be elitist, a problem one might also say that Hollywood faced in its early decades.

In Barrymore/Larry's second (and only other) scene, it becomes clear that he would fare better if people listened to his voice rather than looked at his body. Larry must convince others to see past his reputation as a washed-up silent-movie actor—past his body—and so perhaps his suicide, his vanquishing of his own body, is already on the horizon. In this scene Max, fed up with Larry's drunken resistance, unloads the truth on him: "You never were an actor. You did have looks, but they're gone now. You don't have to take my word for it. Just look in any mirror; they don't lie." Max enjoins Larry to gaze at his "pouches and creases" in the looking glass next to them but Larry remains silent, still, and in perfect profile, both in the room and in reflection. We feel the indignities of aging, reminded, too, of Barrymore's former glory. Max exits, telling him, "You're a corpse and you don't know it. Go get yourself buried." Barrymore makes Larry wince at "corpse," signaling that Larry may be discovering the desire to kill himself in this moment.

Larry drunkenly approaches the mirror and gazes at himself, silent, before collapsing in despair at the sight. After being informed he must leave the hotel in which he lives (because of lack of funds), Larry decides to poison himself via the gas fireplace. In a scene that's several minutes long, and without speech, he goes about the necessary business: sealing the room, tearing up photographs, and so forth. He dresses in front of the mirror and arranges the mise-en-scène, lighting his body just so. Cukor tells us:

> In the scene where he was going to kill himself one had to feel that he wanted to die beautifully, like Greta Garbo. We started the scene, he crossed the room to plug up the chimney and turn on the gas . . . and I said to him: "Jack, he should not even be able to commit suicide. He has always bungled everything and now some awful indignity should happen to him." Then Jack walked across the room again . . . right in the middle of the carpet was a stool and he tripped on it, went spilling all over the floor—an awful middleaged, ungraceful sprawl . . . the touch was just right. So unconventional. (Long 24)

As Larry drifts off, and then away, it is in perfectly lit profile. If *A Bill of Divorcement* allegorizes Barrymore's transition from silent to sound star,

Figure 9.2 Larry Renault carefully organizes the setting and lighting for his final repose in *Dinner at Eight* (George Cukor, MGM, 1933). Digital frame enlargement.

Dinner at Eight indicates the tragedy of the loss of the glory of his silent days, the profile days. If a star cannot make a comeback—cannot resurrect himself—he is already dead.

ROMEO AND JULIET

Barrymore's third and final collaboration with Cukor was *Romeo and Juliet*, a prestigious production on which producer Irving Thalberg—whose wife Norma Shearer plays Juliet—seemingly spared no expense. Cukor had meticulous researchers, twelve hundred cast members, and script conferences supervised by Harvard professor and Elizabethan theater authority John Tucker Murray. Cornell professor William Strunk oversaw rehearsal and filming (McGilligan 106). Despite this surge in budget and scope, *Romeo and Juliet* remains a Cukor film. It shares common ground with *A Bill of Divorcement* and *Dinner at Eight*: stories of family and loyalty, generational divides, and an overt concern with the relation of film and theater performance. It opens with a series of moving portraits of the cast and then features a tapestry that dissolves into the stage world and thence into the diegetic world.

Figure 9.3 Costume, lighting, and blocking collude to picture Barrymore/Mercutio as a star within the world of *Romeo and Juliet* (George Cukor, MGM, 1936). Digital frame enlargement.

This sequence marks the film as being not about history but about the history of theater and theatricality.

Barrymore is Mercutio, Romeo's most dramatic and sympathetic friend: again a secondary character whose tragic death colors the lives of the main players. Mercutio is the "star" in this Elizabethan world, the one whom all the passersby hail and admire. We might see his casting as prioritizing the voice, given that, at fifty-four, Barrymore's body was indisputably too old for the role (even if Shearer was in her mid thirties as Juliet and Leslie Howard in his early forties as Romeo). Mercutio enters singing and, when he speaks, Barrymore makes clear that there is irony embedded in Mercutio's every word.

This is a jocular cad, yet mercurial, able to switch to a sincere tone in a flash. In this way, Barrymore manages to create a sense that Mercutio is metaperforming, despite the action not being scripted as such. We know he's thinking, playing games with those he encounters. Barrymore's performance brings the character in line with much of Shakespeare's themes of passing and verbal identity—"Tis by his voice he should be a Montague," Tybalt famously declares, after all. At the level of performance, Cukor translates into American idiom the British accents with which Shakespeare was, and is, typically performed for an American audience, as when, for example, a bumpkin character sounds as though he hails from the southeast of the United States. Within this verbal system, and contrary to the other actors' plodding delivery, Barrymore's lilting, agile expressions stand out. The levity he brings to Mercutio—through which is created a layer of ironic metaperformance—is nowhere more apparent than in his death scene. Mercutio tosses off "A plague on both your houses" as no more than an empty cliché, without malice, something to say when one wants the last word and can divine no riposte. Barrymore's Mercutio welcomes death, as though it suits him, as though he was already spirit. This is a light performance, yet one at which only a man in a dark place could have arrived.

Perhaps it may not surprise us to know, then, that Barrymore was in personal decline. Reminiscent of Hilary, he was forced to reside in a sanitarium near MGM during filming. According to McGilligan, Cukor not only cared for Barrymore but was bothered by the fading of the man's stardom:

> Cukor insisted, over the years, that Barrymore stayed "absolutely on the wagon" throughout the picture, but the actor was nonetheless difficult to handle, and held up photography with his gaga antics. At times, Thalberg had to be summoned to the set to intimidate Barrymore into speaking the lines as written. Cukor did not give up on Barrymore. The downfall of a great artist always aroused the samaritan in him. Indeed, the director considered Barrymore for a part in *Camille*; and within a year, partly on Cukor's advice, Selznick would cast Barrymore—and fire him—as the lead in William Wellman's version of *A Star is Born*. (106–7)

THE AMERICANNESS OF STARDOM

Cukor once unequivocally praised Barrymore, saying that "his ability to project himself into a dramatic character, and then let that character completely transcend his own individuality; and then, to interpret it, down to the last fine shade of mood—that genius is possessed by no other actor on the screen today" (Power-Waters 197). There is in Cukor's comment the notion, familiar to actors, that performing involves a kind of death, the self-erasure of individuality. But, of course, the transcendence is not complete. Given that stardom took hold of the United States during its most fervently Christian decades, it is difficult to divorce "the movie star" from the Christian idea of God, of a God that is both Jesus and Holy Father, and whose claim to the status of deity rests upon a metaphysical mix of myth and mortal.

Across their three collaborations, Barrymore and Cukor think about the danger of mistaking stardom for actorly talent, and the danger of looking to movie stars—until then a silent film phenomenon—as godlike saviors, figures in whose image we fancy we might make and remake ourselves. Also present across these films is a concern with death and a concern with the possibility of living on. These concerns are related. Stardom promises life after death, a kind of immortality, yet stars are also *born*, as dramatized in Cukor's famous 1954 film. In this respect we might recognize an affinity with the nation that gave rise to this kind of fame. In an oft-quoted passage, Stanley Cavell notes that, unlike European nations that enjoy deep ties to the past, the myth Americans peddle is that, even as America acts invincible, it was *discovered*, and, "since it had a birth, it may die. It feels mortal" (345). Hollywood stardom is usually dated back to 1910 when Carl Laemmle (who would later cofound Universal Studios) placed false notices of the tragic death of "the Biograph girl" in a streetcar accident. When it was revealed that she was alive and well, the nation rejoiced and suddenly everyone knew the name of Florence Lawrence. Hence, Hollywood stardom has always had a messianic Christian flavor which is also endemic to the religious fervor of the United States.

Stars are not just Christlike for having supernatural origins. They are actors who, in continuing to work, are reborn in successive stories. It is essential that we know that stars existed in a historical present—knowledge inherently promised in a medium such as film. When we revisit their performances onscreen, experiencing them as alive, we experience a resurrection, a seeming perpetual reenactment of the Christ myth. But stars also exist in our imagined future. They promise more. We trust that they will appear in more movies, give us more lives, precisely because they are stars. In turn, we expect that their own lives will continue—and so can our idolization of them. Barrymore and Cukor raise the curtain on this ideology. In *A Bill of Divorcement*, it's the *returned* being who matters. Coming back from death, Hilary becomes *more* real, no longer an ideal image, and, in the process, damns Sidney to unhappiness. In *Dinner at Eight*, Larry achieves not romantic immortality through dying but immortal pity. In *Romeo and Juliet*, however, Mercutio/Barrymore is not attached to life and, instead, welcomes death. In this way, Barrymore and Cukor use the example of Barrymore—once advertised by Warner Bros. as the world's greatest living actor—to discourage identifying stars by their promise of a glorious future still to come. The films tell stories that metaphorically suggest this everlasting ongoer may not go on and, even if he should return, his subsistence would clearly not be good.

Together in Hollywood, Barrymore and Cukor offer up the radical notion that death may be simply death.

CHAPTER 10

Handling Time: The Passing of Tradition in *A Bill of Divorcement*

Daniel Varndell

> Certainly I believe that ghosts communicate with those who stay on earth. And when I come back, don't stand and gape. Be hospitable to my shade.
>
> *John Barrymore*

"Setting down words to explain Jack Barrymore," his brother Lionel pointed out, "is like seeking the mystery of Hamlet himself in the monosyllables of basic English" (Kobler, x). Erik Erikson sees the temptation to solve the riddle of Hamlet's "inscrutable nature" as a pointless endeavor if for no other reason than because Hamlet's inscrutability *is* his nature. Far from explaining his "condition," Erikson stages the riddle of identity crisis in the play as one that hinges on Hamlet's always being "on the verge of slipping into the state [of madness] he pretends" (*Identity* 236–7). Unlike the foolish critic, an actor would never attempt to "explain." Rather, there is, writes Steven Berkoff, a sense that every actor who plays him must take the conundrum of Hamlet "within his own breast," where "to touch these words is to set alight a small flame within himself," such that "when you play Hamlet, you play yourself and play the instrument which is you" (vii–viii).

As an "instrument," John "Jack" Barrymore communicated something vital in his Hamlet. While most contemporary reviews were positive, the overwhelming feeling was that—irrespective of the shortcomings of these nascent performances—his was not just a Hamlet for the new generation but one heralding a historic "turn" in theatrical performance. As Ludwig Lewisohn noted in 1922, Barrymore spoke to his generation in a way they had not been spoken to before. "His bearing and gestures have the restrained but intense expressiveness of the bearing of modern men who live with their nerves and woes in narrow rooms" (Mills 190). Barrymore, Stark Young remarked (also about the 1922 performance), "seemed to gather together in himself all the Hamlets of his generation, to simplify and direct everyone's theory of the part. To me his Hamlet was the most satisfying that I have ever seen, not yet as a finished creation, but a foundation, a continuous outline." At its best, Young said, it was like "a fundamental pattern so simple and so revealing that it appeared to be mystical; and so direct and strong that it restored to the dramatic scene its primary truth and magnificence" (Wells 195, 200). After Barrymore's death twenty years later, his friend Arthur Hopkins said of his Hamlet that it was like watching "the unfolding of the pattern" in which "the unseen and unheard was being communicated" (Fowler 208). Here is a curiously paradoxical image: an unfolding pattern revealing a secret to be passed down through the generations, and yet, since inscrutable, communicating only something of style not content.

In writings on Barrymore's cinematic work, however, opinions vary. William K. Everson notes that from his 1921 performance in *The Lotus Eater*, Barrymore was "now beginning to cultivate a deliberate classic–romantic image" (173). In contrast, David Thomson avers that Barrymore is "an actor who cannot believe in acting in the way that his romantic audience did. None of his own weapons—handsomeness, rhetoric or flamboyance—actually convinces him. Acting becomes a trap and 'John Barrymore' an onerous part that he alternately mocks and falls short of." Only a single masterpiece (*Twentieth Century*) in his *oeuvre*, Thomson concedes, "illustrates the helpless pursuit of himself" (28). While David Shipman describes John Barrymore as having been "regarded, quite simply, as a great actor," he frames this comment with the opening statement that

> the legacy of the Barrymores, John, Lionel and Ethel, is, as it is available to us today, for the most part singularly unimpressive. They have a golden name. Surviving colleagues still speak of them with awe, and the raves they had in their lifetimes are sometimes called into play. Their work in the theatre may have been magnificent, but on the evidence of their screen work, there is little to be said for any of them. True, they were past their prime. (41–2)

Such barbs are not uncommon in critical approaches to Barrymore's life and work in film. Indeed, there is a sense in criticism on Barrymore that his cinematic work never achieved the quality in technique that his theatrical performances eventually did, that "the unfolding of the pattern" had ceased.

But, given that the only enduring "evidence" of his talent is his screen work, it is little wonder he is often discussed in oxymoronic terms. From the legend of his Richard III and Hamlet to the embarrassing self-parody of his late work, one can run the gamut of critical opinion from "great actor" to "great ham," from the "crown prince" to the "clown prince." The films he made in the early 1930s, however, are justly receiving critical attention. This chapter proposes to look at a film of the mature Barrymore and at what might be called his "unspeakable" side, a side not reducible to the thoughtless epithets—"the greatest Hamlet of his generation" and "a failure and a drunk"—but which aims at our very thinking of him as a classic actor. It focuses on a man who is telling us something that never quite passes across his lips. The chapter considers this "something" in his style in terms of the passing of tradition and, in particular, the communication of secrets from one generation to the next. It will take as its case study George Cukor's *A Bill of Divorcement* (1932), a film in which Barrymore plays a man who, after fifteen years in an insane asylum, returns home to find that his daughter does not recognize him and the woman he loves has divorced him. Barrymore's performance as Hilary Fairfield was rumored to have been admired by David O. Selznick as "the greatest all-time performance on any motion-picture screen" (quoted in Fowler 413) and yet *Bill* is one of his critically neglected films. The story is about filial responsibility and what it means to be a faithful husband and father, to sacrifice one's own needs for the good of others while avoiding the debt of gratitude such deeds beget.

A GREAT SEPARATION

Adapted from the play by Clemence Dane, *A Bill of Divorcement* introduces Barrymore as a war veteran who returns home on Christmas Day, having spent fifteen years in an insane asylum following a mental collapse. When he walks through the door, Hilary's experience of home is one of Freudian *Unheimlichkeit*: the clock has been misplaced and the sofas reupholstered but it is when he gazes into the face of the daughter he never knew that he suffers the greatest shock. Mistaking Sidney (Katharine Hepburn, in her debut) for his estranged wife, Hilary finds himself gently corrected, "I think I'm your daughter." Hilary soon brings Sidney up to speed on his "miraculous" recovery. She, however, cannot bring herself to inform him that his wife, Margaret (Billie Burke), has taken advantage of the "bill of divorcement" passed in the 1920s to allow madness as legitimate grounds for divorce, nor that she is now betrothed to a new man. Hilary intrudes, then, on a family filled with the promise of new (if not, for him, happy) beginnings. Like her mother, Sidney is also intending to marry in the New Year, having accepted a proposal from her beau, Kit (David Manners), with whom she intends to emigrate to Canada. Youthfulness and vitality are in the air as with her new lover, Gray (Paul Cavanagh), Margaret reflects on her changing fortunes: "I feel young with you," says she, adding, "it's wonderful to be free. To have a burden lifted from one's shoulders." Margaret's levity is only marginally affected by aunt Hester (Elizabeth Patterson) who does her best to weigh down the festive frivolity with constant reminders that "Hilary is the master of this house and no one else, your husband Hilary." So, when the master of the house returns, it is as a revenant of a past both burdensome and unfinished. This is heralded by two musical motifs. The first, an unfinished sonata Hilary was composing before the war which Sidney wistfully plays while dreaming that her father will one day return to complete it. The second, church bells ringing, a sound which signals at first the advent of a new marriage but soon transforms into a memento mori of the broken vow (". . . in *sickness* and in health"). In Dane's play, the tradition of the church bells is interrupted by modernity with the ringing of the telephone when Hilary, calling ahead to announce his arrival, has his message misconstrued as a wrong number. One is reminded of the saying that one cannot unring a bell, be it the wedding bell announcing the union of husband and wife or the phone call that echoes, almost knell-like, from the past.

When Margaret eventually informs Hilary that she has divorced him, he threatens an immediate relapse, giving rise to the key moral dilemma of the story. Is it Margaret's duty to give up on new love's promise in order to honor an old marital vow and guide Hilary through his convalescence? Or, does she owe it to herself not to abandon the spirit of her own life with Gray but at the cost of sacrificing Hilary to a living death back in the asylum? "Why, face it, man! One of you must suffer," Hilary's doctor impatiently suggests to the family gathered in the drawing room. "Which is it to be? The whole or the maimed? The healthy woman with her life before her, or the man whose children ought never to have been born?" This last point stills the room. The doctor confirms what Aunt Hester had already implied, that the hereditary insanity was made manifest by shell shock. The historical has prompted the hereditary. (See also Michael Hammond's chapter in this volume.) Hence, Sidney is similarly genetically predisposed; her willful temperament suddenly falls under scrutiny because madness threatens to recast her adolescent rebelliousness as emerging hysteria.[1]

In Dane's play, the sacrifice will be Sidney's alone. Having intentionally driven Kit into the arms of a rival, she commands her mother to go off with Gray, declaring that she will care for Hilary instead. Here is an aspect of what Bruno Bettelheim calls the "conflict of generations" arising because of a "parent who sees his child's main task in life as the duty to execute his will or to justify his existence (which is different from a parent's devotion to an unfinished labor which the child, on his own, later wishes to bring to fruition)." In such situations, "the son who does not revolt when he is expected to devote his life only or mainly to achieving what the parent could not, usually perishes as Hamlet did" (83). While Sidney does not perish as such, she is left emotionally isolated—"I pray you get your punishment" (Dane 90), Hester maligns, calling Sidney "hard as nails" after blaming her for Margaret's departure. Hilary simply despairs: "Gone. Everything gone," he moans; "I'm not gone," Sidney meekly replies. "I don't see ahead. I don't see what's to become of me. There's no-one," he laments further (echoing Lear); "There's me," Sidney tries to remind him. Despite snatching the family brand from burning, Dane's Sidney ends the play with the distinguishing line between madness and pretense vanishing fast. Desperate to win her father's affection, she cries out, "Father, don't believe her! I'm not hard. I'm not hard" (92). The playwright's implication is that Sidney is doomed to spinsterhood (like Hester!); her cake, one fears, will remain dough.

Rebecca S. Cameron points out that "Dane, in effect, transfers the agency in the decision to divorce from the wife to the daughter, who decides that it is her ethical responsibility to break off her own 'unhealthy' marriage," meaning that, despite her final collapse, Sidney "remains the strongest character in the play" (482–3). The only hope for Sidney's childless future appears in the final lines which indicate an initial motion towards paternal love, as "*His arm goes round her with a gesture, awkward, timid, yet fatherly*" (92). It is an uncertain bond, not of marriage but of kinship through heredity. The reinforcement of divorce and ostensible rejection of marriage end the play with the "stifling irony," as Stanley Cavell put it, of the melodrama rather than the "educative conversation" of the remarriage comedy ("The Good of Film" 342). With a burst of sentimentalism, however, and a change in key in this final act, the film departs from its source material in a crucial, inspiring, way.

While Cukor's Sidney likewise drives Kit away for fear of propagating her corrupted genes, it is Hilary in the film who, by feigning madness in front of Sidney, prompts her to send Margaret off with Gray. Returning to her father, Sidney recognizes his act as he quietly observes that perhaps he and Margaret were never meant to be. "Poor Meg," he laments, "I've never really known her at all." It is on this observation that the film departs from its source for, without it, the divorce might be viewed somewhat cynically. Dane's point, Cameron reflects, is that whatever the cost to Hilary, Margaret's right to divorce is affirmed not only because of his madness but also because of the exceptional conditions of war in the shadow of which their vows were taken. "It was the feeling in the air," Margaret explains to Sidney. "They say the smell of blood sends horses crazy. That was the feel. One did mad things" (Dane 10). The marriage contract has not been violated because—as Cameron notes—"it was never valid in the first place" (481). This suggests a nuanced definition of a marriage, one which, as Cavell puts it, is no more legitimized or ratified by a church than by the bell that rings in its honor. Marriage, Cavell writes, "is a diurnal devotedness that involves friendship, play, surprise, and mutual education, all expressed in the pair's mode of conversing with one another, expressing an intimacy of understanding often incomprehensible to the rest of the world" ("Philosophy the Day After Tomorrow" 325). The key shift in *A Bill of Divorcement* occurs through Hilary's own acceptance of this fact whereas, in the play, by contrast, the focus is on Margaret's moment of release as she dares to dream once more of a new life with Gray. Hence, when, in Cukor's adaptation, Hilary despairs that "everything's gone," Sidney's reply—"I'm not gone"—is received with a measure of understanding, illustrating her father's acceptance of Margaret's new relationship. Moreover, the substitution of Sidney for Margaret recapitulates key moments in the film in which Hilary mistakes one for the other. In addition to the initial misrecognition of Sidney for his wife, Hilary also observes that Margaret has changed: "There's something I miss, something you used to have, a kind way with you. The child's got it, Sidney. She's more you than you are. You've grown right up, away, beyond me."

The declaration Sidney makes to stay with Hilary inspires, as did Cordelia's devotion to Lear, an equal measure of reverence and pity (as A. C. Bradley put it) as with bitter resolution her expression conveys a passionate adolescent bridled by filial duty. In the same expression, as she turns her head to hide her tears from her father, there is all the dignity and composure, undercut with just a touch of Hepburn's trademark severity, of a young woman already undertaking a daughter's obligation: her first responsibility being to protect her charge from seeing through her feint. Hilary, however, is already wise to Sidney's act. In the previous scene, he overheard Margaret explaining to Gray that she could not leave with him because Hilary is weak. "I'm losing all I love in you, there's no more to lose," she cried. Hilary quietly stepped out into the night and lifted his eyes to the sky, holding for just a moment before gasping with the barest flicker of a smile. He looked through the window at Sidney and comprehended everything. The next bout of madness to possess him, contrived in order to drive Margaret to leave with Gray, is a performance of absolute nobility and strength of will. This pitiable figure emerges as true love's champion.

Hence, when Hilary asks Sidney why, if she truly loves Kit, she will not leave with him, it is also an invitation (albeit less contrived) to embrace her own plans. Sidney's response, however, reveals a motive other than pity: "We're in the same boat, father." Hilary realizes that he holds in his hands the future of his daughter, thus, the future itself. As he extends his arms to her, she falls into him. Finally, having discovered the protective embrace of a father known only through the sheet music of his unfinished sonata, Sidney is able to reclaim a word she has longed to say: "daddy." This moment demonstrates two softenings: in their world and, by extension, in Hepburn's often shrewish acting style which here, in response to her own defiant adolescence, reveals an early maturity. When she aspirates that word, "daddy," she lets go, as if by separating from Kit she has discovered something new, a union not only genetic but cultural, nurturing, luminous.

Another alteration in the adaptation can be found in some of the dialogue. "What's that?" Hilary asks when Kit is heard whistling for Sidney outside, signifying her last chance to leave with him instead of remaining with her father. "Nothing," Sidney replies, echoing Cordelia once more as she closes the curtains on her future. "I'll make it up to you," Hilary insists—a line spoken by Sidney to her father in the play. "We'll have a good time together, somehow, won't we? We'll be happy together, you and I." One can hear in this sentiment the echo of Margaret's lines from the beginning of the film where, having finalized her divorce from Hilary and looking forward to her "new life" with Gray, her anticipation of their future together is undercut by a lament for lost time since "life only starts when love comes." "Oh Gray," she says—part statement, part question—"we've time for everything, still." The same uncertainty cuts through the scene between Hilary and Sidney as they anticipate what the future will bring. Perhaps they might have drawn comfort from Nietzsche's concept of the difficult separation that always heralds a new day:

> It may be conjectured that the decisive event for a spirit in whom the type of the "free spirit" is one day to ripen to sweet perfection has been a *great separation*, and that before it, he was probably all the more a bound spirit, and seemed to be chained forever to his corner, to his post. What binds most firmly? Which cords can almost not be torn? With men of a high and select type, it will be their obligations: that awe which befits the young, their diffidence and delicacy before all that is time-honored and dignified, their gratitude for the ground out of which they grew, for the hand that led them, for the shrine where they learned to worship—their own highest moments will bind them most firmly and oblige them most lastingly. (6)

For these free spirits the separation from their ties comes suddenly, like the shock of an earthquake. As dawn breaks on this new freedom, the young soul cannot help feeling that she has been torn loose, set adrift on an ocean with nothing left on which to anchor. What stops these free spirits from suffering seasickness?

AN UNFINISHED LABOR

It is with only a minor dramatic shift that Sidney's renunciation of her future with Kit appears as more than a sacrificial gesture. Indeed, the personal catastrophe of her selfless act sheds its tragic character when, having rejected Kit's call by wordlessly drawing the curtains closed and after several seconds of mournful silence, Sidney sidles over to the piano and lets her hand carelessly land on the treble keys. Of course, the notes she hits form the opening bars to her father's unfinished sonata. Roused by the familiarity of the notes, Sidney sits and plays on, stirring something in her father also—a long-forgotten passion controlled and creative, no longer to be dismissed as mere madness. When Sidney plays for him two of her attempts at finishing the sonata, she looks up for his approval, but he interrupts. "No, you silly old thing," he says, sitting beside her on the bench, not quite brushing her aside. He tries a few notes, uncertainly, before brushing his hair across his head—a nervous gesture, perhaps a tic from his days in the asylum. This time, however, his nerve holds as he plays on. "The end of it should be elaborated," he declares, "it should build and build, it should be ecstatic!" Departing from Sidney's descending variations on the theme, Hilary's ending ascends through the chords to reach a crashing crescendo, after which he continues playing with a lightness of touch, with virtuosity and frivolity. Sidney squeals with delight. "Oh, isn't that lovely father, isn't it gay!" "Why not?" Hilary responds, his mood buoyant, "Weren't we born that way?" The movie ends right there, not in relapse and despair but in rebirth. These two aren't destined to sit and rot as they take turns to rue the future each has given away. Rather, they sit as one—a marriage of father and daughter.

The culmination of the rising chords of the sonata provides more than the film's "emotionally satisfying conclusion" (30), as Laurence E. MacDonald puts it. It is a point of transformation, even of transference across the generations. Margaret and Kit fade into the background as father and daughter sit down together to complete a fifteen-year-old musical composition. Next to this melodic union, Kit's unanswered whistle echoes as little more than the ghost of the nascent teen's adolescent crush, in place of which the finished sonata marks the blossoming of a woman's great passion and the beginning of a beautiful friendship—perhaps a symphony (one thinks of Schubert's *Unfinished Symphony*). This fulsome ending to the film through Max Steiner's "Unfinished Sonata" is more than an emotionally satisfying conclusion because Steiner uses the piece as a leitmotif marking a subtle psychological point. If, as Peter Wegele suggests, Steiner's use of "As Time Goes By" in *Casablanca* would be an example of what Carl Maria von Weber called the "reminiscence motif" (26), his signature melody for *A Bill of Divorcement* comes closer to Richard Wagner's early description of the motif as being about

Figure 10.1 A piano tutorial in *A Bill of Divorcement* (George Cukor, RKO, 1932). Digital frame enlargement.

a type of melodic *revelation*. "These melodic moments," Wagner asserted, "will become emotional guides through the complex construction of the drama. With them we will be confidants of the deepest secrets of the poetic intention; we become direct participants in its realization." These "melodic moments," Wagner concluded, are "where we remember the foreboding, while they make the foreboding a remembrance" (Wegele 27). As father and daughter sit at the piano joking around, all fears of a lapse into madness ("It's in our blood") become moot. Instead, at the piano their conversation takes the form of musical composition. As they play together—he as the teacher giving the lesson, she the rapt pupil taking notes—one becomes aware that a secret is being communicated, though not articulated in words. Their shared devotion to music signals an intimacy beyond comprehension, beyond stating: an intimacy and a transfer that is finally only for the hands. It can be called "mad" only because, in its inscrutable transcendence, it cannot be "explained."

Margot Peters points out that, in his performance as Hilary, Barrymore "played out many of his own fears: the taint of hereditary madness that he might have passed on to his own child, the disruptiveness of his presence in his own home, the bouts of madness that were like the bouts of drinking, his extreme vulnerability.' Peters quotes Hilary's speech from early in the film:

"You know we mustn't talk about these things," says Hilary as Jack might himself have said. "It isn't safe, I tell you. When I talk I see a black hand reaching up through the floor. You see that widening crack in the floor to catch me by the ankle and drag, drag"—and the actor loses control as he envisions the forces of darkness pulling him down to destruction. (340)

Whether she means to or not, Peters speaks here as if it is Barrymore who is losing control, as if the very performance itself is slipping into the madness he feared. Gene Fowler, Barrymore's friend and biographer, writes that the collapse into mental illness of Maurice Barrymore, John's father, left a lasting cloud over his son's thoughts. "It echoed," Fowler writes (with some melodrama), "knell-like, again and again in after years to plague his soul" (104). One might concur with Roland Barthes, however, who says of such moments: "No, this is not a relapse, only a last *soubresaut*, a final convulsion of the previous demon" (81) prior to being vanquished. For, if madness still threatens to explode in the sonata scene, it is detectable only in the brief gesture when Hilary runs a shaky hand through his hair as he considers the correct way to end the musical composition his daughter has waited a lifetime to hear. It is the kind of madness Gaylyn Studlar ascribed to Barrymore as his "impassioned vitality."

BARRYMORE'S SECRET

A timeless performance, argues Stanley Kauffmann, is as much about style as it is lineage. "Classic acting," he suggests, "is larger than life" neither in the sense of overacting (as a "ham") nor in placing as its sole aim the quality of verisimilitude; rather, classic acting "sees verisimilitude as a step along the way to qualities more spacious, daring, mysterious, qualities in consciousness, in dissatisfaction and hope that existed before us and will exist after" (55). Kauffmann made these observations in describing Christopher Plummer's performance as John Barrymore in William Luce's *Barrymore* (1996), a fictional depiction of the actor in 1942—one month from the end of his life. The play opens with "Barrymore" renting a theater to rehearse his Richard III, a reprise of his original 1920 performance which, he recalls, was "the first time they took me seriously." In Luce's play, Barrymore intends to use this performance to revivify a career lost to self-parody and tabloid gossip, opening with a plea "to be taken seriously, once more, before the man in the bright night-gown comes for me." As a rehearsal, however, Barrymore's performance betokens his impending demise: in his constant state of inebriation, the actor struggles to remember his lines (he relies on a prompter offstage) and frequently recourses to anecdotal reveries from his colorful past, reminiscences that emerge as the heart of the play. This failed rehearsal, one soon realizes, *is* Barrymore's encore; the curtain on his career being, like his life, ready to fall.

In his review of the play, Ben Brantley observes that, in addition to bearing a stunning physical resemblance to Barrymore, Plummer gave a performance of interpretation and impersonation in which his "glittering, restless eyes directly evoke the Barrymore of the movies." It is a performance that does something remarkable, Brantley concludes, because "it puts Barrymore's very style of acting, at least as we know it from film, in a richly personal and illuminating context" ("A Dazzler of a Drunk, Full of Gab and Grief," *New York Times* [March 26, 1997], 1, online at nytimes.com). One might draw parallels with the self-reflective films of Barrymore's mature period, especially his appearance in "portmanteau" films such as *Grand Hotel* (1932)—in which he plays the Baron who, fallen on hard times, is pressed into petty thievery, and *Dinner at Eight* (1933)—in which he plays silent film star Larry Renault who, having fallen victim to the talkies, still thinks he can live off of his name. In both films, despite basking in the faded glow of past glory, these men are undone. Of the latter performance, Murray Pomerance writes that Larry Renault's death at the end of the film "only highlights his condition for us, makes him an icon of failure, not least because he manages to collect the entire spotlight upon himself in his last, hopeless moment (in a gesture suggested, Cukor tells us, by Barrymore himself)" (195). Pomerance cautions, however, against invoking "performance as biography" as a way to read Barrymore *as* this icon of failure, for there is an antithesis between style and personality which "heightens for the audience an awareness of the awkward poise with which any occupational endeavor—acting or otherwise—must perch itself upon a fluid arrangement of forces, materials, techniques, concentrations, and virtuosities" (194). The "ruling hand" of *Barrymore*, Brantley writes, is to be found in "the pauses between and within the jokes, in which the teller's eyes go glassy with a soul-searching fear. He has seen something unspeakable, and words like failure, ruin and even death don't begin to describe it" (1). It is, as Pomerance puts it, a "mortal performance."

One might ask whether this constitutes a version of T. S. Eliot's problem of disentangling the man from the artist. "The more perfect the artist," Eliot wrote in his essay on "Tradition" in 1919 (the year before Barrymore debuted his Richard), "the more completely separate in him will be the man who suffers and the mind which creates; the more perfectly will the mind digest and transmute the passions which are its material" (18). The expression of emotion in acting is a complex thing. One does not simply turn one's emotions loose nor express one's personality onscreen; a performance is more accurately a kind of escape from both emotion and personality. And perhaps this is the reason, Kauffmann observes, that when Plummer does Barrymore "doing" himself as a younger, more virile, man, it is with "a faint suggestion of a smile as if he is softly confiding a privacy—about great matters" (55). It is the same smile on Barrymore's face as he looks up to the stars before, with Hamlet's "antic disposition," he performs his own madness in front of Sidney.

Whence the "problem of the generations" (177), as John Fowles calls it in his short story "Poor Koko," which reflects on the tendency among the young to use "hopeless *parole* in search of lost *langue*," and for whom "the underlying mistrust is of language itself" (182). The conflict between the generations arises from the failure of the old to communicate its "secrets" to the young. In Fowles's story, an author of some distinction is confronted by a youth who accuses him of being deaf to his generation's woes. The young man's complaint, the author concludes, "was my generation's 'refusal' to hand down a kind of magic" (183). Fowles ends his tale with a warning that, when an older generation loses its bearings, the younger generation is lost with it. This constitutes the tragedy of Clemence Dane's play. There is no legacy for the young to take up into their own breast, no fire to ignite them. When Plummer suggests a smile as he performs Barrymore acting out his Hamlet, it is the smile of the Mona Lisa. It is the tacit acknowledgment that, for all the failures of his performed subject, here was a man who strove in his art to create a better world worthy of the standard required for his successors to invest their own efforts. It is a question of nurturing a "living tradition." In *A Bill of Divorcement* one can see the maintenance of a world of clear standards as Hilary and Sidney sit and play out that unfinished sonata, which now belongs to them both, as Margaret departs to begin her new life.

The German language has a wonderful word, *Überlieferung*, for this sense of taking the care needed to pass one's traditions down through the generations. More than the sense of simply explaining this or that performance to someone, *Überlieferung* implies that what one passes on is a passion crucial in some way to one's life. A passion, say, for performance. It is the delivery of the meaningfulness of that passion that is the gift. What I give is not the performance but myself in my giving, that which disturbs or ignites me to give. It is in this way only that a rich maturity can be discovered. Nietzsche asks: "What binds most firmly? Which cords can almost not be torn?" The free spirit finds the strength required to effect a "great separation" from all that grounds him, such that he might "come into the world."

NOTE

1. Diagnoses of "hysteria" in young women were prevalent in the 1930s (*hysteron*, "womb"), as were discussions of eugenics pre-Nuremberg.

CHAPTER 11

John Barrymore's Sparkling *Topaze*

Steven Rybin

In *Topaze* (1933), principled schoolteacher Auguste A. Topaze, played by John Barrymore, suddenly finds himself in need of a job because, after giving poor marks to a malingering student with politically influential parents, he has lost his teaching position and with it his dreams of attaining an academy medal. An offer shortly comes along from the unscrupulous businessman and politician Baron Philippe de la Tour-La Tour (Reginald Mason)—the father of the disruptive schoolboy whose behavior led to Topaze's dismissal. The Baron promises Topaze that, in exchange for the use of his name in the marketing of a new health beverage, he will receive funding for his scientific researches as well as the academy medal he prizes.[1] The drink, with Topaze's blessing, is to be christened "The Sparkling Topaze." Innocently assured that it will be his research that guides the formula for the beverage, Topaze agrees to the Baron's plan. He will use his research to create a health drink of benefit to the public and it will bear his name. But the viewer knows something Topaze initially does not: the drink possesses no health benefits whatsoever and is designed only to cheat the public of their money. After he learns of the ruse, Topaze receives a real-world lesson in ethics that challenges his schoolroom ideals.

Topaze is adapted from a French play by Marcel Pagnol who directed his own film version in 1951 (with the popular comedian Fernandel in the title role). The original French play is a satire and a moral tale, critical of unwavering ideals in the face of a contingent social world. In the hands of director Harry d'Abbadie d'Arrast and actor John Barrymore, the 1933 American film version becomes something of a comedy of manners, focusing its attention on Topaze's behavior and reactions as he finds his understanding of human ethics challenged by the administrative bureaucratic class that manipulates him throughout the film.

Central to this film version of the story, of course, is the casting of Barrymore whose star persona and biographical legend inscribe at least two playful ironies into the role. The first is that the dutifully sober Topaze, who becomes dizzy at even the slightest drop of drink and who endorses a beverage with ostensible health benefits, should be played by one of film history's most notorious and passionate drinkers (whose health derived very little benefit from his frequent inebriation). This aspect of Barrymore's biography, inescapable for any viewer who knows his legend, inflects the viewer's perception of the title character, particularly during humorous scenes in which Topaze unwittingly finds himself drunk. The second and ultimately more substantial irony is that the mousy Topaze—a man who lives by noble principles but who is modest and meek in his performance of everyday life—should be inhabited by one of cinema's great theatrical presences and one of sound cinema's most commanding elocutionists, not to say a performer of stunning good looks. Topaze the character could not project to the back row of a theater if his life depended on it but Barrymore the actor makes the cinematic projection of his theatrical presence his business and his art.

Barrymore is not miscast in the part, however; Auguste A. Topaze is one of the actor's most delightful film characterizations. It is precisely in the distance between the character and Barrymore's biographical personas, and in Barrymore's underappreciated range as a cinema performer, that his performance of Topaze takes on life and humor. In Barrymore's subtle hands, the viewer discovers a character who himself discovers the power of performative irony, moving away from a position of earnest naïveté by film's end.

PROJECTING TOPAZE

At the beginning of the film, the innocent Topaze takes certain schoolroom virtues as essential axioms governing all human behavior. One sign of this belief in the inherent and unquestionable virtue of these principles is located in the mise-en-scène of the film's early classroom scenes. Various virtuous sayings ("Ill Gotten Gains are Not Worth While," "Money Does Not Bring Happiness"), printed on framed placards, line the walls of Topaze's classroom. Topaze does not claim authorship over these ideals; he merely presents himself as their vessel. He speaks, but does not need to become, their meaning. In other words, Topaze does not take himself as one who must project or perform these virtues for his students. If, for example, he were to project virtue theatrically, in a social space such as the classroom, his performance would be a declaration that goodness is something that must be publicly acknowledged and ratified, something contingent and up for debate. Topaze has no belief in such contingency. His ideals are essential and true, and inherently virtuous. All he must do for his students is point to these truths. Topaze soon discovers, shortly after he is duped into endorsing the phony health drink, that the world is not, in fact, shaped by his ideals. He must now find a way to perform virtue—to declare virtue to a world, outside the schoolroom, which has forgotten it.

In an essay on the display of virtue and villainy in motion pictures, William Rothman reminds us that most films place viewers in intimate relationships with characters, rather than distanced and overtly theatrical ones. This is because in cinema, as Rothman writes, we encounter not figures in a theatrical melodrama but rather "human beings who inhabit a world and hence cannot in themselves be pure exemplars of virtue or villainy" (75). As Rothman points out, this strategy is distinct from the tradition of nineteenth-century melodrama (from which narrative film as a medium derives), a tradition in which the melodramatic performer overtly and unambiguously declares herself an exemplar of either virtue or villainy. In his essay, Rothman demonstrates that in cinema, by contrast, good and evil are demonstrated not only through the theatricality of performance alone but also through more subtle "encounters between the camera and the human subjects whose privacy it penetrates" (75). Rothman's observations about film art resonate with our understanding of Topaze as a character. Though he begins the film as a naïve innocent, he is purely cinematic in not behaving as a pure exemplar of virtue because he does not understand why virtue would need to be demonstrated, or made an example of, in the first place. He inhabits a world in which virtues must be taught and recognized, to be sure, but he does not yet know that in the larger social world, in which morality has become ambiguous and uncertain, these virtues must also be performed. In keeping with the words Rothman uses to discuss film characters who, at certain moments, must declare their own virtue to the gaze of the camera, Topaze must learn to nominate himself as an exemplar of virtue in his social world. He will do this, by film's end, after he is exposed to its villainy.

It is an actor who possesses fully the ability to project both virtue and villainy in the melodramatic tradition of the theater, of course, here playing Topaze. Melodramatic performance is not uncommon in John Barrymore's silent films. Where Barrymore's sound films, including *Topaze*, add textures of the everyday through the actor's nuanced vocal presence and personality, Barrymore's silent films sometimes rely on his unparalleled ability to occupy melodramatic tableaux and convey essential gestures of virtue or villainy. Perhaps the finest example of this is *Dr. Jekyll and Mr. Hyde* (1920). In this film, Barrymore projects clear qualities of both virtue and vice through gesture, facial expression, makeup, and positioning. Made during his period of greatest success on the stage, *Jekyll and Hyde* offers a relatively theatrical experience (compared to the actor's later sound films), with Barrymore not so much inhabiting an everyday, diegetic world as translating melodramatic gestures and expressions from the stage to the apparatus of the film camera. The film relies throughout on profile shots of Barrymore to convey the essential goodness and virtue of Dr. Jekyll (moral correlatives, the film suggests, to the actor's own beautiful physiognomy) and on melodramatic gestures and expressions (complemented by makeup which distorts both his face and his fingers), often projected in close-up, to convey villainy in his scenes as Mr. Hyde.

The very experiment Dr. Jekyll is conducting in the narrative involves testing the thin line between human virtue and villainy, a line that is blurred when he drinks a formula concocted in his laboratory. By contrast, Topaze sees the line between virtue and villainy as thick and definitive, and as one that should not be blurred through the consumption of drink. Where Dr. Jekyll's experimental drinking opens up the evil side of human nature, the concoction that Topaze endorses is intended (at least as far as Topaze knows) to insure physical and mental health. Because Topaze's entire life, and, indeed, the health-drink project as he conceives of it, is built around principles of virtue, he need not declare virtue in a socially theatrical way. Barrymore's performance in *Topaze* thus abandons the sorts of melodramatic tableaux we see in *Jekyll and Hyde* (and some of Barrymore's other silent films). Instead, *Topaze* moves Barrymore toward quieter, more intimate connections with both viewer and camera, gestures appropriate for a character whose sense of dignity and decorum are themselves rejections of melodrama.

Yet the uniqueness of Topaze as a character in Barrymore's filmography is not relative only to his earlier silent films and stage performances. Barrymore's Oscar Jaffe in *Twentieth Century* (1934) or his Larry Renault in *Dinner at Eight* (1933), two grandly theatrical characters who delightfully and immodestly inhabit the cinema screen, stand in sharp distinction to Topaze's more reserved sense of self. Unlike Jaffe and Renault, Topaze does not project to the back row. Further, unlike Jaffe and Renault, Topaze is not an engagingly vibrant social personality (even as Barrymore's *performance* is itself vibrant and engaging in its very suggestion of the character's lack of these qualities). The larger social world—the world of the bureaucrats and politicians who make a fool of him and whose villainy is placed in comic counterpoint to Topaze's essential, if unremarkable, goodness—is not his stage. His stage is his schoolroom in which he speaks forthrightly, patiently, and only so loud that the child in the back row may pay him attention; and his roles, everyday ones, are as teacher and chemist. In these relatively modest social roles, Topaze's performance is one of calm and patient eloquence rather than declarative theatricality.

In his natural role as a teacher isolated from, indeed oblivious to, the everyday workings of ethically compromised businesspeople and politicians, Topaze thus need not melodramatically declare himself either hero or villain.

Only when he is thrust into the social world—a world that, in its corruption and villainy, at every turn contradicts the virtues of his classroom—does Topaze need to find strategies of declaration in order to make virtue known. The character's triumph is that he is able to do so in ways which allow him to transcend the earnest naïveté that makes possible his downfall in the first place. In other words, Barrymore's performance conveys to us Topaze's discovery, by film's end, of the power of performative irony.

BARRYMORE'S SPARKLING PERFORMANCE

His role as Topaze places Barrymore on the subtle end of his performative range in films, striking a note of great cinematic intimacy with both camera and viewer. In what follows I want to analyze closely three moments of Barrymore's performance in *Topaze* that illustrate how he conveys his character's progression from meek and sincere schoolteacher to a social player who discovers that being earnest is a handicap.

The first moment finds Topaze offered the job of hawking the phony health drink. He arrives at the apartment of the Baron and his mistress Coco (Myrna Loy). Prior to Barrymore's entrance, the Baron and Coco were discussing the need for the Baron to find "an idiot" to endorse his phony beverage. Cue Topaze who has come here to tutor Coco's nephew. The teacher arrives, his rickety walk into the apartment balanced by his cane. In his left arm he clutches three copies of *First Steps in Chemistry*, a book he has authored, and, as he sits down and is invited to a cocktail, he cradles these books in his lap. As the conversation ensues, Barrymore's primary gestures, in addition to the cradling of the books, involve occasional adjustments of his pince-nez as he responds to the Baron's questions, and a polite straightening of his necktie when asked by the Baron to outline his qualifications in science. Stationed in the center of the shot between Loy and Mason, Barrymore uses these delicate gestures to indicate his character's sober, intellectual refinement as well as his nervousness in matters of social interaction. Topaze is a character secure in his achievements but who is perhaps not as experienced in performing this security for other adults. Yet he sees no need to declare socially his achievements or his virtues. Indeed, if he should ever *have* to declare socially his virtues, this scene suggests he would not be good at doing so; he is a nervous, fiddling, fidgety presence, as Barrymore suggests with comic aplomb throughout the scene.

But, like Dr. Jekyll, Topaze's behavior will be changed by the consumption of a drink. Offered an aperitif, he politely accepts and, not knowing the custom whereby one nurses one's drink for a while, imbibes it with one gulp. From this point forward in the scene, Barrymore's performance works to suggest how drink slowly tears down Topaze's secure defenses. Struck by his sudden

Figure 11.1 John Barrymore, sparkling under the influence, in *Topaze* (D'Abbadie D'Arrast, RKO, 1933). Digital frame enlargement.

and complete metabolism of the alcohol, Topaze clutches his necktie to his mouth, keeping inside whatever the drink might prompt him to declare. A cutaway shot shows the Baron ostensibly reading *First Steps in Chemistry* (he is, in fact, tittering at Topaze's own failed attempt at understanding the first steps of social chemistry, in this case how to nurse a drink). Seeing this first crack in Topaze's already fragile social façade, the Baron continues to chip away at it, asking whether Topaze has a family: and, "Women? What about women?" "Women?" Topaze responds quizzically, the high pitch in Barrymore's voice suggestive of his character's utter innocence. "I mean," the Baron rejoins, "have you some wife, or whatnot?" "No, no, no sir—no wife," Topaze responds, "and no whatnot, I assure you!" The Baron and Coco respond with polite, but genuine, laughter.

This is a sparkling moment for the man who will soon endorse the "Sparkling Topaze," because, for the film's viewers, as for Coco and the Baron, it is genuinely entertaining; the meek schoolteacher has become something of a confident social performer. Though Barrymore's performance suggests everywhere in the scene that Topaze meets every social interaction with earnest response, in this moment his earnestness has unwittingly found him an audience. "No whatnot!": Topaze could never conceive of having any sort of social relation interfere between himself and his teachings, and between himself and his ideals, such as a mistress like Coco. But, in unknowingly finding himself a successful social player here, in the moment—a man who might win an endearing laugh through pitch of voice and heartfelt response—Topaze begins to progress, with the help of a drink, from schoolteacher, secure in his ideals, to social performer, and one distinctive enough to win the charms of Coco and the confidence of the Baron. Importantly, in this moment, Topaze does not sacrifice what is essential about his personality in order to give this performance. And the preservation of his personality will become important to the character's triumphant final scene.

Nevertheless, at this early point in the film, Barrymore's Topaze is still secure in his virtue and unaware that he need perform it: he believes that what he is doing is for the social good and thus an extension of his already established character. Later in the film, in the second moment of Barrymore's performance I want to bring into view, we see an important evolution in the character. When Topaze discovers that he has been duped, Barrymore's performance will need to convey Topaze's discovery that virtue is not inherent in the social world. In his laboratory, and having overheard a conversation about the phoniness of the drink, Topaze examines a sample of the "Sparkling Topaze" and discovers it is not the formula he has endorsed. He rushes out of his laboratory to collect more samples from the unwitting public. As he does, the camera follows him. As Topaze walks past the Baron and Coco, Barrymore slows his walk and the camera, in turn, slows its movement. Placed behind Barrymore's shoulder, the camera looks on as Coco lowers her head in shame. Here, in conjunction with Barrymore's measured gait, the camera conveys the character's disapproval of those who have tricked him. Barrymore continues stepping forward, but now in a backwards motion, as he keeps his gaze on these social villains. The moment conveys Topaze's recognition that vice exists "out there." He is not yet at the point of projecting virtue but he has arrived at the moment which reveals to him that, in this film's world, virtue is not self-evident. It will require a declaration.

After Barrymore confirms his laboratory test—every bottle of Sparkling Topaze contains the same phony formula—he ambles out into the city streets in a daze. Though he is completely sober, this expressionistic sequence brilliantly conveys the toxic mental effects of his unfortunate discovery. He stops at the doors of a shuttered art gallery, stepping behind the bars to its front gate as if to protect himself from the surrounding world. In a series of shot/reaction shots, the film shows us Topaze's new view of social reality. He gazes at a series of billboards surrounding the street. On each there is an advertisement for the Sparkling Topaze. Before our eyes (and as seen through the filter of Topaze's mental vision), these advertisements transform themselves to reveal their inherent dishonesty. Three signs encouraging the public to "Drink Sparkling Topaze" become "Topaze is a Thief" and, as Barrymore runs to get away from these haunting images, a series of superimpositions on the visual track presents images of a disapproving public come to get their revenge on the hapless chemist.[2]

Just as the images become more expressionistic in this sequence, Barrymore's performance becomes more ostensive, even a touch melodramatic (in its silent visual power the sequence recalls the expressive tableaux of some of Barrymore's silent films). As visions of shattering Sparkling Topaze bottles are layered over the actor's presence, Barrymore runs in place and repeatedly rolls his fingers through his hair in terror, as if his character's unfortunate discovery had channeled him directly into a horror movie. In the film's final act, Barrymore's performance will now have to work to project Topaze's virtue. Having discovered the degree to which his good character has been taken advantage of, Topaze will now have to take the social stage and project goodness to the public. In response to the Baron's villainy, virtue will now need to become performative. But Topaze's triumph is that he does not sacrifice his self-identity or his earnestness in this performance. He is able to declare virtue without resorting to melodrama.

In the film's final sequence, the third moment of Barrymore's performance I want to discuss, Topaze returns to his schoolroom. He has been given the academy medal that he prizes, from the Baron and a group of equally crooked politicians and businessmen, and is now to address the students in a celebratory speech. The purpose of the speech is to reinforce belief in an institution—the schoolroom—that he now knows to be a false conveyor of ideals only contradicted by the outside world. Further, the discovery that this medal was awarded to him as a result of his unintentionally villainous act of fooling the public with the false claims behind the "Sparkling Topaze" has shed Topaze of his innocence, and stripped the medal of its meaning.

What has changed in this final scene, and what is beautifully conveyed by Barrymore's performance, is the manner of Topaze's self-presentation. In place of his naïve earnestness, he has discovered a self-aware, presentational irony, signaled initially through a change in physical appearance and costume. In place of his usual professorial attire—a tidy goatee and a modest jacket—Barrymore now appears mostly clean-shaven (with only a polite moustache) and in an elegant jacket and tie. He has made these changes in his person in order to give a self-conscious social performance as a man of the world, rather than present himself as a shabby, self-contained schoolteacher; he now occupies a position as a member of the political and business class that his work on the "Sparkling Topaze" has won him. Yet, in the scene, "politician" and "businessman" are not the social roles Topaze earnestly performs. He takes on the guise of these institutional figures only so as to demonstrate ironically the distance between his schoolroom ideals and the realities of the "real world."

The key expressive prop in the sequence is Topaze's pointer, a professorial object he uses in the film's early scenes to instruct his students in moral ideals. Now, wizened by the realities of the larger world, Topaze will use it to demonstrate the emptiness of the social roles as politician and businessman that he finds himself presently performing. In the scene, Topaze is to award the Baron's son with an academic distinction he does not deserve. In other words, he has been instructed to abandon his earlier ideals in favor of an empty political gesture. And he goes through the motions dutifully, instructing the boy to come forward and answer a series of questions about the Three Punic Wars. Barrymore's vocal performance is not terribly different here in comparison to the film's early classroom scenes. He speaks eloquently and only loud enough to be heard in the back row of the small classroom. And his use of objects is consistent with the earlier scene; he holds his pointer in hand as a schoolteacher does, prepared to give instruction. Indeed, he goes through the questioning of the malingering student—who, of course, does not know the answers to any of the questions—as might any patient teacher.

But, as Barrymore here expresses him, Topaze has learned the social power of irony and of irony's power in performance. He now no longer performs the role of *earnest* schoolteacher but takes on the role of a man who seeks to demonstrate, for the public gathered in the classroom, the very fraudulence of the political and social role he has won through the con of the "Sparkling Topaze" beverage. Importantly, the very point of the demonstration, which is meant to illustrate how little this student deserves the academic award he is to receive in the ceremony, is consistent with Topaze's earlier ideals. He is still intent on conveying that "Ill Gotten Gains are Not Worth While." But his manner of performance has changed. He is now a self-aware social player, able to declare ironically—to his students, their parents, and various administrators and public figures—that the role he has won in society is without merit or substance. In place of his earlier earnestness, the now world-weary Topaze has discovered the performative power of irony.

And yet, in this climactic moment, Topaze (and *Topaze* the film) still does not go in for melodrama. Arguably, the only melodramatic sequence in the film is the earlier expressionistic montage in which, having discovered his unintentional complicity in thieving the public of their money, Topaze imagines bottles of Sparkling Topaze crashing all around him. What is valuable about Barrymore's performance in the quietly powerful *Topaze*—a film filled with straightforward, quiet action instead of heavy emphasis through underscoring and ostensive performance—is that it reminds us of the actor's relative range in films during this period. In cinema, of course, Barrymore is still capable of grandly theatrical moments, as in *Twentieth Century*, and of disturbingly expressionistic displays of villainy, as in *Svengali*. Yet, even in those films, there is a kind of knowingness, in some cases lightly ironic, to Barrymore's display: we watch *Twentieth Century* in the knowledge that, through his very theatricality, Barrymore is, to some extent, making fun of his earlier stage persona, and we watch *Svengali* with the knowledge that the actor, so beautifully performing the villain onscreen in this sound film, did so (and so beautifully, there, too) in the silent era with *Dr. Jekyll and Mr. Hyde*. Having established a secure career in films by the early 1930s (in large part through his mastery of the kind of vocal personality and performance needed in sound films), Barrymore could play on the public's memory of his earlier roles. This self-awareness, of course, would be an aspect of his career that would only intensify as the decade wore on, with films such as *The Great Profile* and *Playmates* explicitly (and, in the case of *Playmates*, somewhat despairingly) referring to Barrymore's extra-filmic existence and public reputation.

In the context of his early sound films, however, *Topaze* still stands as unique, and perhaps the most underappreciated of Barrymore's ironic film performances during this period. The meek schoolteacher would be, in many respects, the most innocent of all the characters Barrymore would ever play and, in the character's disregard for drink and in his lack of interest in women, perhaps the most distant from Barrymore's own biographical legend. But the film reminds us that Barrymore the actor could discover a wide range of emotion in his performances, even emotions that strike a pitch of earnest innocence very far from the actor's own public reputation. Indeed, that the sophisticated, world-renowned actor playing him should still be able to find that right pitch of innocence in the characterization of a man who, having looked villainy in the face, discovers the power of irony, is perhaps the most moving irony of all.

NOTES

1. During the time period of the story, it would not have been at all unusual for an elementary school teacher such as Topaze also to be engaged with scientific laboratory research.
2. John Carpenter would later use a similar effect in *They Live* (1988), with "Rowdy" Roddy Piper unmasking subversive messages in billboard advertisements through the power of a special pair of sunglasses.

CHAPTER 12

"Planes, Motors, Schedules": *Night Flight* and the Modernity of John Barrymore

Will Scheibel

"All you care about is planes, motors, schedules," cries Simone Fabian in *Night Flight* (1933), reproving the managing director of the Trans-Andean European Air Mail for his lack of compassion towards his pilots. "When they land, when they take off," she continues, waving at the map of South America behind him in his office, "just a map with a lot of lights on it!" Simone's husband Jules is one of those airmail pilots, en route from Punta Arenas, Chile to the airline's headquarters in Buenos Aires. After flying off course in a blinding rainstorm and with only minutes of fuel left, he and his wireless operator jump from the plane to their oceanic grave below. John Barrymore plays Rivière, the authoritarian director of the fictional airline, who has just informed Simone that her husband is lost. "We're doing everything that can be done," he assures her sternly. "Unfortunately, we don't know just where to look. In the last message we picked up, he said he couldn't land. He was still over the sea, but he didn't know how far from shore." When Simone reminds Rivière, desperately, that she is Jules's wife and loves him, Rivière replies, "Can't you see that's of no importance . . . when there's work to do?" Cold and mechanical, resistant to "tears and hysterics," Rivière is Barrymore at his most ruthlessly antiromantic. Positioned opposite Simone, whose sentiment, he informs her, "is only in the way now," Barrymore's Rivière represents the masculine gendering of an industrial and managerial modernity.

Barrymore, "The Great Profile," was one of the preeminent actors of Hollywood cinema during the 1920s and early 1930s. There is much to be said of the techniques and traditions with which he created his roles, not only in films such as *Dr. Jekyll and Mr. Hyde* (1920), *Don Juan* (1926), *Grand Hotel* (1932), *Dinner at Eight* (1933), and *Twentieth Century* (1934) but also on stage—his *Hamlet*, which ran on Broadway from 1922 to 1923,

Figure 12.1 Cold and mechanical, resistant to "tears and hysterics," Rivière is John Barrymore at his most ruthlessly antiromantic in *Night Flight* (Clarence Brown, MGM, 1933). Digital frame enlargement.

was regarded as the greatest of his day (see Fowler and Morrison for earlier work that deals with some of this material). This chapter views a different face of Barrymore that, given his reputation as an actor, may come from a less likely perspective but it provides an opportunity for us to look closely at his film performances within a uniquely *cinematic* frame. As Andrew Klevan has argued, film performance is "an internal element of style in synthesis with other aspects of film style and explores the achievement of expressive rapport" (i). In *Night Flight*, we shall see how Barrymore both inhabits and embodies the space of Rivière's office through his "internal relationships within the film," as Klevan describes film performance in the context of mise-en-scène (i).[1] Of primary interest for my analysis are not Barrymore's biography and extratextual influences but his looks, expressions, gestures, voice, and placement onscreen, the experience of watching which may be articulated through description. To quote Klevan, performance is constituted by "multifaceted relationships—not always prominent—to the surrounding dramatic environment" (ii), and *Night Flight* is rich with moments in which the film reveals how to interpret Barrymore. Barrymore, in turn, reveals how to interpret the film.

Indeed, *Night Flight* is a film that never had the opportunity for proper assessment within Barrymore's filmography and, until 2011, had been out of circulation since its first theatrical run in 1933 and 1934 (Robert Osborne, "Introduction to *Night Flight*," Turner Classic Movies [August 10, 2012]). Director Clarence Brown and executive producer David O. Selznick adapted this MGM aviation melodrama from the bestselling 1931 novel of the same name by French author Antoine de Saint-Exupéry, today best known for *The Little Prince* (1943). Saint-Exupéry based *Night Flight* on his own experiences as a pilot for Aeroposta Argentina (a subsidiary of the French airmail carrier Aéropostale) which he went on to recount in his 1939 memoirs *Wind, Sand and Stars*. The novel earned him international recognition after winning the Prix Femina, a major French literary prize awarded annually by an all-female jury, and attracted interest from Hollywood. MGM secured only a ten-year license from Saint-Exupéry who hated the film and refused to renew the rights (Osborne). Then, while flying over the English Channel in 1944 on a reconnaissance mission during World War II, he disappeared and the remains of his aircraft were not discovered until 2000 (Lou Lumenick, "DVR Alert: Lee Tsiantis and *Caught* on TCM," *New York Post* [March 17, 2011], online at nypost.com). Warner Bros., owner and administrator at the time of MGM's pre-1986 catalogue, restored the film from the original camera negative in 2009 and finally cleared the rights for an April 2011 public exhibition at the TCM Classic Film Festival in Hollywood, a June 2011 DVD debut from Warner Home Video, and an August 2012 world television premiere on Turner Classic Movies (Lumenick, "DVR"; Lumenick, "DVD Extra: Long-MIA *Night Flight* (1933), *The Constant Nymph* (1943) on the Way After TCM Fest Bows," *New York Post* [February 14, 2011], online at nypost.com; Osborne).

CLASSICAL ACTOR, MODERN FIGURE

A longstanding "Holy Grail" for cinephiles of old Hollywood, *Night Flight* boasts an all-star cast from the MGM stock: Lionel Barrymore as Robineau, the humane airline inspector; Robert Montgomery as playboy pilot Auguste Pellerin who must carry a life-saving serum across the Andes during a polio outbreak in Rio de Janeiro; Clark Gable as Jules Fabian whose rendezvous with Pellerin in Buenos Aires is aborted by a fatal storm; William Gargan as an unnamed Brazilian pilot who, in Fabian's place, relays the serum to Rio; and Helen Hayes and Myrna Loy as the concerned wives of Fabian and the Brazilian pilot, respectively. John Barrymore's character, Rivière, was inspired by the real-life operations director of the Aeropostale, Didier Daurat. Though marketed as an airborne, epic-scale *Grand Hotel*, the film disappointed at the box office, even after the studio edited its over two-hour preview length to a lean eighty-five-minute running time (Lumenick, "DVD Extra: Lost *Flight* Surfaces After 78 Years," *New York Post* [June 7, 2011], online at nypost.com). The production was fraught with difficulties as well. Owing to the number of office and bedroom scenes, Selznick hired aviation-film veteran John Monk Saunders to do uncredited work on Oliver H. P. Garrett's script, bolstering Gable's role and the flying sequences while the polio framing device was added to lend greater dramatic urgency to the pilots' mission—a subplot that served Selznick again in *Made for Each Other* (1939) and supposedly originated from a childhood incident involving his brother Myron (Lumenick, "DVD Extra: Lost"). Despite the various problems, Brown (himself a pilot) and cinematographer Elmer Dyer captured some extraordinary aerial footage over the Rocky Mountains (Lumenick, "DVD Extra: Lost") which alone makes the film worthy of rediscovery.

But let's get back to that office, a key site of dramatic action both in the original script and the completed film, where the modernist problems of mobility, speed, and economy are negotiated and made visible. The space is presented through a kind of stylized realism and austerity, often from a camera perspective either behind or in front of Rivière's desk which bisects the room horizontally. Sitting on the desk are the assorted technologies of radio and telephone communication that mediate the drama above the clouds; this establishes the office as a point of connection for the film's interlocking stories while keeping the characters apart. Dotted with lights that correspond to the various air bases around the Andes, a wall-sized map of South America towers behind the desk; to its left is a window, allowing Rivière to oversee takeoffs and landings; and to the right hangs a smaller map of South America and Western Europe over a correspondence desk where he charts transatlantic mail delivery between the continents (a model airplane is displayed on this second desk, metaphorically indicating the control he wields over his pilots). As he remarks late in the film, "Everything must be carried out to the minute as I planned. If there's any change, I decide it."

Rivière is both the administrator of the office and the incarnation of its meticulously designed order. Therefore, he is never seen outside of this space (he cannot exist anywhere else, the film seems to suggest, as if no other space can manifest him). The office becomes a space where the film itself is "clocked" and "mapped." If Rivière is a metonym for the office, then the office is a metonym for the airmail industry. Moreover, as Rivière diegetically organizes the flight schedules that propel the twenty-four-hour events of the narrative, the very construction of the film follows a tight, formal "schedule" of its own. Tom Conley points out that "the 'modern age' begins with printed maps" (253) and that "the modernity of cinema is tied to the way the film's locational powers, like those of a map, are configured and even theorized within its own form" (255). We shall see how Rivière's map places us in the social and geographical location of South America and how the film's cartographic function through its zones of narrative action makes us hyperconscious of the ways in which modern industry, technology, and communication manage space and place.

The opening sequence begins with an apparently extradiegetic map of South America and a close-up of Rio de Janeiro before an iris opens on the Brazilian National Clinic where a distraught mother attempts to comfort her paralyzed infant son in the midst of a polio outbreak. After physician Dr. Decosta learns by phone that the nearest serum is in Santiago, he is informed that it could arrive via European Air Mail in less than twenty-four hours— just in time to save the boy's life. The map returns, this time as a transitional image, wiping across the screen with a close-up of Santiago as another wipe reveals the Santiago doctor on the phone with Dr. Decosta, confirming that the serum will be on board the mail plane. Referring to the inaugural night flight that we are about to witness, he adds, "Lucky thing this new service has started, eh?" A box addressed to the City Hospital in Rio is stamped and dropped into a mailbag before we finally meet one of our heroes, Pellerin, who departs from Santiago to Buenos Aires.

Rivière's introduction in the next scene performs the function of narrative exposition as he explains the mechanisms of the film's structure through the course of the night flight schedule, retroactively providing greater context for this network of maps and phone calls that culminated in Pellerin's takeoff. Standing in medium shot behind his desk, Rivière smokes a cigarette and dictates to his assistant seated in front of the desk in the foreground of the shot. This master shot identifies Barrymore by his instantly recognizable profile cut against the map of South America, a map that is now fixed within the diegesis of the film and frames him in the shot, suggesting the global might of his airline company contingent upon, as he puts it, "the rigid attention on the part of every man in the organization." Yet, as Rivière continues his dictation in robotic monotone and walks stiffly toward the map in the background, the deep-focus cinematography dwarfs him and undermines his patriarchal authority. With his staccato speech patterns and puffs of smoke, he is consistent with his motorized world. "The entire operation of night mail service in South America," he continues, "is dependent on the most exact adherence to the plan laid down." Rivière has reduced his pilots to nothing more than "planes, motors, schedules" whose significance is determined by a "map with a lot of lights on it" but he, too, is dehumanized by this environment as a mere cog in the machine of his own company.

Cut to a close-up of the map as the camera traces Fabian's flight north from Punta Arenas "over 1,500 miles of difficult country" and Pellerin's flight east from Santiago which, though it "crosses the Andes in daylight," nevertheless "beyond that point must be in darkness." Rivière's dictation clarifies not only "the peculiar hazards involved" in the two flights but the importance of both planes arriving in Buenos Aires before midnight: "There must be time for both of these planes converging on Buenos Aires to clear their mail and transfer that destined for Europe to the plane to the north." The stakes of the flight schedule are now explicit. On a more implicit level, Rivière's map signals France's colonial domination over Latin America in the nineteenth and twentieth centuries. The map outlines a legacy of conquest and control, trade agreements and European financial investments that cast the modernization of Latin nations in the light of European patronage and cultural influence. In this way Rivière's office gives an imperial context to masculine, managerial authority.

Despite the draw of the film's cast, Gable and Montgomery neither share a scene with each other nor one with John Barrymore. The romantic leads of Gable and Hayes are also never able to share a scene together (we come close in two moments: one in which Simone gazes at a photograph of her husband framed above her radio, another in which, under emotional distress, she pretends to have dinner with him at home upon hearing of his delay in arrival at Buenos Aires). As a result, Rivière's schedule is a source of both narrative pleasure and frustration, regulating the parallel stories of Gable/Montgomery, Gable/Montgomery/Barrymore, and Gable/Hayes, that are never allowed to intersect. On one hand, the parallel stories create a sense of anticipation: will these characters get together and what will happen if they do? On the other, the delayed gratification is never released: these characters *cannot* get together because of Rivière's pressures to time their work to his schedule. There is an implied justification for this narrative structure in Rivière's final declaration, "Every pilot, mechanic, mail handler, and clerk must be held strictly accountable for any failure in his work." He walks back toward his desk, his head cast down as if he is unable to recognize his assistant as a person, and he stops when he is framed (again) and centered by the map to remind us that he will be equally regulated by this system of management.

The Rivière character comes out of a long tradition of gender symbolism in historical narratives of modernity that characterize its innovations and experimentations with metaphors of masculinity. In her book *The Gender of Modernity*, Rita Felski argues that "individual or collective human subjects are endowed with symbolic importance as exemplary bearers of temporal meaning" (1). When historians or theorists of the modern era dramatize or personify their subjects as male or female, she continues, they shape the ways in which those narratives are told and impact our understanding of the past. That which is "made new" is often gendered male or attributed to autonomous men. Felski insists, "Gender affects not just the factual content of historical knowledge—what is included and what gets left out—but also the philosophical assumptions underlying our interpretations and the nature and meaning of social processes" (1). For example, her reading of Marshall Berman's well-known *All That Is Solid Melts Into Air* suggests that, by citing Goethe's Faust as "the exemplary hero of the modern age" (1), Berman identifies modernity with "dynamic activity, development, and the desire for unlimited growth" (4), and equates modernity with masculinity. *Night Flight* celebrates the airmail industry's interwar development of night mail service and, as company manager, Rivière is figured according to Felski's modernist/masculinist mythic ideal: the "accelerating momentum of industrial production, rationalization, and domination over nature" (4).

Yet, the film ultimately remains ambivalent about Rivière's definition of industrial progress, and Barrymore's unemotional performance suggests that Rivière is as much a function of the office as are his instruments of scheduling. If the heroes in the narrative are male pioneers of aviation, nevertheless the film attributes aviation heroics not to engineers of technology or managers of industry but to the pilots themselves, old-fashioned adventurers who tamed the unknown, uncharted wilderness of night with its "unfathomed dark" that claimed the lives of their predecessors. As the epigraph tells us, the film is a testament to the "human courage" of night flight pilots who "stride the high, dark clouds . . . bearing hope to the anxious . . . strength to the week . . . solace to the dying." In the final scene, Fabian's plane rises from the waters in a ghostly superimposition effect, only to be joined by a horde of other superimposed planes soaring into the heavens. It was their "human courage," says the coda, "that men died . . . so others might live . . . and so, at last, man's empire might reach triumphant to the sky!" While the scheduling he enforced helped make the inaugural night flight possible, this final scene supports Simone's reproach that his pilots are more than "planes, motors, schedules." Rivière's masculinity is therefore made official in contrast to the courageous masculinity of his pilots as well as in contrast to Simone's sentiment which the film vindicates in its melodramatic resolution.

OFFICIAL MASCULINITY

Barrymore performs what I am calling an "official masculinity" as an extension of Rivière's office, and most clearly realizes this spatial character through his interaction with other performers in the office. When Rivière decides to "make an example" of pilot Pierre Roblet (Harry Beresford) by firing him for one instance of "carelessness," the two men stand in long shot facing the wall-sized map and are separated by Argentina. The cartographic wedge between them visualizes not only Rivière's emotional distance from his pilots, figuratively the distance of an entire country, but also the impersonal nature of their relationship which Rivière can conceive only as a professional negotiation through maps and schedules. "You might have caused a crack-up, a couple of deaths, loss of the mail, disruption of the whole service," he barks. The exact circumstances of Roblet's mistake are never explained, attention shifting instead to Rivière's assembly-line thought process that is leaving Roblet helpless. Pleading with Rivière to reconsider, the pilot informs him that he has worked in aviation since 1910 when he assembled the first plane in Argentina. Filmed in medium shot, the shot/countershot dialogue sequence reveals Barrymore parallel with Argentina as two lights pierce through the map, "doubling" Rivière with an official counterpart. Roblet speaks of his wife and children to which Rivière replies, "Sentiment can't enter in."

As the scene concludes, Roblet exits the office and Rivière appears to continue mapping the schedule for him but his narration primarily serves as a means of directing the viewer to the time and place of the film's action in the upcoming sequence. Losing himself in the map, Rivière stands before it in long shot, taking inventory of the topography: "You ought to have known better than anybody what we're up against flying at night, with mountains, fogs, and jungles down to the sea. Hundreds of miles with no place to land." The map serves as a kind of magic mirror, for both Rivière and the viewer, and a close-up of Santiago plots a narrative coordinate as Rivière continues: "It's bad enough over the Andes in the daytime. Flying blind in clouds, going 120 miles an hour, not being able even to see your own wing tips, with mountain peaks all around you and air currents like elevators shooting you up and down." An iris opens on Pellerin flying over the Andes experiencing the very conditions Rivière has just described.

Pellerin quickly reports that he may be delayed in an effort to avoid a cyclone and we cut back to Rivière sitting at his desk in an intimidating, low-angled medium shot as he speaks into the radio. Positioned between the radio in the foreground and the map in the background, he is a node in the office's transmission and reception of information, another intermediary awaiting calls and messages. As if to repress knowledge of "the peculiar hazards" he pointed out in his previous scene, he responds to the control tower operator, "Delayed? He mustn't be! The European mail plane has to leave here no later than midnight!" Rivière's threat to fine Pellerin 200 francs for lateness reminds the viewer of the stakes of the flight schedule and further delineates the purely administrative terms of his relationships with his pilots.

A cut to a reestablishing shot reveals Inspector Robineau seated in front of Rivière's desk, listening to the manager insist that asking the impossible always yields "more than if you haven't asked for it." Once again, Rivière is drawn almost compulsively back to the map and Robineau follows him. Recreating the composition from Rivière's meeting with Roblet, the camera shoots the two Barrymores facing the map in long shot, their separation (by Argentina again) setting up their divergent methods. Rivière opens a window to see a dense cloud of fog but his mind immediately moves to the demands of the schedule. Asking about the status of a plane bound for Paraguay which is due to leave in five minutes, he threatens to fine the pilot and revoke his punctuality bonus if the takeoff is delayed. Thinking of the pilot's safety in the fog, Robineau questions the justice of Rivière's order to which Rivière asks callously, "What have I to do with justice?" Further still, he refers to the pilots as "lazy, careless, and easily frightened." Before trailing off, he adds, "They're like a lot of children. If I'm not hard with them . . ." During his conversation with Robineau, we see a telephone in one shot and an intercom in another. Both props have been placed on his desk in the foreground, linking Rivière to the world outside this office only through technologies that are, in turn, mediated by operators. The circuit of communication between Rivière and his pilots is lined with injustice and misinformation, and remains subject to interference.

One of the film's distinct pleasures for audiences at the time would have been to see the brothers Barrymore perform side by side. The older Lionel, a legendary scene stealer, was said to have embellished Robineau's eczema irritation by scratching himself incessantly—in a later scene, after Rivière tells him to "stop scratching," he leaves the office dejected and sneaks a scratch under his buttocks. Clarence Brown allegedly lost a ten-dollar bet that Lionel could not upstage John (Jay S. Steinberg, "*Night Flight* [1933]," Turner Classic Movies, online at tcm.com). One-upmanship aside, the slouching, twitching, grimacing Robineau expressively contrasts with the deadpan Rivière who sits and stands as erect as an office fixture and moves as precisely as hands on a clock. Rivière seems to feel nothing, neither physical irritation nor relief. Moments of satisfaction are immediately denied ("Everything's going smoothly . . . too smoothly") and, unlike his pilots, he has nobody in his life (even Robineau alludes to a wife at one point, showing Pellerin a photograph). When Robineau jokes about killing himself if his itching does not stop, Rivière quips back, "Stop? A friendship like that? I wish I had such a loyal companion."

After Pellerin lands in Buenos Aires and Robineau joins him for dinner, Rivière teaches the inspector a lesson by forcing him to fabricate grounds on which to fine the pilot. To the extent that Rivière accepts the pilots' hatred as part of his job, he reprimands Pellerin in front of Robineau for succumbing to his fears and turning back in a squall after noticing engine problems (Rivière admits to Robineau that the pilot made the right decision but he wanted the man to overcome being afraid). "Admire them if you want to. Love them even. But never let them know it," he advises, cautioning Robineau that friendship with pilots weakens the authority and impossible standards of training that he should uphold as the inspector in order to prepare them for the dangers of night flying.

Following Robineau's first confrontation with Rivière is a peculiarly interesting scene between John Barrymore and character actor C. Henry Gordon (a fellow stage veteran) as airline president Daudet. Typically cast as a villain in the 1930s, Gordon here plays a smarmy bureaucrat who warns Rivière that night flying through fog puts the company's reputation at risk. "If there's an accident, the plane burns, the mail destroyed . . . it will spoil our record," he says, reminding Rivière that the company has not been responsible for an accident or a delay in five years. For Daudet, the safety of the pilots is simply a "public obligation." Rivière, however, sees lead time as a matter of life and death. Night flying may be a new, more efficient mode of transportation but only if he maintains his schedule. Daudet questions whether night flying in South America is simply an effort to compete with Europe and the United States, to which Rivière responds, "We lose time. Hours every night. We're always held back by fog and darkness. It's a matter of life and death to us. The lead we gain by day on ships and railways is lost each night." Both men are driven by official company records which secure Daudet's public political image and Rivière's pride in a success rate.

The composition of this scene conveys the power dynamic between Rivière and Daudet, reinforcing Rivière's insatiable appetite for global management. In a rare shot from behind his desk, approximating Rivière's perspective, Daudet sits to the left of a row of silhouetted board members (their exact identities and location in the space are never made entirely clear, one of several ways in which the hierarchical organization of the office privileges Rivière). Daudet corners Rivière against the window, as the fog rolls thickly in the background, and insists that the planes should be grounded. Walking past Daudet from the window to the map of South America, Rivière takes credit for the company's reputation and economic growth, beginning with flying the Andes, and the camera reframes him in medium long shot with the map behind him (again, Rivière is parallel to Argentina, mirroring the map of that country). We cut to a long shot of Rivière, leaving Daudet offscreen. Gesturing to the enormity of the map, he boasts of forcing the company to expand to cover 20,000 miles, which Daudet confirms. "You can't stop me now, yet you even try it," he shouts and walks back to his desk into a medium shot. He threatens to resign if the planes do not fly on schedule, banging his left hand against his desk and waving his right across loose papers that flutter to the ground. The office—map, desk, and accessories—is not just a space but also a vehicle for Rivière's articulation of self through expressive objects. "I've never made a failure of anything yet, and you're not going to make this my failure now," he asserts, slamming his cigarette case on the desk, at which point Daudet rushes back into frame to reassure him.

For all of Rivière's steely eyed, monomaniacal ambitions, he remains, in the end, just a company man. "Fog, darkness surrounds us like a prison," he comments to Daudet looking out his office window. Though he is referring to the pilots, the film implicates his character as a melancholy, alienated prisoner of his own managerial design whose desire for geographical expansion paradoxically encloses him further. As he yells at Daudet, "But if walls can be driven back, I can do it! Always the world would stop when the sun went down ... no more!" That darkness increasingly surrounds Rivière the closer the film reaches Fabian's climactic death. Practically disappearing into the office space, he is lit only by his desk lamp when he learns that Fabian has encountered a storm. Shadows cover his eyes and the top of his head as he sits at his desk. When he rises, what had been hidden is now illuminated, while shadows envelop the rest of his face and body. Rivière appears to us only in fragments of chiaroscuro (first a mouth, then a pair of eyes) and, as he walks to the window, we share his gaze into the blackness outside that not even the light of the full moon can penetrate.

The film's most profound revelation is the way it ultimately finds an alternative to Rivière's "planes, motors, schedules" in Simone's "sentiment," her "tears and hysterics" that the affective experience of modernity stereotypically disavows. Justus Nieland has argued that modernist feeling is "often understood as either a flat rejection of emotion as conventionally experienced and expressed, one that takes the form of an inhuman antagonism to sentimentality and rhetoric, or as some late and lamentable revival of romanticism" (1). Yet, he shows how modernists were deeply concerned with the *feeling* of life in the public sphere. *Night Flight* offers a counterpoint to Rivière's "office" story with Simone's parallel "bedroom" story that creates a dual narrative in which the melodrama of masculine industrial management is displaced by the romantic–domestic melodrama of the Hollywood "woman's film."

The realization of Fabian's fate is the source of the film's melodramatic pathos, and the emotional catharsis of his plane rising from the water belies Rivière's hostility toward sentiment. If *Night Flight* generates suspense through the derring-do of the pilots who work to follow Rivière's schedule, we are also held in anticipation by Simone's virtuous waiting for the safe arrival of her husband. Ending with Fabian's memorialization redeems Simone's emotional and psychological subjectivity by acknowledging the poignancy of her romantic love for her late husband and the missed moment of their reunion. When the newspapers cover Fabian's disappearance, Daudet forbids Rivière to proceed with the flight to Rio but Rivière lies that the Brazilian pilot has already left Buenos Aires ("You can't stop all the clocks in the world from ticking," he muses). The film awards Rivière a qualified reprieve as the Brazilian pilot takes off in defiance of his earlier accusation of cowardice, successfully delivering the serum on schedule. Left alone in the dark of his office with his giant map, Rivière will reset a new timetable as the wife of the Brazilian pilot (Myrna Loy) begins her waiting. The image that lingers in our minds as a point of identification is Loy looking up at the night sky, her face glistening with tears.

NOTE

1. Paul Stock has explored the relationship between office space and ideology in the James Bond films. Though his subject and methodology are substantially different from mine, his thinking about the metonymy of a cinematic office has influenced this chapter.

CHAPTER 13

Barrymore and the Scene of Acting: Gesture, Speech, and the Repression of Cinematic Performance

Barry Langford

Over a twelve-month period beginning in August 1926, three star vehicles for John Barrymore, all costume melodramas directed by Alan Crosland and set in highly romanticized studio-fabricated versions of medieval or early modern Europe, were released on to the United States market: two productions under Barrymore's munificent contract at Warner Bros., *Don Juan* (1926) and *When a Man Loves* (1927), and the first in his new three-picture deal at United Artists, *The Beloved Rogue* (1927), a fanciful account of the career of medieval balladeer and cutpurse François Villon and remake of the 1920 Fox film *If I Were King*.[1]

Don Juan—which was a considerable box-office success—has a significant place in cinema history as the first film released with a synchronized recorded score and sound effects, and the film's critical reception was predictably dominated by commentary on the novelty of the Vitaphone process rather than on Barrymore's performance as the legendary lover. The two subsequent films are, by contrast, both far less remembered[2] and, upon their original release, also fared less well either at the box office or critically, meeting with decidedly lukewarm reviews. A particularly notable contribution to the chorus of critical disapprobation was Stark Young's near-eulogy for Barrymore's serious acting career, published in September 1927 in *The New Republic*:

> Since the *Hamlet* we have had the sex appeal movies... Of these moving pictures of Mr. Barrymore's last years, these puzzled people, looking at them and wondering afterward, can only observe that they are rotten, vulgar, empty, in bad taste, dishonest, noisome with a silly and unwholesome exhibitionism, and odious with a kind of stale and degenerate studio adolescence. Their appeal is cheap, cynical and specious. The

only possible virtue in Mr. Barrymore's progress, as these films show him, is a certain advance in athletics; he is more agile, he leaps, rides and hops to a better showing, an advance encouraged no doubt by the competition with Mr. Douglas Fairbanks' appeal . . . Artistically, the only thing we could say about Mr. Barrymore's performances is that he brings to them remnants of his tricks and mannerisms that stiffen them slightly and perhaps convey the sense of acting to a public that has seen but little of it . . . The little measure of its superiority over most movie acting, in sophistication and technique, is only another way of saying how low Mr. Barrymore has sunk. (98–9)

The immediate object of Stark's disdain was *When a Man Loves*, an adaptation of *Manon Lescaut*—Barrymore's bare-chested, cage-fighting stunts therein probably earning the "sex appeal movies" label—but the notice takes in this swashbuckling, action-oriented, and (in theory) audience-pleasing phase of Barrymore's film career more generally. The lack of overt reference to Barrymore's alcoholism notwithstanding, Stark's verdict of an irretrievable downward artistic trajectory is obviously an early draft of what would—within half a decade, as Barrymore's physical, mental, and professional decline became all too unavoidably apparent—be cast in stone as the received version of his career: the heights of his prime on the classical stage followed by precipitate and irreversible downturn; a rake's progress in which the movies are, at best, a noxious catalyst, at worst the Mephistophelian agent of Barrymore's downfall. This cautionary narrative traces Barrymore's tragic downward arc from the heights of his Broadway and, above all, Shakespearean performances immediately after World War I, climaxing in his legendary early 1920s *Hamlet* in New York and London, followed in short order by his abandonment of the stage for fabulously lucrative Hollywood contracts and—as the inevitable sequel—a swift degeneration bottoming out in the depths of self-parodic alcoholic ruin in his final Hollywood films before his premature death in 1942.

As Marion Keane has noted, firmly embedded in this account is a traditional critical prejudice that estimates the value of screen performance as inherently inferior to that of the stage: "Chronicling behind-the-scenes intrigue in Hollywood and often only cataloguing the titles of his films, Barrymore's biographers do not argue for the idea that film acting is a lesser endeavour than stage acting: instead, they take it for granted" (171–2). Stark Young's contemporary notice quoted above indicates this bias was not confined to Barrymore's later biographers but was already actively at work in his contemporary reception as what would become the canonical narrative of Barrymore's tragedy began to crystallize. It also typifies the bad faith by which this "theater-centric" prejudice seeks partly to conceal itself. That is, while the review excoriates Barrymore for acting (badly) in bad movies, in truth it seems that the possibility of any other kind of (American?) movie—and certainly of any other kind of movie acting, certainly any "worthy" of Barrymore's gifts—is actually canvassed.

Exactly what does the badness of Barrymore's performances consist in? It's never specified. What, by contrast, is very clear is the a priori assumption that film acting precludes the expression or even preservation of the qualities that made Barrymore such a legendary artist in the legitimate theater. That acting for the screen might entail a different—rather than simply an inferior—toolkit of acting skills is a proposition never seriously entertained. The necessary externalization of interior condition, for example—especially important, of course, in silent film—is reduced to a gross physicality or crude athleticism (leaping, riding, and hopping); film as a medium can do nothing but counterfeit Barrymore's quondam artistry, debasing the coinage of his genius for a vulgar spectatorial constituency that knows no better and never could ("perhaps convey the *sense* of acting to a public that has seen but little of it" [emphasis added]).

Keane takes forceful and persuasive issue with this school of critical thought, arguing that, even when Barrymore's screen performances receive critical acclaim (such as his role in William Wyler's *Counsellor at Law* [1933]), such endorsements are effectively limited by operating under an unstated self-denying ordinance by which Barrymore's screen acting is critically validated only to the extent that it conforms to conventional standards of masculine propriety (lack of histrionic display, emotional restraint, and so on as well as reflecting a broader mid-century turn away from ornamentation and demonstrative excess. By undertaking a careful exegesis of Barrymore's modes of performative masculinity ("performative" here employed in a double register: both the straightforward denotation of professional acting performance, and the concepts of gender performativity outlined by Judith Butler)[3] in films such as *Beau Brummel* (1924), Keane suggests that this backhanded praise for some of Barrymore's later work really negates the more unconventional enactments of masculinity and self-fashioning by which Barrymore's most memorable performances—onstage and on screen—are characterized (see Studlar 90–149).[4]

Just to complicate matters, Barrymore himself seems to have shared the generally low estimation of the quality of his screen work. A well-known anecdote related by his biographer John Kobler finds Barrymore lurking in the balcony during a public screening of *The Beloved Rogue*: midway through the show "unable to contain himself any longer, he startled the audience by shouting, 'Call yourself an actor? My God, what a ham!'" (Kobler 231).

But was Barrymore any better a judge of his own work than contemporary or later professional critics? That *The Beloved Rogue* is silly and trivial is hard to dispute. The same year in Weimar Germany, Bertolt Brecht was incorporating (uncredited) snatches of Villon's verses into *The Threepenny Opera*.

Since adolescence, Brecht had found in Villon a role model of the bohemian, antibourgeois, protoproletarian artist and had earlier in the decade fueled his first theatrical antihero, Baal, with splenetic *ressentiment* drawn in equal measure from Villon and Baudelaire (see Ewen 69–70; 177–8).

The Beloved Rogue scenarist Paul Bern's Villon, by contrast, is that distinctly Hollywood type of rebel, the prosocial outlaw in the Robin Hood vein whose minor violations of law (petty theft and fraud and disturbing the peace—not, as the historical record indicates, larceny and murder) and lack of due deference are expressions less of Baalesque nihilism and transgression than unquenchable lifeforce and indomitable individualism, and are, in any case, wholly compatible with love of country and support for hereditary absolute monarchy (if not necessarily for the superstitious and spiderlike Louis XI himself, juicily impersonated by Conrad Veidt). The film implausibly depicts Barrymore's Villon as a literary celebrity in his own lifetime, venerated alike by the common folk and the nobility (almost everyone he meets, from whatever social stratum, in this preGutenberg world hails him as "France's greatest poet," as if Villon's lays were readily available at the local bookstore), a man whose irrepressible vitality and lust for life lead him repeatedly to transgress social proprieties and codes, at the peril of his liberty and even his life. But Villon's essential natural nobility ultimately wins through, saving the kingdom, winning him King Louis's grudging approbation and a wife of noble blood. As a star vehicle for Barrymore, as Young notes, the movie pushes him further into the vein of a Fairbanks-style swashbuckling action hero: Barrymore—at forty-five, still strikingly youthful and lithe—is provided with numerous opportunities for stunt work from comic knockabout to heroic fisticuffs and swordplay.

Yet *The Beloved Rogue*'s foolishness notwithstanding, if Barrymore's reported deprecation of his own performance is true, it seems at this distance in time much less justifiable. In fact, Barrymore's acting is more likely to impress the modern viewer as—within the conventions of silent-film male heroism—strikingly lacking in the expected stagy mannerisms but rather as relaxed, both physically and expressively supple, and very much at ease before the camera's gaze: certainly comparing very favorably with Conrad Veidt's scenery-chewing gurning as Louis or the wide-eyed theatrics of Marceline Day as Barrymore's love interest, Charlotte de Vauxcelles. For the most part, certainly, Barrymore gives the impression of taking the material no more seriously than it deserves: yet, at the same time, the performance in no way resembles the willfully self-abnegating parodic turns of Barrymore's final years, most (in)famously *The Great Profile* (1940). However silly a picture *The Beloved Rogue* is, it is also fast-paced fun and, in the main, Barrymore's performance, matching Fairbanks in his own time and anticipating Errol Flynn a decade later, seems well keyed to the material. It's not immediately clear what Barrymore could have seen that so offended his self-regard.

But there is another dimension to *The Beloved Rogue*, one that, in fact, foreshadows the painful later spectacle of *The Great Profile*: an early version, albeit masked, of what Jeanine Basinger calls "playing yourself as a concept" (99). The film's portrait of a profoundly gifted artist brought low by his venal appetites—and cursed in his self-destructiveness with a yet more painful self-awareness—seems to invite the viewer's identification of performer and character. Not for nothing does Michael A. Morrison use one of *The Beloved Rogue*'s intertitles, "one must sorrow that a man of such genius should be a drunken clown," as the epigraph to the final chapter of his study of Barrymore's career as Shakespearean actor (261). The association is not hindsight: as we have seen, while the ravages of the 1930s still lay ahead, by this point in his career, the judgment of Barrymore's *nostalgie de la boue* was already forming and, indeed, hardening.

This reflexive dimension to *The Beloved Rogue* is particularly and powerfully present in the pivotal sequence of Villon's banishment early in the film. Crowned "King of Fools" by the Parisian mob, Villon insults Charles of Burgundy, cousin, courtier, and rival to the king, to his face. For this act of *lèse-majesté*, Louis spares Villon's life but takes sadistic pleasure in banishing him from the environs of Paris (the city he perceptively, if improbably, acknowledges as the source of Villon's poetic inspiration). To this point in the film, Barrymore's performance has demurred not only tragic style but mainstream romantic heroism, too, featuring a striking degree of capering, high jinks, and quasi-*commedia dell'arte* buffoonery—more Harold Lloyd than Douglas Fairbanks (though Lloyd's Joe College character would never be found committing burglary which is how we first meet Villon). The invitation to read this exaggerated farcical pantomiming as Barrymore's self-conscious undercutting/refusal of his viewers' expectations and desires, whether of manly heroism or romantic elegance and sensitivity, is underlined by his first close-up of the film which presents a grotesque deformation of his famously noble profile: an absurdly elongated "nose" in the form of an icicle that Villon dons to escape watchmen when he and his crew, Little Jehan and Nicholas (whose diminutive size and rotundity, respectively, serve to emphasize Barrymore's own elegant proportions), are almost caught thieving. While, narratively, the gesture establishes the film's predominant comedy action mode, thematically and also metatextually, it points up Villon/Barrymore's willful deformation of his own (outer and inner) beauty. That, once Villon is formally elected King of Fools, he delivers his pronouncements from semiformal stagelike structures—first, the scaffold permanently erected in the square before Notre Dame that foreshadows what increasingly seems Villon's own predestined doom; later, from the base of an equestrian statue—seems also to make an association between Villon's degraded artistry and Barrymore's own.

Figure 13.1 The spectacle of degradation in *The Beloved Rogue* (Alan Crosland, Feature Productions, 1927). Digital frame enlargement.

In the sequence immediately following Villon's elevation as King of Fools, two paired but contrasting close-up one-shots[5] invite the viewer to dwell and reflect upon the spectacle of his abasement and its consequences, and upon Barrymore's inhabitation of the character in successive ecstasy and agony of degradation. The first, seven seconds in duration, reveals Villon fully bedecked as King of Fools and fades up on a surprising—even shocking—reveal to camera[6] of Barrymore's celebrated visage masked and transformed by the grotesque makeup that constitutes the oafish tokens of his "office": a clown's mouth, jackass's ears, a bald-pate wig complete with miniature offset crown, and a sot's nose. In the last (echoing the earlier but more broadly and unproblematically comic), his icicle schnoz seems a particularly marked blight on Barrymore's famously noble profile (all the more so perhaps for any viewer in on the open secret of his alcoholism). Seemingly relishing his abasement/elevation, Barrymore's mouth curves into an idiot's grin matching the painted-on clown smile as he gazes, first and unnervingly (the strangeness intensified by the grotesque transformation) directly to camera, then to his right and upwards, to his left, and back again to his right. Eyes unfocused, his head movements jerky and apparently unmotivated, he bats his eyelashes in an idiotic parody either of maidenly decorum or possibly—this is clearly suggested—of the gaze of a martyred saint in devotional art.

Trying to draw a clear line between character and actor here seems a futile exercise. Clearly the *character* Villon is himself performing the spectacle of his own degraded apotheosis, embracing the carnivalesque spirit and the antiauthority with which it endows him as the fulfillment of his own transgressive nature, one he embraces and celebrates. Though the image is contextually located amid the frenzy of a drunken, ebullient mob, the exclusion of anyone else from this shot suggests Villon's inhabitation of this identity. Though formally vouchsafed to (imposed upon) him by others, it is nonetheless fundamentally unique, even solitary. A certain solitariness is one of the features Keane identifies as importantly constituting Barrymore's star persona; she notes, too, repeated blinking as a characteristic signifier of confusion when the (actual or reported) world of others fails to match the perception of the world Barrymore's characters have formed for themselves (see Keane 189–91). Here, in a highly self-conscious display, Barrymore's own performative repertoire of tics and gestures is appropriated by a character who is himself performing idiocy. Yet, in place of the careful play of interiority and external display Keane anatomizes in Barrymore's performance in *Beau Brummel*, Villon/Barrymore here offers a determined absence withdrawal—more precisely, an evacuation—of actual (mental or emotional) content. Villon, obviously, is acting but, in acting, is he actually thinking or communicating anything at all? In the disturbing near masochism of the retarded glee Villon/Barrymore pantomimes here, and in the ecstasy of abasement he discovers himself to inhabit, judgment on the baseness of (his) performance is unavoidably invited and, in the same moment, delivered: a tale, indeed, told by an idiot, signifying nothing.

But the second, much longer, close-up in turn complicates this implicit reflexive judgment by mercilessly working through, at the level of narrative content, its inevitable consequences (isolation, self-loathing, and despair) while simultaneously challenging its validity (through the merciless, even borderline masochistic, rigor and psychological acuity of Barrymore's screen performance).[7] Following Louis's pronouncement of the sentence of banishment, royal troops disperse the carnivalesque mob venerating Villon. Barrymore sits stunned and dismayed at the foot of the equestrian statue, emblem of regal authority, Villon's temporary license to appropriate which has been so readily revoked by the real power of the armed state. As before, he is set apart from those around him. Whereas previously, however, that separation was partly by virtue of his (in the film, stated and assumed rather than demonstrated) genius, partly (as King of Fools) by sheer otherness, here Villon/Barrymore is consigned to the isolation of despair. His companions variously try to engage with, and console, him but to no effect: he largely avoids their eyes or stares blankly past them. Once again, his gaze seems drawn upwards, as if meaning and/or consolation are to be discovered, if at all, in another sphere than he is compelled to inhabit. One by one, his associates exit the frame until, finally, he is left alone. It is here—some twenty-four minutes into the movie, in a single shot held uninterrupted (bar a brief insert of Barrymore's hands clutching fistfuls of wet snow he will use to wipe off his makeup) for *ninety-five long seconds*—that *The Beloved Rogue* allows us our first sight of Barrymore in a mode of tragic authenticity rather than antic burlesque. Again, Barrymore first gazes directly at the audience, as if implicating us in his wretchedness; then, as if struck by a thought, he reaches up to touch his face: his fingers alight on the bulbous drunkard's false nose and a momentary confusion passes across his face as if he had temporarily forgotten his circumstances. He stares about him in all directions, not with the blank idiot's gaze of the earlier shot but with a yearning desperation, but nothing his gaze lands on can bring him solace. He smears away his makeup with those handfuls of snow and the corner of his cloak; piece by piece he tears off the tokens of his "office," the bald-pate wig and tiny lopsided crown; but the recovery of his "true" self offers no consolation, if anything. the reverse. In the intractable reality he has courted by the choices he's made, Barrymore discovers an authentic abjection deeper and more irredeemable than the abjection he performed as King of Fools. The image fades to black.

Of course, *The Beloved Rogue* briskly recovers from this bleakness and, in short order, Villon is catapulting cabbages, barrels of beer, and ultimately himself over the rooftops of Paris and into noblewomen's boudoirs. But the spectacle of the performer despairingly stripping away the garish props, the tokens of his self-abnegation, to discover beyond them only a still-deeper emptiness, is deeply disturbing and haunts Barrymore's performance through the rest of the film—is directly echoed, indeed, in Villon's shame at his own fraudulent claims to his mother and, perhaps indirectly, in the otherwise incongruously graphic torture scene. The idea of faithlessness—to others but, above all, to oneself and one's artistic vocation—hovers over the film. It's therefore a conundrum that, at least in his performance, in this one sequence, of a man lost to himself and his art—rightly described by James Card as "absolutely ineradicable from memory" (161)—Barrymore demolishes the notion that his screen acting was overly histrionic or stagy; yet, as did others, he himself dismissed it as the work of a "ham." Moreover, the film's reflexive aspect—its portrait of the *artiste maudit*—clearly aligns it with the judgment Barrymore's own artistry *within* the film contradicts. It may be, indeed, that more truth lies in this contradiction itself than in its facile resolution. But can the contradiction at least be explained?

While Keane's rigorous scrutiny of Barrymore's acting style undoubtedly calls out key critical prejudices, at the same time it raises further questions about the cultural construction of cinema as a scion of the theater whose answers arguably lie deeper than simple snobbery toward an upstart medium (a snobbery of the kind cinema itself would subsequently display toward television, and, in due course, television towards online entertainment). An important problematic, obviously by no means confined to Barrymore's case but very apparent here, is overlooked—more accurately, it goes unstated—in Keane's analysis: that is, the shift not only from the live stage to recorded moving-image performance but from the gestural mode of the silent era to sound cinema (or, more accurately, given that live musical accompaniment was a ubiquitous part of the cinemagoing experience throughout the silent era, cinema of the spoken word).

Keane herself does not make this linkage. In her direct comparison of Barrymore's performances in the silent *Beau Brummel* and the sound *Counsellor at Law*, the absence of spoken dialogue in *Beau Brummel* is not even noted as a factor in Barrymore's construction of his performance (dialogue intertitles are discussed for Keane's analytical purposes as if they were spoken utterances). The restraint in Barrymore's acting style, which she notes as the basis for the (as she maintains, misguided) critical tendency to valorize *Counsellor* over *Brummel*, is noted simply in relation to the script and Wyler's direction rather than as a function (in whole or in part) of the transition to spoken-word cinema. But, given the obvious privileging of stage over screen that Keane notes in critical tradition, there would seem to be a ready correlation with the valorization of Barrymore's (early, that is, before the complete collapse of his reputation following the highly publicized personal crises of 1934–35) sound-era roles: for what did the advent of the optical soundtrack entail if not the restoration of the stage actor denied him during the silent era, his speaking voice? If, as Keane argues, it is associated back to Barrymore's celebrated "serious" work in the classical theater, by leaping over his decade as a major star of the silent screen, the "toned-down" quality of his work in a film such as *Counsellor at Law* implicitly rebukes the overstated gestural histrionicism that supposedly marred his silent film performances and which, perhaps, the muting of his vocal talents exacerbated.

Yet if the (admittedly scant) evidence is anything to go by, Barrymore's Shakespearean performances were some way removed from the kind of restrained self-sufficiency discernible in *Counsellor at Law*. Aside from the 1933 *Hamlet* screen test, Barrymore's turn as Richard of Gloucester (from *3 Henry VI*, III. iii) in Warner Bros.'s 1929 *The Show of Shows*—a showcase for the vocal performance skills of Warners' contract players in the new era of sound film to match MGM's successful *Hollywood Revue*, released earlier the same year—is the only moving-image record we have of his legendary Shakespearean acting skills from (albeit close to the end of) his stage-acting heyday. The evidence, however, is unpersuasive to a modern eye. Rather than either psychological depth or classical gravitas, Barrymore's exaggerated, stagy delivery, with broad facial contortions and eye movements, recalls ripe contemporaneous screen hams such as Dwight Frye's turn as Fritz in Whale's *Frankenstein* (1931); the *Babes in Toyland* makeup doesn't help matters. In fact, notwithstanding the generally positive critical response to the performance, this appearance—far more than the action-hero antics of *The Beloved Rogue*—seems far more deserving of Barrymore's apocryphal self-denunciation as a "ham."

It seems that, rather than restoring to Barrymore's performative quiver the unique arrow that separated him from other stars of the late silent era— his incomparable capability with the spoken word—the advent of recorded speech on film may, in fact, have presented Barrymore with a challenge to which he was unable to rise: that is, whereas during the silent era of stylized pantomime performance, Barrymore had of necessity developed an acting style quite different in significant ways from the style with which he had made himself an international acting celebrity, a style indeed better accommodated to the camera's particular registration of nuanced facial expression, glances, and motivated gesture, the sound era presented a new conundrum. With his expressive speaking abilities now restored to his armory, could Barrymore find an acting mode for sound cinema that modulated his rich vocal timbre for the necessarily restricted range of "believable" spoken intonations that matched his adjustment of his physical and facial register in the silent period?

The popular history of the transition to sound of course abounds with largely apocryphal accounts of careers destroyed by the optical recording of the actor's voice (famously burlesqued in *Singin' in the Rain*'s nasally Brooklyn screen siren Lina Lamont [Jean Hagen]). Perhaps the best known of these tragedies of sonic lapsarianism is the supposed collapse of Greta Garbo's onscreen paramour John Gilbert's heroic romanticism when optical sound recording allegedly exposed his weak piping voice. Though few of these tales stand up to much scrutiny, they are an important part of the folklore of Hollywood's Golden Age. While film history abounds with obvious examples of acting careers where an idiosyncratic delivery became a crucial part of the actor's screen persona (James Cagney, for example), there are fewer corresponding heroic narratives of careers rescued by the revelations of sound though there are a few of triumph over the medium ("Garbo talks").

One need not subscribe to cinephiliac versions of film history in which the advent of recorded sound is sometimes represented as a fall from an Edenic Golden Age of cinematic purity in order to acknowledge that—as anyone who has attended a screening of a significant silent feature in a well-preserved or restored print with appropriate musical accompaniment can readily testify—the enduring mystique of silent cinema owes much to the extraordinary power of the gestural and pictorial language developed by actors, particularly in the late silent (*c*. 1923–8) period. Conventional historical accounts point to the way in which the remarkable expressive cinematic lexicon of the late 1920s, making extensive use of both a mobile camera and a range of non-naturalistic devices (such as double exposures) to communicate inner states of mind, was physically and demonstratively constrained by the advent of sound. Though the initial immobility of sound cameras was quickly superseded, the shift to a new regime of verisimilitude in the spoken-word cinema largely suppressed not only most of the expressive devices of the late silent era but also the melodramatic gestural performance style that had underpinned silent cinema.

The paradox is that while, for modern cinephiles, recorded sound, specifically dialogue, can seem a corruption of "pure" silent cinema, for middlebrow critics in the silent era itself, it was the *absence* of the authorizing presence of the actor's voice, implicitly or explicitly, that branded silent acting as inauthentic: all the more so when the actor in question, such as Barrymore, could be represented as betraying a legacy of "serious" theatrical acting in favor of mutely (but lucratively) mugging for the movie camera. Does this reveal a critical "theatro-centrism" that, in a minor key, we can align with the logocentric Western philosophical traditions which, according to Derrida, treat the spoken word as the marker of absolute metaphysical presence and treat writing with suspicion for its malleability and interpretability? From an ontological perspective, and less on account of its vulgarity than because of its reproducibility and interpretability (its capability of *difference*), the film medium itself stands in the same second-order relationship to the supposed "authenticity" of (necessarily unique and irrecoverable) theatrical performance.[8] "Theater," in contrast, allows for, as Derrida puts it, the "dream . . . of full presence, the reassuring foundation, the origin and the end of play" (Derrida 292).

Of course, if this were true, then logically Barrymore's later spoken-word performances ought to have been received even less favorably (for tarnishing the originary authority of the imaginary locus of speech by recording it and rendering it a second-order reality). But the tangible *distance* between the restrained, more colloquial acting styles Barrymore adopted in his final years for sound film and the highly stylized (yet, because irrecoverable, nonetheless authentic) grand style of his Shakespearean performances, and the galloping collapse of Barrymore's capabilities as the 1930s progressed, culminating in the painful self-parody—"shredding himself for money," as Basinger memorably puts it (99)—of *The Great Profile* allows for *this* speech to be at once devalued as itself but valued as a faint echo of the "real" (always already lost) Barrymore. Card speculates that Barrymore was afflicted by a "deep doubt" of the ultimate merit of what he had accomplished in his most serious [cinematic] efforts" (163). The evidence of *The Beloved Rogue*, in which he deftly acts out self-estrangement and degradation *by* the camera *for* the camera, suggests that this self-limiting, even self-denying, ordinance was, indeed, at the heart of Barrymore onscreen.

NOTES

1. *The Beloved Rogue*, though the last-produced of these three films, was released on March 12, 1927, five months earlier than *When a Man Loves* on August 21.
2. *The Beloved Rogue* was thought to be lost until it became known in 1968 that a print was in Mary Pickford's personal archive of UA productions during her control of the company.
3. See Butler. Keane does not cite her: this is my supplementary gloss on her reading.
4. Gaylyn Studlar argues that from his "matinee idol" origins through his celebrated performance as *Peter Ibbetson*, up to and including his Fairbanks-esque Hollywood star vehicles of the late 1920s, Barrymore characteristically performs a version of masculinity that is simultaneously normative and transgressive and straddles "safe" (noble, wounded, and sensitive) and "dangerous" (sexually aggressive and uncontained) models of male romantic heroism.
5. In keeping with prevailing studio stylistic conventions, close singles in *The Beloved Rogue* very rarely move in closer than a medium "bust" close-up. Unless stated otherwise, in the close textual analyses here "close-up" indicates this framing—what in modern parlance would be termed "MCU."
6. The relatively prolonged shot also allows the viewers to confirm for themselves that this sot with the misshapen visage is, indeed, still *John Barrymore*.
7. The question is whether medieval carnival—in Bakhtin's classic analysis—entailed merely a term-limited license to burlesque institutional authority with no *real* surrender of, or challenge to, power—indeed, whether the act of granting such license itself reaffirms, rather than undermines, state power (as Villon fails to appreciate); or whether, as Michael Holquist argues, "the sanction for carnival derives ultimately not from a calendar prescribed by church or state, but from a force that preexists priests and kings and to whose superior power they are actually deferring when they appear to be licensing carnival" (see Bakhtin xviii).
8. I mean to suggest not that theater *is* in any meaningful sense a site of originary meaning but simply that it can perform this rhetorical and ideological function in theatrocentric criticism. On the use of theatrical metaphors in Derrida's own work, see Schröder.

CHAPTER 14

"I Never Thought I Should Sink So Low as to Become an Actor": John Barrymore in *Twentieth Century*

William Rothman

No one can watch—and listen to—John Barrymore in Howard Hawks's *Twentieth Century* and fail to recognize that his is a stupendous performance. With every physical gesture, facial expression, and vocal inflection, he marshals unexcelled acting technique, control, and timing to "nail" the charismatic, monstrous, yet strangely likable Oscar Jaffe. Oscar is always playing to an audience, not striving to make himself intelligible to others—or to himself. Drawing on knowledge gleaned from the theater—not the world's—stage, he is forever passing off as spontaneous lines of dialogue and behavior he scripts for himself to use, to his advantage, in his everyday life. He lives as if he were the star in a play he is writing, producing, and directing.

Sometimes, he acts so as to pass himself off as a man simply being himself, as at the train station, by disguising himself as a veritable Colonel Sanders to fool the detectives on the lookout for him (see Figure 1). At other times, the acting strives for melodramatic effect, as when he tries to convince Lily Garland, née Mildred Plotka (Carole Lombard), that, if she leaves him alone to go to a party, he will kill himself. (Many Barrymore characters, such as Hamlet, are subject to melancholy so profound that, at some point, they contemplate—or even commit—suicide.) At his most theatrical, demanding the spotlight, Oscar acts as if the play of his life has the gravitas, the elevated poetic language, of Shakespearean tragedy. He is this way every time he fires his right-hand man Oliver Webb (Walter Connolly) by pronouncing sentence on him, declaiming in a portentous voice and with a grand sweep of his arm, "I close the iron door!" Or when, his glazed eyes looking past Oliver as if captivated by a vision of another world, he says that, in the Passion Play he imagines himself producing, he has "at last found a story that is worthy" of Lily. Or when he says to Lily that the play will climax with her delivering "one of the greatest speeches

170 WILLIAM ROTHMAN

Figure 14.1 Six delicious moments from *Twentieth Century* (Howard Hawks, Columbia, 1934). Digital frame enlargements.

in the history of literature." Or when, after acting his way past the detectives, he declares, in a grandiloquent voice, "I never thought I should sink so low as to become an actor."

In this last example, there is dramatic irony in these words being spoken by Barrymore, the greatest actor of his generation, but also in Oscar's saying this without a trace of irony of his own, as though, if it is obvious to us that he has been acting nonstop all along and is acting now, he doesn't know this about himself. Ostensibly, he is speaking to Oliver but he is so captivated working his own performance that he loses sight of the fact that he is acting and that the audience he is playing to is . . . himself. As his musing approaches its inevitable, self-justifying conclusion that his genius is revealed most fully by his "magnificent failures," Oscar keeps distractedly pulling putty from his nose (see Figure 14.1.2). Hawks frames him in profile here, perhaps to remind us that Oscar, so comically lacking in self-knowledge, is John Barrymore, known by the public as "The Great Profile" but also as a great tragedian famous for playing characters who know themselves not wisely, but too well. A visual effect of this alignment between framing and acting is to make Oscar's nose appear to grow longer and longer, as if he were Pinocchio telling a lie. Barrymore's acting alone could not achieve this effect; it is dependent on the way Hawks has the camera frame him which, in turn, depends on the way Barrymore addresses himself to the camera. In this regard, this moment is paradigmatic of the fact that, throughout *Twentieth Century*, Barrymore's performance in bringing Oscar's theatricality to life is inseparable from his relationship with Hawks's camera. In a stage play, it is not possible for an actor, or the character he is playing, to have a relationship with the camera; there is no camera.

A NEW ACT

Ben Hecht and Charles MacArthur based the screenplay they wrote for Hawks, who was the film's producer as well as its director, on their 1932 Broadway play of the same name (which they had adapted, in turn, from *The Napoleon of Broadway*, an unproduced play by Charles Mulholland). In their play, the action begins when the main characters board the 20th Century Limited, the elegant passenger train advertised as "The Most Famous Train in the World," on its run from Chicago to Manhattan. Hawks insisted they add an entirely new first act providing a backstory to the Oscar–Lily relationship, and rode herd on them to ensure they held their cynicism in check and granted Oscar and Lily at least a modicum of emotional depth. To this end, Lily was changed from a haughty grande dame to an aspiring actress with humble roots. The changes went a long way toward transforming a frivolous farce into a virtual prototype for the romantic comedies Stanley Cavell calls "comedies of remarriage," especially Hawks's own *His Girl Friday* (1940).

In *Twentieth Century*'s first thirty-five minutes, we gain sympathy and respect for Lily, as does Oscar. No matter how badly his possessiveness, jealousy, and narcissism cause him to treat her, I find myself fervently wishing to believe, and at times believing, that there is a real part of Oscar that sees and truly values the "gold" in her soul; that his desire to "mine" that gold is not entirely self-serving; and that she is not *completely* crazy for loving him—just as in *His Girl Friday* Hildy (Rosalind Russell) isn't *completely* crazy for loving Walter (Cary Grant). Then again, in Archie Mayo's 1931 film, Barrymore's Svengali loved Trilby, too, and how did that turn out?[1]

Without the script changes he demanded, Hawks's film would have been, like the play, a knockabout farce with brilliant dialogue, perfectly offering Barrymore a showcase for his formidable comic skills. (It was considered a stretch when Barrymore, who had gained recognition in comedies, took on the dramatic roles that culminated in his triumphs as Richard III and Hamlet.) I'm not sure, though, that Hawks would have got his signature on a contract—Harry Cohn wouldn't back the film without Barrymore—to play a self-styled genius a total phony which was Hecht's and MacArthur's view of Oscar. As Barrymore incarnates him—as Hawks films Barrymore incarnating him—Oscar *is* a con artist but one who has conned himself into believing in his own genius. But a phony genius isn't all Barrymore's Oscar is. He also *is* a genius. But what kind of genius?

His Girl Friday ultimately declares Walter Burns, who behaves almost as badly as Oscar, to be worthy of the mantle of the male leads of remarriage comedies who are moral in their own ways. Is Oscar Jaffe Walter Burns's kind of genius or Svengali's entirely manipulative kind of genius? *Twentieth Century* avoids unambiguously answering this question. Perhaps this is a strength of the film. To me, it's a weakness. But neither Barrymore's acting nor Hawks's direction is to blame. The culprit is the screenplay. The fast-paced action on the train is uproariously funny but hews so closely to the cynical spirit of the Hecht–MacArthur play that it's only fitfully responsive to the ambiguity and depth with which the first act endows Lily and Oscar. One exception occurs when Lily finds herself in what Oscar calls "the creative mood" and, with his encouragement, comes up with her own ideas for the Passion Play production, matching him inspiration for inspiration. Her ideas may be as ludicrously over the top as his and they both may have hidden agendas but, in joyously pursuing their shared goal of creating theater, they are engaged in a conversation of equals worthy of a remarriage comedy. Here, *Twentieth Century* offers us a tantalizing glimpse, all too brief, of the film it might have been had it made a cleaner break with the cynicism of the play and, without sacrificing humor, found fruitful ways to make the rest of the film resonate more deeply with its first act.

I devote the remainder of this chapter to a close reading of one section of that first act. That is the best way I know to express, and to back up, my guiding intuition that in bringing Oscar Jaffe to life, Barrymore's performance, attuned with Howard Hawks's camera, showcases the man's theatricality but, further, that Barrymore's acting is precisely cut to the measure of film, not theater.

HOW TO SCREAM

Oscar is rehearsing a scene that climaxes in Mary Jo's scream. They come to the point where "Uncle Remus" (George Reed) informs her that her "daddy has just shot Mr. Michael." "Bang Bang!" Oscar cries out, raising his cane as if it had metamorphosed into the murder weapon. "Sway, sway," he anxiously cues Lily. "Come on, Uncle Remus," he says with urgency, so impatient is he to get to the scream that he believes will confirm his hunch that Mildred Plotka has what it takes to be a star. "Oh Lordy, Lordy, Miss Mary Jo," Uncle Remus says, dutifully speaking his line as he shuffles in. Hawks cuts to a shot with "Uncle Remus," Oscar, Lily, and, playing Emmy Lou (Mary Jo's "little chum," Oscar calls her), Valerie Whitehouse (Mary Jo Matthews) (the same Valerie Whitehouse Oscar will try to make a star after Lily leaves him). In synchronization with Lily's long, deep intake of breath in preparation for the rafter-shaking scream he is anticipating, Oscar spreads his arms wider and wider, like an expanding balloon, as if to make room for the capacious scream to come. When Lily emits only a pathetic little sound, Oscar's arms lower slowly, the balloon deflating, his gesture punctuated by the dull thud of his cane hitting the floor. "What was *that*?" he asks derisively, "That . . . *squeak*!" Throwing his script to the floor in frustration and disgust, he vehemently announces, without looking at Lily, "We're going to stay in this theater until Miss Garland learns to scream. Dismiss the cast!"

One by one, the cast and crew pass through the frame until only Oscar and Lily are left. Breaking down, Lily collapses in a chair, cries "I can't stand it any more," and lowers her head in shame and exhaustion. With still greater contempt in his voice, Oscar calls Lily a "squalling amateur" and demands that she stand up, adding disgustedly, "Take that *hump* out of your back" (a sly *Richard III* reference?). In a tight close-up on Lily, with Oscar capping his series of insults offscreen: "You're not demonstrating *underwear* any more!" Lily finally looks up, fiercely meets his gaze, and rises to her feet, the camera reframing with her movement to transform the close-up that had isolated her into a two shot in which Oscar and Lily face off. He is staring intently at her (though the angle doesn't permit us to see his eyes or discern his expression) as she fights back. "I've taken all the bullying from you I'm going to. No man living can kick me around like that for eight hours until I can't see straight. I'm a human being, do you hear? A human being!"

The camera slightly reframes to a three shot as Oliver tries to soothe Lily's ruffled feathers. With Oscar still watching her intently, Oliver says, patronizingly, "Now, now, Miss Garland . . .," and tries to put a consoling arm around her. She rebukes him. "My name is Plotka. It's a good name, too." Turning sharply to face Oscar, she adds, "Just as good as Jaffe!" Pulling at her hair in frustration, and all but in tears, she completes her peroration. "I wanted to be an actress, but I won't crawl on my stomach for any man. You ... you find somebody else." Angrily, she exits the frame screen right. But Oscar—whose expression is now visible for the first time in the shot—reacts very differently. In the aftermath of Lily's emotional outburst, his eyes are wide, as if he is still transfixed, entranced, by what he has seen and heard. Perhaps more to himself than to Oliver, and in a hushed, calm voice we had never heard from him before, a voice that makes an astonished Oliver stare at him dumbfounded, he says, "She's marvelous, just as I thought! Fire, passion, everything! The gold is all there . . ." In an altered voice that registers that he is again thinking soberly and is determined to keep his eyes on the prize, he adds, "But we must *mine* it." As Lily, offscreen, softly sobs, Oscar slips silently out of the frame to join her. In a shot with Oliver in the background looking on, Oscar walks up to the sobbing Lily who is putting on her coat. When she turns to leave she sees Oscar, standing in silence close to her, his expression inscrutable. Lily seems to have a momentary impulse to embrace him or perhaps to resume berating him. Instead, she simply lowers her head as the camera moves in to frame them more closely. Gripping her arm, Oscar says, firmly but gently, "Lily Garland, I only heard one thing: that you want to be an actress. That's all I want, too."

All the time he is speaking this sentence, Lily's head is still bowed and she is quietly sobbing. Saying, "Look at me" and cradling her face in his hands, Oscar gently tilts her head up and, when she responds by raising her eyes to meets his gaze, there is a cut to a closer, more intimate two shot (see Figure 14.1.3). Though the camera angle, which favors Lily, again keeps us from seeing Oscar's eyes, we sense, from her eyes, that she is powerfully drawn to his and that he is moved by the exquisiteness of her face which this framing so eloquently registers. His fingers barely grazing her cheek, he says, in a gentle, slightly awe-struck voice, "Duse had that modeling."[2] Is Oscar hiding lustful thoughts, simply putting on act whose real goal is getting her into bed with him? Perhaps. But Barrymore's performance, filmed as Hawks films it, makes it impossible for me to believe that deceiving her, seducing her, is all he is doing. I cannot doubt that Oscar means what he saying, that his words are acknowledging the genuine luster of the "gold" that he is seeing—and we with him—in this woman's face. (Lily's face is Carole Lombard's face, after all.)

Oscar's next line ("Now we're going to teach little Mary Jo how to scream"), spoken as his hands are cradling Lily's cheeks, signals a shift. He is still speaking to a beautiful woman with Duse's modeling who wants to be an actress and whose "gold" he is determined to "mine." But his actual words and his tone of voice suggest, rhetorically, that he is addressing "little Mary Jo," the character he wants Lily to play. Lowering his hands from Lily's face he asks, "Do you trust me, child?" It is a woman, not a child, who answers, "Yes." Lily's "Yes" signifies that she accepts Oscar as the man she trusts to preside over her education, her creation, as an actress. Oscar *will* "teach little Mary Jo how to scream." He *will* transform Mildred Plotka into the actress, the star, Lily Garland. In this sense, he *will* prove worthy of her trust. But will he will also betray it? We shall see.

Authorized by Lily's "Yes," Oscar abruptly changes his demeanor. Casting aside all gentleness, he declares in an impassioned voice, "I'm going to find the soul that's there and release it . . ." As he speaks, his hand pokes her repeatedly to punctuate his words and give them emphasis. As he continues, ". . . so it'll fly further . . ." his arm rises, as if to mime his words as well as punctuate and emphasize them. As he brings his sentence to a close, ". . . soar up to the top gallery!" his raised arm soars even higher. Is Oscar acting here? Of course. Nonetheless, Barrymore endows Oscar's performance with such passion, such sheer physical force, that I find myself unable to doubt that, at this moment, he is genuinely inspired, *possessed*, by the vision animating his words, the vision his words are conjuring: that he fervently wishes for Lily, too, to become possessed by this vision; and, fervently, believes that his genius will find a way to make this happen so they will go on to make great theater together, the kind of theater that—like all great art, perhaps—has the power to liberate—"release" is Oscar's more evocative word—the human soul. To state the obvious: Barrymore personally shared Oscar's belief that great theater has the power to make souls soar. Had he not had that faith in theater, he could not have been the great Hamlet he was—or the great Oscar Jaffe he is. (I don't know whether Barrymore, a man of the theater, had an equal faith in film. Hawks, a true man of the cinema, surely did.)

In now turning abruptly to Oliver and ordering him to go all the way up to the top gallery to listen for the anticipated rafter-shaking scream—an order that, as usual, Oliver only grudgingly obeys—Oscar is breaking, or rather, as it turns out, putting on hold, the ecstatic mood captured and cast by his words to Lily. (Barrymore characters are wont to have a talent for getting right back into a mood they had put on hold, as if returning to a dream from which they had been rudely awakened by the need to attend to some mundane practical matter.) By literalizing his own poetic metaphor—Lily's soaring will rise up to the top gallery—Oscar is following a line of thought, in a sense, making a logical connection, bringing his soaring language down to earth. He sustains the metaphor when he turns back to Lily and, shaking his fist for emphasis, says, "Now, you're going to lift Mr. Webb out of his *seat* with your scream!" Squeezing her arm, his voice at a high pitch of excitement, he adds, "Come on! I'll take all the other parts."

His assistant, Max Jacobs (Charles Lane), interrupts Oscar's concentration by asking whether he wants the manuscript. Oscar snaps back, in a voice dripping with contempt, "I *slept* with that manuscript for six months!" That's the difference between the two men. For Max, theater is merely a business;

he doesn't have greasepaint running through his veins. Oscar does. That's the kind of genius he is. Theater *thrills* him. He lives for that thrill. But he can't create theater on his own. Hence the crescendo of excitement in his voice as he says to Lily, seamlessly seguing into the ecstatic mood he had put on hold, "Come on now, dear. Take off your coat. We're going into *action*! There are 2,000 people out there!"

Oscar can't wait for the action to begin. He rushes over to Lily, sits her down in a chair, and, hovering over her, says, excitedly, "We'll go back a little ways so when we come to the scream, you'll be in the mood." He pats her cheeks with both hands and then runs to the place where Emmy Lou is to make her entrance, the camera following him and excluding Lily from the frame. "Now, Emmy Lou comes on." The camera pans left with Oscar, imitating Emmy Lou's gait and speaking in the girl's mild, squeaky, exaggeratedly Southern voice: "Mary Jo, Mary Jo, where are you, Mary Jo? Your daddy just met Michael. They're on the lawn." In Mary Jo's voice, he says, "Emmy Lou, what are we all going to do?" Then: "Bang! Bang!"

Oscar stares into Lily's eyes with a Svengali-like intensity. "Remember the pause. Sway. Keep swaying." She obeys. "Come on, Uncle Remus," Oscar says with mock impatience, as if that character was being played by another actor, not himself. In a moment, we shall understand that he says this only to buy time to do something he was planning all along. He rushes screen right, the camera following him, to the chair on which Lily had draped her black coat which has a white flower pinned to it. Leaning down and reaching for the flower, he casts a quick look back to make sure Lily won't see what he is up to. In a beautiful extreme close-up in which the perfect flower stands out against the lustrous black of the coat, Oscar's fingers reach for the mother-of-pearl tip of the hatpin, then pull the pin out with one sure, swift motion, causing the flower to fall out of the frame, a perfect symbol for Lily's impending loss of innocence (see Figure14.1.4).

Oscar quickly spins around. For the briefest instant, we glimpse an expression of almost maniacal glee, before he hunches his back and, now in character as Uncle Remus, shuffles over to Lily and says, in that stereotypical "stage Negro" voice, "Oh Lordy, Lordy, Mary Jo! Your daddy has just gone and shot Mr. Michael!" Turning away from "Uncle Remus," Lily raises her hands to frame her face, opens her mouth wide, and takes a deep breath—all exactly as she had played the scene in the earlier run through. Will her scream be different this time? At this moment of high suspense, there is a cut from the two shot of Lily and Oscar to a second extreme close-up, this one of Oscar's hand holding the hatpin. Like a rattlesnake coiling to strike, his fingers tighten into a fist to grasp the pin more forcefully, the palpable strength of his grip registering, expressively, the real violence of the act he is about to perform, however comical we might find it. It is in the next shot—a reprise of the setup that preceded the close-up insert—that the strike takes place. At the instant Lily is primed to scream, Oscar stabs the hatpin so hard into her rear end that the real pain she feels—the pain he means that she should feel—causes her to produce exactly the rafter-raising scream he wanted. Ecstatic, he shouts, more to himself than to Lily, "Perfect! Marvelous!" and punctuates his words by kissing his hand, throwing his head back and, looking up to the heavens, raising his hand as high as it can go, as if to send the kiss soaring to the heavens in gratitude to a guardian angel or lucky star. Oscar doesn't do this to achieve a particular effect; it's a spontaneous expression of what he really feels. But there's ambiguity, perhaps dramatic irony, in his performance of this gesture. Is he really acknowledging providence or Lady Luck, even Lily, for making possible a triumph he couldn't have achieved on his own? Or is he exulting in what he *does* believes he has achieved on his own, achieved solely by his own genius, in the same spirit in which, today, athletes perform fist pumps to exult in their own physical prowess?

We cut to Oscar sitting in the top gallery with, far off on the stage and small in the background, Oscar and Lily. Lily is simply staring at Oscar who momentarily pulls himself away from her and shouts, "How was it, Oliver?," his voice altered by an echo effect to underscore the real and symbolic distance between audience and performer, between the world and the stage. Barely awake, Oliver answers, "O.K. from here" and begins dutifully clapping but the import of what we have just witnessed is lost on him, as usual. What *did* just happen?

In the next shot there is a lapse in continuity. Lily no longer stands facing Oscar. She is on the floor, her head bowed, with Oscar standing over her, applauding. Oliver's applause seems to segue seamlessly to Oscar's applause, an effect that serves to make the jump cut less noticeable. Hawks's direction in this period is ordinarily so precise that it is unlikely, even with the tight shooting schedule, a lapse in continuity was caused by a mistake in coverage, or that it simply went unnoticed, especially at so critical a moment. My suspicion is that the gap between the two shots—Oliver clapping in the balcony; Lily on the stage floor—had once been filled by some frames that Hawks and editor Gene Havlick decided to leave on the proverbial cutting-room floor. Does this jump from Oliver to Lily make any difference? No, if we simply enjoy *Twentieth Century* as a frivolous farce. Yes, if we take the film's Oscar seriously in human terms, as Barrymore surely did. The gap between the shots denies us a way to know how Lily—who doesn't collapse after her scream but simply stands motionless looking at Oscar (feeling what? thinking what?)—came to be on the floor, her head bowed, no longer meeting his gaze (and why?).

Applauding Lily, Oscar says directly to her face, "Splendid! Excellent! Brava!" Brava!" Now she looks up but feeling what? Thinking what? Without allowing us time fully to take in her expression, Hawks cuts back to the previous setup with Oliver in the foreground (still, or again) listlessly applauding, his applause echoing that of Oscar in the background who is continuing his litany of praise to Lily ("Magnificent! Brava! Brava! Brava!"). Then Hawks employs a wipe, together with a sound overlap, to effect a transition to the well-dressed audience at the play's premiere performance, filling the theater's once-empty seats, applauding warmly as the final curtain rings down on the opening-night performance.

Remarkably, this wipe wipes out all the rehearsals, all the hard work—usually a focus of movies about theater people—that it took for Lily to go from her scream to her triumphant debut. Perhaps even more remarkable for a film about theater people, the wipe also wipes out the performance that makes Lily a star. Indeed, in the entire film we *never* have an opportunity to observe, even for a moment, Lily onstage, acting. Though we have no way of judging her acting for ourselves, the shot of the applauding theater audience is presented without irony. We are given no grounds to doubt this audience's judgment, hence no reason to doubt that Oscar has succeeded in mining the "gold" in Lily, in presiding over her metamorphosis. As a man of the theater, Oscar may not be a Shakespeare but he's evidently not a fraud, either. When large bouquets of flowers are brought to the stage for her, Lily receives them with grace and humility. There's no suggestion that she hasn't earned this reward. But hasn't Oscar earned a reward, too?

ALONE

In the unsettling shot that follows, Oscar is alone, perched high on a spiral staircase behind a corner of the stage (see Figure 14.1.5). He is framed frontally in expressionistic shadow, dressed all in black from hat to shoes, as he had been the night he feigned suicide. This shot is followed by a high angle, from Oscar's point of view, of Lily bowing once again as the audience continues to applaud her and the curtain begins to come down. This shot contrasts so starkly with the preceding shot of Oscar that it intensifies our sense of his depressed withdrawal. In the shot of the audience that follows, the lowering curtain casts a shadow that progressively darkens the frame, as if this gathering darkness was an objective correlative to Oscar's inner darkness. The next shot, from the audience's point of view, begins with darkness, until the black theater curtain parts for Lily's final curtain call. This is followed by a reprise of the shot of the solitary Oscar gravely taking in the scene of his protégée's triumph.

It occurs to me that these haunting shots of Oscar are responding to the final shot of Lloyd Bacon's *42nd Street* (1933), in which Julian March (Warner Baxter), the producer/director of a Broadway musical whose triumphant opening-night performance has just ended, sits alone and unrecognized on a metal staircase at the side of the theater as the last members of the audience, cheered and uplifted by the show, straggle out of the theater and head homeward into the night as the image fades to black. With a shrug, March accepts his aloneness as a price worth paying for knowing that he has done his part, in the depths of the Depression, to bring joy to the audience and jobs to the cast and crew. March's mood is bittersweet. Oscar's mood is much darker, and also more inscrutable.

The dark mood that the shots of Oscar capture and cast is created, in part, by Hawks's expressionistic lighting and composition. Hawks frames Oscar here in a manner befitting a sinister, cold-blooded killer. The absolute stillness of Barrymore's Oscar here is in the starkest possible contrast to his manic behavior in the immediately preceding sequence, which climaxed in Lily's scream. There, he was a dynamo of nervous energy, of nonstop motion, as he almost always will be once the action moves to the Twentieth Century Ltd. But now he takes in Lily's triumph with the dark, unfathomable gaze of a great tragedian, viewing her from a place outside the human circle, as if he were haunting the world, not living in it. He could be Svengali, or the treacherous, murderous Richard III, or Hamlet, contemplating suicide.

For all the farcical dimension of the Hecht/MacArthur screenplay, there is a depth to Barrymore's Oscar that enables him to throw himself body and soul into the farce and, at the same time, transcend it: a haunting awareness of mortality, of the inevitability of death and loss, of the ephemeral nature of everything he holds precious. There is the sense of the potential for tragedy that is universal in the human condition. But his sense of the tragic is compounded by the harrowing fear, particular to Barrymore, that he was personally fated for madness. Barrymore brings to Oscar a depth that, even with the revisions Hawks demanded, the screenplay does not consistently acknowledge, a depth Hawks's camera consistently reveals, and a depth Barrymore consistently reveals to Hawks's camera, as he had revealed it to William Wyler's camera in *Counsellor at Law* and, before that, George Cukor's camera in *A Bill of Divorcement* (1932) and *Dinner at Eight* (1933).

Once Lily is backstage Oliver has the chutzpah to say to her, "I always knew you could do it," as he ushers her to her dressing room. Soon after that, Oscar brushes off well-wishers who want to congratulate him and, framed with his back to the camera, walks purposefully, his arms hanging limply at his sides, with a gait as grim as his black clothes, toward Lily's dressing-room door. We may recognize his gait as the classic "monster" walk of the expressionist theater of the early twentieth century, most familiar to American audiences as Boris Karloff's in *Frankenstein* (1931). It is also George O'Brien's walk, as his character approaches his loving wife with the intention of murdering her, in Murnau's *Sunrise* (1927), a film that strongly influenced Hawks's style in his early sound films; the walk of James Arness as the monstrous alien in *The*

Thing from Another World (1951); and, most pertinently, Paul Muni's walk at the end of *Scarface* (1932).

In a gorgeous shot worthy of von Sternberg, Lily is beside a round mirror bordered by lights. "Was I all right? . . . Was I what you wanted?" Oscar walks slowly toward Lily, expressionless, giving nothing away. (This is one of a number of shots in the film in which Barrymore's greatness as a dramatic actor is manifest not by the way he expresses his character's thoughts and feelings but, rather, by the way he vacates his face of all nameable expression, the better to reveal his character's unfathomable depth.)

Lily waits expectantly and hopefully for Oscar to declare himself. He tips his hat and says, in a voice devoid of irony, "I came to pay my respects to a great actress." Wiping away tears, he bows down and literally kisses the hem of her garment. Can this gesture possibly be sincere? Can he believe that she is sucker enough—can she be sucker enough—to take it at face value?

As Lily sits wiping away tears, we see her and Oscar both doubled, symbolically, by their reflections in the mirror. He turns screen right to Lily's maid, saying, "Go outside, Sadie," which cues a cut to Sadie, shutting the door behind her with a smirk that she seems to direct to us, as if calling upon us to second her disgust for the cynical scene of seduction she has no doubt Oscar is authoring. This attitude can't help but influence our response to Oscar's eloquently worded and voiced attestation to Lily: "The beauty and glamour that were mine for a little while during those rehearsals now belong to the world forever and ever more."

As Oscar speaks these eloquent words, we hear knocking—very distracting, that knocking—that provokes him to turn and say, abruptly dropping his lofty tone, "Are you there, Mulligan?" We hear the offscreen voice of Mulligan, whoever he may be, answering in the affirmative. Oscar turns back to Lily, instantly recapturing the elevated mood—being as adept as Chaplin's Tramp at turning on a dime is one of the gifts many Barrymore characters have in common—and leads her or, rather, her figure framed in the mirror, to the door. He opens the door, briefly revealing Mulligan, before Hawks cuts to the cut-out star, viewed from Oscar's and Lily's shared point of view, that Mulligan had been nailing to the door. Over this shot of the star, we hear Oscar's offscreen say, "This once hung on *Bern*hardt's door."[3]

"How marvelous," says Lily, softly and breathlessly. "I almost wish it weren't there," replies Oscar, his voice trembling. "Why?" Turning to Lily, Oscar says, again with no tangible irony in his voice and with the camera slowly moving in toward them, "It's the golden mark that sets you apart from the world, beyond the reach of any one man to have and to hold." Oscar lowers his eyes and looks almost in the direction of the camera, as if the full import of his words—that she is now beyond his reach—is dawning on him as he speaks them. "No, don't say that—it frightens me." The camera is still slowly moving in as he says, hesitantly and without meeting her gaze, "Would you . . . —" His voice cracks, as if he is fighting back tears: ". . . Would you . . . let me kiss you goodbye?"

ACTING AND OVERACTING

Here, for the second time in the film, Oscar strikes me as overacting. Earlier, he performs a phony death-bed scene to trick Lily into signing a contract. In both scenes, I find myself wondering how Lily can possibly fail to see that Oscar is acting. I can't believe she's that gullible or blind. But neither can I believe that Barrymore has simply misplayed these crucial scenes. Then perhaps Lily does *not* fail, or not *simply* fail, to see through Oscar's act. And perhaps there's some reason Oscar overacts in these scenes and nowhere else. What if he wants Lily to know that he desires her but is unwilling or unable to declare his feelings directly? (How does a man so practiced in faking sincerity speak sincerely?) And what if he isn't *simply* acting when he calls the star on Lily's door the "golden mark"—the mark of the "gold" he has mined?—that "sets her apart from the world," thus beyond his reach? Could his overacting be symptomatic of an anxiety this idea arouses in him, perhaps because he fears that it is he, not Lily, who is fated to be "set apart from the world"? What else could Oscar have been thinking about when Hawks framed him in those expressionistic shots that did, indeed, "set [him] apart from the world"? In "Experience," Emerson writes: "I shun father and mother and wife and brother when my genius calls me." That true artists are married to their art, hence out of the reach of others, is an idea that Barrymore's Oscar—or Barrymore himself, or Hawks, for that matter—might cavalierly dismiss.

When Oscar again meets Lily's gaze, his eyes are beseeching. So are hers. Almost imperceptibly, she nods her head and answers, barely audibly, "Yes," echoing her answer to his earlier question, "Do you trust me, child?" Then, her "Yes" meant she trusted him to teach her to be an actress, and this he has done. What does her "Yes" mean this time? She trusts him to kiss her. But she doesn't want this to be a *goodbye* kiss. She wants this kiss to mean nothing less than "I do." Leaning close, he kisses her tenderly on the lips but then . . . pulls away. Burying her head in his shoulder, she implores him, "Oh Oscar, don't leave me now!," adding, "I'm nothing without you and never will be." In retrospect, we can recognize the dramatic irony, the prophetic dimension, of this last line. It will turn out, in ways neither Lily nor Oscar can possibly anticipate, that truer words were never spoken. And if it had been Oscar speaking those words to Lily, not the other way around, they would be no less true.

At this point, Hawks cuts, devastatingly, to Oscar's foot, silently and surreptitiously pushing the door shut. Then to a shot, with the closing door progressively blocking our view, of Oscar, his eyes wide open and with an inscrutable, and indescribable, expression—an expression unreadable by us and unseen by Lily whose face is still pressed against his shoulder. With no need for a cut, the shot ends with the camera framing the star on the now closed door (see Figure 14.1.6). The image fades out, bringing to an end the film's first act—the act Hawks insisted on having from Hecht and MacArthur.

Do we really know that Oscar is simply betraying Lily's trust when he closes that door? Does it make a difference that she wishes him to be her lover not just her director? She doesn't wish to be "beyond his reach." Her wish is for Oscar to "have" and to "hold" her. She will learn the hard way what those words "have" and "hold" mean to this man.

Be careful what you wish for.

NOTES

I am grateful to Marian Keane for all she has taught me about Barrymore over the years.

1. On *Svengali*, the reader should see the chapter by Diane Carson in this volume [eds].
2. Eleanore Duse (1858–1924), an Italian actress regarded as one of the greatest of all time.
3. The French actress Sarah Bernhardt (1844—1923), "the Divine Sarah," Duse's equal in greatness and fame.

CHAPTER 15

Barrymore Does Barrymore: The Performing Self Triumphant in *The Great Profile*

R. Barton Palmer

Produced by Twentieth Century-Fox, *The Great Profile* (1940) showcases the last significant screen performance of John Barrymore who, for comic effect, plays a thinly disguised John Barrymore bearing the very theatrical name of Evans Garrick.[1] Yet the intriguing way in which he here constructs a version of his older and in-decline self has never drawn the critical attention it well deserves. This is both understandable and regrettable. *The Great Profile* takes for its title a sobriquet that Barrymore had enthusiastically adopted earlier in his career, marking it as autobiographical, which must have been a calculated marketing decision on the part of the studio. And the film refers more or less directly to recent events in his life as he slipped from stage and screen eminence into what some of his admirers regarded as alcoholic degradation and embarrassing incompetence in handling his personal affairs.

Yet Barrymore does more in this film than register on celluloid all of the warts of his currently failing self—career in jeopardy, latest marriage on the rocks, bankruptcy threatening because of huge sums of money owed to creditors, and his health on a downward spiral as a result of constant overindulgence in drink, leading to "benders," memory blackouts, and the DTs. A one-dimensional autobiographical approach to *The Great Profile* of course reflects the most fundamental of category errors, confusing art and life, while failing to acknowledge that Barrymore here constructs a slanted fictional version of what he had become even while (as an actor with not just one but two bodies like any other) he remains legible as "himself," that is, as a presence in full control of what he shows to moviegoers. Acting out marital discord is very different from enduring and participating in it, as Barrymore would have been able to point out. In other words, the film dramatizes, even as it exemplifies, Barrymore's performing self, imaged here triumphant over unpromising circumstances in a vehicle that was confected for him by a major studio. Evans Garrick offered a strong contrast to the less than worthy roles he had recently been offered by Hollywood in productions such as *Hold That Co-ed* (1938). With *The Great Profile*, in fact, Darryl F. Zanuck and Fox gave Barrymore the opportunity to make something entertaining and, if in an unusual way, positive compared to what was happening to him in the last years of a career now as notorious as it had been amazing.

Most important, perhaps, Barrymore's competent and trouble-free participation in *The Great Profile* refuted the then publicly bruited view that he was "through" as a star because his worsening peccadilloes made him unreliable. Provocatively, Barrymore's supposed permanent fall from entertainment-industry grace is a proposition that the film, with a telling sense of *mise-en-abîme*, advances as its narrative hook. Overcoming difficulties which are largely self-created, Garrick in the end is shown as profitably channeling—at least for the moment—his well-known character flaws, with some help from favoring circumstances. He achieves renewed professional success because of, rather than in spite of, them. There is thus no little humor, however grim, in this story, which emphasizes above all the star's perseverance in continuing a career that he loved while rejecting "reformation" in the spirit of remaining true to himself. The film's production tells a different story, reflecting Barrymore's renewed dedication to the rigors of screen acting, with its longueurs, discontinuous performance, and inflexible production schedules. Shooting on *The Great Profile* wrapped five days early because the star, using blackboards on which dialogue he could not memorize was written in large letters, did not muff his lines or miss cues. Little was required in the way of reshooting even though the role was challenging. This madcap comedy required Barrymore to devise and sustain a complex performance, especially in the frequent ensemble scenes that often required well-timed movements, with instantaneous changes of voice, mood, and expression. From all reports Barrymore found the project inspiring. As one of his biographers, John Kobler, remarks, he "plunged into it with manic zest," and that energy certainly shows through in the release cut (350). Perhaps Barrymore realized that this was autobiography in the optative mood. After all, the film does sketch out the kind of immediate and positive professional future that Barrymore might still reasonably hope for; the film was a useful advertisement that he was still a capable and reliable performer, even if rapidly declining health, due to chronic alcoholism, quickly threatened his professional future in the aftermath of its release. Even so, despite these physical limitations, his last project, *Playmates* (1941), allowed Barrymore to offer yet another version of the hammy Shakespearean who had seen better days that he had first created in *Profile* for Walter Lang, this time in a comic romp with radio personality and band leader Kay Kyser. David Butler's *Playmates* is essentially a sequel to *Profile* and thus a testimony of sorts to what some others in the industry thought were the profitable elements of that earlier production.

Critics, however, have generally seen little value in either the film or in Barrymore's incarnation of Evans Garrick. *The Great Profile* did not do well at the box office but that is an unfortunate and all too common fate that can have many authors. To be sure, filmgoers might have been put off by the way in which its autobiography cuts too close to the bone; this certainly is the major complaint of later commentators. Though impressed by the star's energetic performance, Kobler plays amateur psychologist and suggests that Barrymore was interested in the role only as an "outlet for the expression of his self-contempt" (350). Similarly, Margot Peters opines that, toward the end of his amazing career, Barrymore had "nothing to sell now but his own degradation" (443). Lacking respect for one of America's most accomplished and celebrated classical actors, "Hollywood," she declares, "offered him large sums only on the condition that he make a fool of himself" (443). This is a strange comment, indeed, because it assumes, contrary to all the evidence, that Barrymore had previously been determined to present to the public a dignified version of himself.

But, like everything written about one of Hollywood's most distinctive and unconventional personalities, Peters's book chronicles how his life had, from early on, been marked by a continuing series of scandals and well-publicized "incidents" about which he never showed much embarrassment. What other Hollywood and Broadway notable, after all, developed and sustained a reputation for urinating in public whenever the urge to do so struck him? In any case, who could blame the American commercial filmmaking establishment for scheming to make money from what they had good reason to expect would please audiences which was Barrymore lampooning his own well-known weaknesses and idiosyncrasies? Self-mockery, as any student of comedy would readily admit, is not necessarily degrading. Was Barrymore exploited by an industry to which he had at times delivered enormous profits? Yes, of course, but was he then more of a pathetic victim of heartless colleagues than any star among the hundreds who passed through the system? In any case, it is important to note, as even Peters and Kobler acknowledge, that in this project Barrymore assumed considerable power over the images of himself he allowed to be put on celluloid.

It seems accurate to say, in fact, that, in *The Great Profile*, Barrymore adopted a quite appropriate approach to "performing" (which included, but was not limited to, "acting") as he made the most of what he had left to give his public, including a lightly fictionalized version of recent events that had made headlines for months. It was reasonable to expect that these foibles might be of great interest to many moviegoers, even as, in a characteristic Hollywood gesture, what had proven to be popular on the legitimate stage was given a second life in the cinema. An important element of his performance in the film is that he reverted to forms of comic acting that he had mastered in his pre-Shakespearean Broadway career, in such forgettable productions as *The Fortune Hunter* (1909) and *A Slice of Life* (1912). Unlike the other characters in the film, his Evans Garrick is consistently self-dramatizing—all exaggerated gestures and postures, pop-eyed reactions, rapid shifts between a transparently phony "educated" English punctuated by less-calculated colloquial outbursts revealing that his otherwise more dignified presentation is simply a pose. As is appropriate for his character, Barrymore constantly acts acting, with few if any sequences in which the "inner" Garrick can be sensed emerging; especially stagy are his several conventionally comic portrayals of drunkenness which feature unsuppressed belching and loud bursts of inappropriate song. Peters writes that "Jack was a willing victim" in such proceedings who, in his appearance as Evans Garrick, took "perverse delight in vomiting upon himself in public" (443). And yet such unembarrassed buffoonery could be seen as having Shakespearean antecedents (see Falstaff, Sir John). In fact, the self-important Garrick, all ego and puffery, seems an actorly version of the *miles gloriosus*, one of the Elizabethan drama's most pervasive stock comic characters.

By "vomiting upon himself," Peters undoubtedly also means the several gags in unabashed bad taste that provide moments of shocked surprise: Barrymore appearing at one point in his union suit underwear or clowning around in a wheelchair in an obvious lampoon of brother Lionel. It is significant that these gags are elements of Garrick's performance on stage; they are in every case greeted with uproarious laughter and applause by the story world's theater audience. But Peters might also be referring to the way the actor is enlisted to poke fun at the tradition of Victorian acting, all standard gesture and declamation, whose claim to aesthetic preeminence he had debunked during his spectacular career two decades earlier (following a long-established American performance tradition he had taken on the roles of only Richard III and Hamlet). If this was vomiting, metaphorically speaking, it was very much in line with the disrespectful fashion in which Hollywood for decades had lampooned Shakespearean tragic acting which provided the country with its only truly highbrow dramatics until the emergence of Eugene O'Neill and the Provincetown Players at the end of the 1920s.

The film opens with a scene at the Garrick mansion in which his agent, Boris Mefoofsky (Gregory Ratoff), angry at his client's contract-breaking misbehavior, tells Garrick that he is now "washed up" as far as Hollywood is concerned, with his bank account empty, the landlord ready to evict him for non-payment of his rent, and his wife Sylvia (Mary Beth Hughes) having departed to seek a Reno divorce. Sylvia was to star with him on the film version of *Macbeth* but that project shut down when Garrick disappeared on a three-

THE PERFORMING SELF TRIUMPHANT   187

Figure 15.1 In *The Great Profile* (Walter Lang, Twentieth Century-Fox, 1940), Evans Garrick first appears in the film with his cheeks heavily rouged, still dressed for his role in the studio production of *Macbeth*, just canceled after his three-day absence from the set. Digital frame enlargement.

day drunk. Lang's film discovers a comic resolution to this career and personal impasse when a quite serious young playwright, Mary Maxwell (Anne Baxter), appears with a script in hand, with a starring role written just for him. The play is titled *Beloved Transgressor*, a neoromantic reference to its main character, a French painter who, embracing a modernist antirealism, has been viewed as an outlaw by the self-appointed curators of the art world. Garrick is not interested when he is told that it has a "message" but then he learns that Mary's well-heeled fiancé Richard (John Payne) would be the production's backer. Garrick quickly imagines that promising her a role in the play will get Sylvia to return (which she quickly does) and that the couple's reconciliation will be eased once they start receiving regular paychecks. Mefoofsky, who is deep in hock to his bookie, is also pleased, seeing Richard as a cash cow he can milk for money to pay off his gambling debts. Like Garrick, he, too, is facing professional ruin and the new production will put him back into business while the mob leg-breakers pursuing him will be called off once the bookie gets his money, that is, if a somewhat reluctant Richard comes through with a big check. (He doesn't, which sets up one of the film's final gags.)

Despite constant fighting between Sylvia and Garrick, the production proceeds and bookings are arranged. On opening night, however, the star finally has it with both Maxwell's pretentious drama of an artist in decline and Sylvia's amateurish acting (he constantly maligns her as an "acrobat" which, in truth, she was when they met). Bored by the play and frustrated by what he thinks is his spouse's ineffective performance, he gets drunk and returns for the second act only intermittently in character. Being "straight" in a play whose author insists on its serious "message" is boring the audience silly but Garrick's interruptive antics get playgoers rolling in the aisles while Sylvia, thoroughly disgusted, departs—again—for Reno. Against all the odds, the play becomes a hit though Mary Maxwell is disconsolate that her script was abandoned in the middle of the premiere performance. She insists that the production be shut down. Flattered by reviews that praise his genius in sponsoring such an unusual project, however, Richard persuades her to reform Garrick on the theory that, if he remains sober, he will remain in character. She embraces the role as his savior. She has him move into her apartment, a gesture he quite naturally mistakes for romantic interest.

Flattered and pampered, Garrick resumes the role as written, if somewhat reluctantly, but once again audiences are bored to tears. Only when, for a second time, has he had enough of what he thinks is pretentious nonsense does the production once again dissolve into audience-pleasing improvisation. Now drunk and quite belligerent, he resumes his backstage battling with Sylvia, returned to the show in a jealous fit after hearing that Mary is enamored of her erstwhile husband. But before the performance can begin, Mefoofsky, disguised as a dark-skinned Carmen Miranda, is pursued across the auditorium by a bewildered gangster who has caught on to the agent's trick. Before the audience can absorb the full import of this strange pursuit, yet another surprise performance interrupts "the play": Garrick has arranged for a troupe of acrobats to take the stage and, in the tableau they create, he takes a role supporting an ecstatic Sylvia on his shoulders (no stunt double for Barrymore in this scene but he manages the trick). The film ends with Garrick acknowledging that Sylvia has achieved success in a different kind of performance art. He validates this art, and her, by his participation in the sculpture, supporting her in the most literal of senses. In proper Hollywood form, the film ends with a somewhat touching reconciliation between the hitherto estranged husband and wife, even if it is hard to manage how the play might go on in the face of such thoroughgoing disruption by an irrepressible individualist like Garrick.

To be sure, the star comes to realize that it's smart to plan a tender moment in order to please an irate spouse, which is reformation of a sort. But otherwise he learns the lesson that learning the lesson is often a mistake. Being yourself and flouting the rules that make no sense to you is the key to success. Mary begs him to "behave" and learn how to prefer milk to whisky but drink, releasing his inhibitions (such as they are), seems the key to his creative improvisations. The result is that theatergoers are bored by the unrelieved seriousness of her play and his performance in it which is thoroughly *contre coeur* and so seems to one and all. Garrick's vehicle for self-reclamation, *The Beloved Transgressor*, provides him with the opportunity to validate his mischievousness which has everything to do with performance instincts that are applauded by an appreciative audience. At the end, the stage has been completely cleared of Maxwell's dreary play, to be filled instead with a spectacle that is as pleasing as it is unanticipated.

Though it seems that the first version of the script did not reference Barrymore directly, it was rewritten explicitly to reconfigure in fictional form the famous star's recent performance in a hit stage play, *My Dear Children*, which was written by two unknowns, Jerry Horwin and Catherine Turney. *The Great Profile* can be most usefully viewed as the last phase of the unique stage phenomenon that was *My Dear Children* of which it can be seen as providing something like an important record. It is no accident that the production at the heart of *The Great Profile* is not cinematic but theatrical because the kind of performance it dramatizes must be live, involving audiences that find themselves entertained by the aleatory, the unexpected, and the unscripted in ways that only self-admittedly improvisational traditions (such as The Second City) customarily provide. Each performance must proceed with the likelihood of its being interrupted or altered in some unexpected fashion. Just to take one example from a repertoire of similar comic moments, at the end of an often-interrupted performance of *The Beloved Transgressor*, Garrick slips off the stage into the orchestra pit from which he then energetically emerges sounding "Hurray for the Red, White, and Blue" on a bugle he has somehow found.

In contrast, because of Barrymore's mischievous interruptions, no performance of *My Dear Children* was precisely the same as any other. To be sure, nothing quite so spectacularly unexpected happened during the unexpectedly long run of *My Dear Children* as the transformation of the stage into a platform for human sculpture. And yet from its premiere at the McCarter Theater in Princeton on March 29, 1939, the play simply did not run according to a script that Barrymore could not remember, thought inadequate, or simply enjoyed subverting in an amazing number of different ways, of which Kobler provides an interesting inventory:

> ... clowning, mugging, grunts, snorts, rumbles, yawns, bleats, belches, leers, sheers, smirks, ogles, roars, squeaks, eye-rolling, eyebrow-twitching, strutting, mincing, pouncing, staggering, hop-skip-and-jumps, profanity, obscenity and general horseplay. (329)

The play's inaugural performance earned Barrymore five curtain calls. It quickly became clear that what had started textual life as a "vapid farce" was transformed by its star into "a freakish smash hit unique in theater annals" (Kobler 329). But that was in more or less liberal New Jersey. The managers of more conservative venues in the Midwest were alarmed by the continuing publicity about Barrymore's antics (almost every night furnishing different material for the gossip columnists) and cancellations followed but the play opened to such acclaim in Chicago that transference to Broadway became inevitable. There, in the first months of 1940, it ran for 117 performances at one of New York's most respected playhouses, the Belasco. Barrymore's bankability was restored; the offer from Zanuck followed soon after, and *The Great Profile*, carefully calculated to take advantage of the play's strong legs at the box office, was quickly produced and released. Still in need of money and eager to maintain a foothold in the business, Barrymore, from all reports, was pleased to accept Zanuck's offer to appear in the film that was named after him and thus told audiences what to expect. The opening credits paid him yet another compliment as, in an unusual move, his name appears above the title, to the accompaniment of a female chorus crooning "Oh Johnny, oh Johnny oh!," a song that first became a hit in 1917 when Barrymore was one of Broadway's most established matinée idols. Zanuck and company were intent not only on evoking the recent but also the distant past.

My Dear Children is a rather conventional domestic comedy in which an aging Shakespearean ham, Allan Manville, obsessed with his youthful success in the role of Hamlet (a portrait of him *en costume* is prominently displayed onstage) presides over a chateau in the Swiss alps where his three adult daughters visit with predictable results in the vein of a sub-Shakespearean *King Lear*. Barrymore's performance, if that is the correct term, was not only theatrical in the traditional sense but improvisational in the minimal sense that he "filled in" as needed when he could neither remember the dialogue nor hear the assistant feeding him lines from offstage. He did inhabit the role of Manville, at least most of the time during the run of the play but he also performed metatheatrically, violating the existential divide of the "missing fourth wall," and this is what audiences found fascinating. Continually, and unpredictably, he stepped out of character and, as "himself," addressed the audience. His performances as Hamlet and Richard III had caused a sensation nearly two decades earlier and, once again, Barrymore was the talk of the theatrical world. Everyone who was anyone in the entertainment business made it a point to catch his performance.

Suddenly a third-rate drama became interesting, not at all for itself but for the performance platform it provided its irrepressible star. Applause, laughs, and gasps of surprise inevitably fed Barrymore's desire for further improvisation. Even during performances in which he more or less abided by the script (helped by assistants in the wings who fed him lines), playgoers were kept on the edges of their seats, never knowing if, when, and how their evening at the theater would be punctuated by some onstage incident that might make the morning papers and be remembered for years afterward (as, indeed, many were: see Kobler 329–8 and Peters 411–42 for what many would regard as "juicy" details). Barrymore was aided in this subversive endeavor (which made a fortune for all involved) by the evolving circumstances of his crumbling marriage to wife number four, Elaine, whose idea this play was, though she had no reason to suspect that her husband would take the approach he did to making it interesting for himself. She hoped that appearing with her husband in a stage production which would ameliorate their financial troubles would also permit them to spend more time together and renew their romance. Her career would receive a needed boost, as would his. But, during the life of the play, this parallel narrative developed with quite different twists and turns. Elaine moved in and out of the cast following a series of more or less public arguments; on one evening, when she had been replaced onstage, she even ostentatiously joined the audience, provoking murmurs of surprise, at least among the assembled cognoscenti, and providing yet another center of interest for that performance. It would not have escaped the notice of critics and playgoers alike that Barrymore's mischievous and disrespectful riffing on the playtext, which was often dependent on the strictly aleatory (the loud seating of a latecomer, for example), was flamboyantly autobiographical, as week after week during the play's run he enacted the "bad boy" self that he had cultivated as a public persona for more than three decades. That this improvisation seemed to express scorn for the poor quality of the playtext fed the narrative of the eminent Shakespearean forced by the weight of his own malfeasance and moral failure to debase himself by doing low comedy, with his periodic stepping out of character readable as a high-tone rejection of the property's mediocrity and yet another assertion of his better self in these otherwise dismal proceedings. One could argue that there was no little autobiography, however indirectly evoked, in these gestures of subversion.

The spectacle of Barrymore playing an aging Shakespearean ham in *My Dear Children* was observed by a fascinated Orson Welles who was prompted to say that, if he knew a young child interested in a stage career, he would take him to see Barrymore in this role; here was a man "who knew everything about acting" (quoted in Kobler 334). *Life*'s review offered a convincing analysis of what was making *My Dear Children* such a popular show: "People flock to see [Barrymore], not for polished performance, but because he converts the theater into a rowdy histrionic madhouse. Sometimes he arrives late. Sometimes he is tight. Usually he forgets his lines. But he always puts on a great show" (*Life* 7: 23 [December 4, 1939], 50). America's leading theatrical critic, Brooks Atkinson, praised Barrymore's unusual approach to entertaining theatergoers, observing that he was "still a superbly gifted player on a tired holiday" ("John Barrymore Returns to New York After 17 Years—Acts Chief Part in My Dear Children," *New York Times* [February 1, 1940], 25).

The Great Profile was not, strictly speaking, an adaptation of *My Dear Children*. It was, instead, what theorist Julie Sanders suggests is an "appropriation": a "new" work that, while it "signals a relationship to an informing sourcetext," also "affects a decisive journey ... into a wholly new cultural product" (26). What exactly is that cultural product? Ordinarily, appropriations involve the borrowing (imitation or remaking) of story, theme, and characters from a source that is not reproduced but evoked; the new work thus functions as a sort of oblique adaptation of an original with which it does not exactly share either a title or an identity. *The Great Profile* is only in part an appropriation of this sort; at its fictional center is a play, *Beloved Transgressor*, that bears a close resemblance, if only at points, to *My Dear Children*. Most significant, of course, is that an aging artist in crisis is the central character in both plots. But, surely more important is that *The Great Profile* appropriates the essence, and many of the details, of the production history of *My Dear Children*, which, with only a bit of exaggeration is, as Kobler notes, "unique in theater annals." *The Great Profile* was fashioned to hook filmgoers by its comic engagement with recent entertainment business history. It is a performance in which Barrymore the actor and Barrymore the man play complementary roles difficult to distinguish from one another, a coincidence of life and art that, in a larger sense, is the view of celebrity and stardom that the film takes as its theme.

What the feature-film medium could appropriate from this extraordinary theatrical event finds a second life in *The Great Profile* which is thus of substantial interest to any proper assessment of Barrymore's unique acting career. There seems no reason to dispute the judgment of theater historian Michael A. Morrison that Barrymore's "Shakespearean performances were among the modern theatre's towering achievements" (xii). But, early in his stage and film careers, Barrymore also achieved substantial success in light comedy and melodrama, with his turn toward classical acting coming during his performance in Edward Sheldon's production of the romantic comedy *Princess Zim-Zim* (1911) when the playwright, correctly assessing his leading man's unusual talent, convinced Barrymore to reconceive his career. According to producer Arthur Hopkins, Sheldon put the "finger of destiny" on Barrymore as the pair entered into what Eric Barnes characterizes as "one of the most incongruous relationships in the theater" (Barnes 73, where Hopkins is quoted as well). As Morrison reports, Sheldon recognized that the "facile comedian" was "far more intelligent than the average actor" and determined to "challenge his abilities in serious roles" (49). But, however prescient he may have been, even Sheldon could hardly have foreseen that Barrymore would turn out to be the next Edwin Booth or Henry Irving. That amazing capacity for performance (including a not inconsiderable athleticism) is still on display in *The Great Profile*, despite the ravages of dissipation and the evocation of his recent marital and professional troubles. As miserable as his life had no doubt become, what better tonic could there have been than turning his own troubles and triumphs into comedy? Why assume, as does Margot Peters, that Barrymore was lying in order to save face when, after completing *The Great Profile*, he told a reporter that "I loved doing this film" (quoted in Peters 444).

Barrymore, and of this there is no doubt, loved performing on stage or before a camera as much as "playing" the public role that, with considerable glee and lack of inhibition about what others considered his moral failings, he had constructed over decades for himself and had no intention late in life of abandoning. There is no evidence in his considerable biographical record to suggest that he ever felt ashamed of what he did or what, as a result of what he did, he had become, as he slipped beyond middle age. After all, to the very end of his career, he was in demand, even if his declining health limited his opportunities, making it impossible for him to do the role of Sheridan Whiteside in the film version of the Broadway hit *The Man Who Came to Dinner*, in which Bette Davis was to star. At Davis's insistence, Barrymore was tested for the part but he was too dissipated to bring it off.

It would suit conventional ideas about how public figures should behave if Barrymore had shown himself conscious of "having wasted his talent" or offered some such self-flagellating judgment, and one can sense the frustration of journalists and his biographers that he failed to feel shame. Despite obvious signs of approaching collapse, common to many in a generation that insisted on smoking and drinking itself into early death, Barrymore was undeterred by the box-office failure of *The Great Profile*, which was reprised, if in only in a minor and less antic key, in *Playmates*. There, he and Kay Kyser play "themselves," and the plot centers around Barrymore's not very successful attempts to teach hip-talking Kay the basics of Shakespearean performance, as, once again in a Hollywood film, low culture collides with high to humorous effect. As in *The Great Profile*, Barrymore's performance evokes his declining fortunes and need to pay a huge debt, this time to the IRS. Once again, the actor is enticed by the prospect of a new production, a mounting of a Shakespeare play in which he would star with Kyser. After much harmless mayhem and silliness, the play does come off—and, *mirabile dictu*, it proves to be *Romeo and Juliet* thoroughly modernized and done as a swing musical. *Times* reviewer Bosley Crowther pronounced an accurate judgment: "a laboriously contrived mélange of comedy, farce and music". To be sure, Shakespeare and the century's greatest American Shakespearean actor become the disrespected objects of a satiric diminishment that, in the inimitable Hollywood manner, refuses any hint of sanctimoniousness. No one who knew him would ever have accused

Barrymore of having no sense of humor, especially about himself. There is no better proof of this than *The Great Profile*.

In the event, Zanuck had misread the market. That the film underperformed at the box office, however, means only that its representations and impersonations were not broadly endorsed by the paying public, not, of course, that this playful pseudoautobiography lacks importance to an evaluation of the last stages of Barrymore's career beyond "sad" evidence of a decline that might have been resisted. Instead, I suggest that crucial to the film's disappointing reception was the fact that the cinema was incapable of restaging the qualities central to the success of its stage source, *My Dear Children*, which was entirely dependent on the nature of Barrymore's serial performances in a production that "ran" for more than five months in a series of venues and required successive repetitions intended, by convention, to be as similar to one another as possible, with production and rehearsals setting norms that were thereafter assiduously to be followed, insuring uniformity of a sort (see Burns 28–39 for an illuminating discussion of the social conventions that govern theatrical performance and spectatorship). Barrymore stood this convention on its head, making every performance of the play an adventure in unexpected and often startling alterations, moving the audience to wonder what outrageously frame-breaking ad-lib he would offer them next. *My Dear Children* became an exercise in metatheater, as violations of accepted rules (an activity at which Barrymore had developed considerable expertise, starting in childhood) were not part of the drama per se (note, for instance, the Prologue addressing the audience about the illusionism involved in stage presentation before the first act of *Henry V* properly begins) but elements of its realization through performance that escaped the control of the script, its director, and the unspoken injunction that the invisible physical barrier between stage and audience not be violated. *The Great Profile* could provide a fictionalized record of such formal deconstruction but, despite the energetic exertions of Barrymore, not of the pleasurably disorienting experience of participating in it.

NOTE

1. This is perhaps a reference to David Garrick (1717–79), the playwright, theater owner, actor, and impresario who was the the dominant figure of the eighteenth-century British stage and heavily influenced modern theatrical practice. The Garrick theaters in London, Chicago, and New York City honor his contribution to the art form.

Works Cited

Adams, Carol J. *The Sexual Politics of Meat: A Feminist–Vegetarian Critical Theory*, 20th Anniversary Edition. New York: Bloomsbury, 2010.
Bakhtin, M. M. *Rabelais and His World*. Trans. Helen Iswolsky. Bloomington: Indiana University Press, 1984.
Balázs, Béla. *Theory of the Film (Character and Growth of a New Art)*. Trans. Edith Bone. New York: Arno Press, 1972 © 1948.
Barnes, Eric Wollencott. *The Man Who Lived Twice: The Biography of Edward Sheldon*. New York: Scribner's, 1958.
Baron, Cynthia. "Performances in *Adaptation*: Analyzing Human Movement in Motion Pictures," *Cineaste* 31: 4 (Fall 2006), 48–55.
Baron, Cynthia and Sharon Marie Carnicke. *Reframing Screen Performance*. Ann Arbor: University of Michigan Press, 2011.
Bartenieff, Irmgard and Martha Ann Davis. "Effort-Shape Analysis of Movement: The Unity of Expression and Function," in Philip Eisenberg, Irmgard Bartenieff, and Martti Takala, eds, *Research Approaches to Movement and Personality*. New York: Arno Press, 1972 © 1937, 17–27.
Barrymore, John. *Confessions of an Actor*. London: Robert Holden & Co. Ltd, 1926.
Barthes, Roland. *A Lover's Discourse: Fragments*, Trans. Richard Howard. New York: Hill and Wang, 2010.
Basinger, Jeanine. *The Star Machine*. New York: Vintage, 2007.
Behlmer, Rudi, ed. *Memo from David O. Selznick*. New York: Random House, 2000 ©1977.
Benjamin, Walter. "Little History of Photography," in M. W. Jennings, H. Eiland, and G. Smith, eds, *Walter Benjamin: Selected Writings*, Vol. 2. Cambridge, MA: Harvard University Press, 1999, 507–30.
Berkoff, Steven. *I Am Hamlet*. London: Faber and Faber, 1989.
Bettelheim, Bruno. "The Problem of Generations," in Erik H. Erikson, ed., *The Challenge of Youth*. New York: Doubleday Anchor Books, 1965, 76–109.
Brantley, Ben. "A Dazzler of a Drunk, Full of Gab and Grief," *New York Times* (March 26, 1997), online at www.nytimes.com Accessed April 21, 2016.
Burns, Elizabeth. *Theatricality: A Study of Convention in the Theatre and in Social Life*. New York: Harper & Row, 1972.

Butler, Judith. *Gender Trouble: Feminism and the Subversion of Identity*. London: Routledge, 1990.
Cameron, Rebecca S. "Irreconcilable Differences: Divorce and Women's Drama before 1945," *Modern Drama* 44: 4 (Winter 2001), 476–90.
Card, James. *Seductive Cinema*. New York: Knopf, 1994.
Carden-Coyne, Ana. "Ungrateful Bodies: Rehabilitation, Resistance and Disabled American Veterans of the First World War," *European Review of History* 14: 4 (2007), 543–65.
Cavell, Stanley. "Philosophy the Day After Tomorrow," in William Rothman, ed., *Cavell on Film*. Albany: SUNY Press, 2005, 319–32.
———. "The Good of Film," in William Rothman, ed., *Cavell on Film*. Albany: SUNY Press, 2005, 333–48.
Church, Hayden. "The Youth of Sherlock Holmes," *Strand* 63 (January–June 1922), 355–60.
Conley, Tom. "Getting Lost on the Waterways of *L'Atalante*," in Murray Pomerance, ed., *Cinema and Modernity*. New Brunswick, NJ: Rutgers University Press, 2006, 253–72.
Cole, Toby and Helen Krich Chinoy, eds. *Actors on Acting: The Theories, Techniques, and Practices of the World's Great Actors, Told in Their Own Words*. New York: Three Rivers Press, 1970.
Crafton, Donald. *The Talkies: America's Transition to Sound 1926–1931*. Berkeley: University of California Press, 1999.
Dane, Clemence. *A Bill of Divorcement*. London: William Heinemann, 1921.
———. *Recapture: A Clemence Dane Omnibus*. London: William Heinemann, 1932.
Davenport, Guy. *Objects on a Table: Harmonious Disarray in Art and Literature*. Washington, DC: Counterpoint, 1998.
Davis, Richard Harding. *The Dictator*. New York: Scribner's, 1909.
DeAngelis, Michael. "Doubling in the Cinema of George Cukor: *The Royal Family of Broadway*, *A Bill of Divorcement*, *A Double Life*, and *Bhowani Junction*," in Murray Pomerance and R. Barton Palmer, eds, *George Cukor: Hollywood Master*. Edinburgh: Edinburgh University Press, 2015, 90–106.
DeCordova, Richard. "Genre and Performance: An Overview," in Barry Keith Grant, ed, *Film Genre Reader*. Austin: University of Texas Press, 1986, 123–39.
Derrida, Jacques. "Structure, Sign and Play in the Discourse of the Human Sciences," in *Writing and Difference*. Trans. Alan Bass. Chicago: University of Chicago Press, 1978), 278–93.
———. "Whom to Give to (Knowing Not to Know)," in Jonathan Rée and Jane Chamberlain, eds, *Kierkegaard: A Critical Reader*. Malden, MA: Blackwell, 1998, 151–74.
Doherty, Thomas. *Projections of War: Hollywood, American Culture, and World War II*. New York: Columbia University Press, 1993.
Doyle, Arthur Conan. *The Adventures of Sherlock Holmes*. New York: Harper and Brothers, 1892.
Dulac, Germaine. "The Essence of the Cinema: The Visual Idea," in P. Adams Sitney, ed., *The Avant-Garde Film: A Reader of Theory and Criticism*. New York: New York University Press, 1978, 36–42.
Eliot, T. S. "Tradition and the Individual Talent," in *Selected Essays*. London: Faber and Faber, 1958, 13–22.
Erikson, Erik H. *Identity: Youth and Crisis*. London: Faber and Faber, 1983.
Everson, William K. "John Barrymore's Sherlock Holmes," *Films in Review* 27: 2 (February 1976), 107–9.
———. *American Silent Film*. New York: Da Capo Press, 1998.
Felski, Rita. *The Gender of Modernity*. Cambridge, MA: Harvard University Press, 1995.

Fletcher, Adele Whitely. "Across the Silversheet: The New Screen Plays in Review," *Motion Picture* 24: 7 (August 1922), 67–8, 113.
Fowler, Gene. *Good Night, Sweet Prince: The Life and Times of John Barrymore*. New York: Viking, 1944.
Fowles, John. "Poor Koko," in *The Ebony Tower*. London: Vintage Books, 2006, 143–84.
Freud, Sigmund. "Some Character-Types Met with in Psycho-Analytic Work," *The Standard Edition of the Complete Psychological Works of Sigmund Freud*, Vol. XIV (1914–16). London: Vintage, 2001 © 1916, 309–33.
Galsworthy, John. *Justice*. New York: Scribner's, 1910.
Garton, Joseph. *The Film Acting of John Barrymore*. New York: Arno Press, 1980.
Gaycken, Oliver. *Devices of Curiosity: Early Cinema and Popular Science*. New York: Oxford University Press, 2015.
Gunning, Tom. "'Those Drawn with a Very Fine Camel's Hair Brush': The Origins of Film Genres," *iris* 19 (1995), 49–61.
——. "Tracing the Individual Body: Photography, Detectives, and Early Cinema," in Leo Charney and Vanessa Schwartz, eds. *Cinema and the Invention of Modern Life*, Berkeley: University of California Press, 1995, 15–45.
——. "In Your Face: Physiognomy, Photography, and the Gnostic Mission of Early Film," *Modernism/Modernity* 4: 1 (January 1997), 1–29.
Hart, V. G. Letter to Colonel Jason S. Joy re *Bill of Divorcement*, September 2, 1932, Production Code Administration Records, Margaret Herrick Library, Academy of Motion Picture Arts and Sciences, Beverly Hills.
Harvey, James. *Romantic Comedy*. New York: Alfred A. Knopf, 1987.
Jackson, Donald Dale. "John Barrymore: A profile in just about everything," *Smithsonian* 28: 1 (1997), 88–98.
Jacobs, Lea. *The Decline of Sentiment: Hollywood in the 1920s*. Berkeley: University of California Press, 2008.
Jellife, Smyth Ely and Louise Brink. "'The Jest': The Destruction Wrought By Hate," *New York Medical Journal* CX: 14 (October 4, 1919), 573–77.
Kauffmann, Stanley. "Timeless Acting," *Salmagundi* 114/115 (Spring–Summer 1997), 49–57.
Keane, Marian. "The Great Profile: How Do We Know the Actor from the Acting?," in Carole Zucker, ed. *Making Visible the Invisible: an Anthology of Original Essays on Film Acting*, Metuchen, NJ: Scarecrow Press, 1990, 167–97.
Kinder, John M. "'Lest We Forget': Disabled Veterans and the Politics of War Remembrance in the United States," in Susan Burch and Michael Rembis, eds, *Disability Histories*. Urbana: University of Illinois Press, 2014, 163–82.
Klevan, Andrew. *Film Performance: From Achievement to Appreciation*. London: Wallflower Press, 2005.
Kobler, John. *Damned in Paradise: The Life of John Barrymore*. New York: Atheneum, 1977.
Kozloff, Sarah. "Melodrama," in Lester D. Friedman et al., *An Introduction to Film Genres*. New York: Norton, 2014, 80–119.
Long, Robert Emmet, ed. *George Cukor Interviews*. Jackson: University Press of Mississippi, 2001.
MacDonald, Laurence, E. *The Invisible Art of Film Music: A Comprehensive History*, Second Ed. Lanham, MD: Scarecrow Press, 2013.
McDonald, Paul. "Film acting," in John Hill and Pamela Church Gibson, eds. *Film Studies: Critical Approaches*. Oxford: Oxford University Press, 2000, 28–33.
McGilligan, Patrick. *George Cukor: A Double Life*. New York: Harper Perennial, 1992.
——. "What is 'Great' Acting?," *Cineaste* 31: 4 (Fall 2006), 36–9.

McLean, Adrienne L. "Feeling and the Filmed Body: Judy Garland and the Kinesics of Suffering," *Film Quarterly* 55: 3 (Spring 2002), 2–15.
Maltin, Leonard, ed. *Leonard Maltin's Movie Guide: 2008 Edition*. New York: Signet, 2007.
Mills, John A. *Hamlet on Stage: The Great Tradition*. Westport, CT: Greenwood Press, 1985.
Moore, Rachel O. *Savage Theory: Cinema as Modern Magic*. Durham NC: Duke University Press, 2000.
Morrison, Michael A. *John Barrymore: Shakespearean Actor*. New York: Cambridge University Press, 1997.
———. "The Voice Teacher as Shakespearean Collaborator: Margaret Carrington and John Barrymore," in *Theatre Survey* 38: 2 (November 1997), 129–58.
Naremore, James. *Acting in the Cinema*. Berkeley: Univeristy of California Press, 1988.
Nieland, Justus. *Feeling Modern: The Eccentricities of Public Life*. Urbana: University of Illinois Press, 2008.
Nietzsche, Friedrich. *Human, All Too Human*. Trans. Marion Faber. Lincoln, NE: University of Nebraska Press, 1984 © 1878.
Norden, Martin F. *The Cinema of Isolation: A History of Physical Disability in the Movies*. New Brunswick, NJ: Rutgers University Press, 1994.
Olivier, Laurence. *On Acting*. London: Sceptre, 1987.
Pearson, Roberta E. *Eloquent Gestures: The Transformation of Performance Style in the Griffith Biograph Films*. Berkeley: University of California Press, 1992.n
Peters, Margot. *The House of Barrymore*. New York: Alfred A. Knopf, 1990.
Phillips, Gene. *George Cukor*. Boston, MA: Twayne, 1982.
Pick, Daniel. *Svengali's Web: The Alien Enchanter in Modern Culture*. New Haven: Yale University Press, 2000.
Pomerance, Murray. *The Horse Who Drank the Sky: Film Experience Beyond Narrative and Theory*. New Brunswick, NJ: Rutgers University Press, 2008.
Pomerance, Murray and R. Barton Palmer, eds. *George Cukor: Hollywood Master*. Edinburgh: Edinburgh University Press, 2015.
Power-Waters, Alma. *John Barrymore—The Legend and the Man*. London: Stanley Paul & Co., Ltd, 1941.
Rothman, William. *The I of the Camera: Essays in Film Criticism, History, and Aesthetics*. Cambridge: Cambridge University Press, 1988.
Sanders, Julie. *Adaptation and Appropriation*. New York: Routledge, 2006.
Schröder, Volker. "Theater and Difference: Derrida and the Scene of Writing," *Papers in Romance* 6: 1 (Spring 1989), online at www.academia.edu/2573215/Theater_and_Difference_Derrida_and_the_Scene_of_Writing_Papers_in_Romance_VI_1_Spring_1989 Accessed August 4, 2016.
Shipman, David. *The Great Movie Stars: The Golden Years*. New York: Bonanza Books, 1970.
Smith, Winchell. *The Fortune Hunter*. French's Standard Library Edition. New York: Samuel French, 1909.
Stock, Paul. "Dial 'M' for Metonym: Universal Exports, M's Office Space, and Empire," in Christoph Lindner, ed. *The James Bond Phenomenon: A Critical Reader*, Manchester: Manchester University Press, 2009, 251–67.
Studlar, Gaylyn. *This Mad Masquerade: Stardom and Masculinity in the Jazz Age*. New York: Columbia University Press, 1996.
"They Thought He Was John Barrymore," *Motion Picture Magazine* 24: 8 (September 1922), 78.
Thompson, Kristin. *Herr Lubitsch goes to Hollywood: German and American Film after World War I*. (Amsterdam: Amsterdam University Press, 2005).

Thomson, David. *A Biographical Dictionary of the Cinema*. London: Secker and Warburg, 1975.
Turvey, Malcolm. *Doubting Vision: Film and the Revelationist Tradition*. New York: Oxford University Press, 2008.
Wegele, Peter. *Max Steiner: Composing,* Casablanca, *and the Golden Age of Film Music*. Lanham, MD: Rowman and Littlefield, 2014.
Wells, Stanley, ed. *Shakespeare in the Theatre: An Anthology of Criticism*. Oxford: Oxford University Press, 2000.
Westwell, Guy. *War Cinema: Hollywood on the Front Line*. London: Wallflower Press, 2006.
Wilson, Garth. *A History of American Acting*. Westport, CT: Greenwood Press, 1966.
Woolcott, Alexander. "Second Thoughts on First Nights," *New York Times* (April 22, 1917), XX3.
Young, Stark. "A Terrible Thing," *New Republic* (September 14, 1927), 98–9.
Zucker, Carole. "The Concept of 'Excess' in Film Acting: Notes Toward an Understanding of Non-Naturalistic Performance," *Post Script* 12: 2 (Winter 1993), 54–62.

Index

Abeles, Edward, 14
Actress, The (George Cukor, 1953), 109
Alberni, Louis, 86–7
Alexander, J. Grubb, 32, 86
Anna Karenina (Clarence Brown, 1935), 111
Arsène Lupin (Jack Conway, 1932), 6, 71, 77, 79–80, 82
Astor, Mary, 49, 72, 73, 103
At What Price Glory? (Raoul Walsh, 1926), 68

Bacon, Lloyd, 59–61, 64, 65–6, 67, 68, 70, 178
Balázs, Béla, 39–40
Barrymore, Ethel, 12–13, 51, 111–12, 124
Barrymore, John Drew Jr., 51
Barrymore, Lionel, 1, 12, 18–19, 20, 78, 83, 89, 115, 123–4, 147, 153, 186
Barrymore, Maurice, 12–13, 51, 116
Beau Brummel (Harry Beaumont, 1924), 1, 6, 26, 47–58, 159, 163, 165
Benelli, Sem, 19
Bern, Paul, 160
Bernhardt, Sarah, 19, 39, 72, 180, 182
Bettelheim, Bruno, 126
Big Parade, The (King Vidor, 1925), 69
Bill of Divorcement, A (Clemence Dane play), 32, 111, 125, 134
Bill of Divorcement, A (George Cukor, 1932), 6, 24, 32, 111–13, 115, 118–19, 122–3, 125, 127–34, 179
Black Pirate (Albert Parker, 1926), 72
Blackmail (Alfred Hitchcock, 1929), 79
Bow, Clara, 10

Brecht, Bertolt, 159–60
Bridgman, George, 13
Brinke, Louise, 27
Brown, Clarence, 147, 153
Brownlow, Kevin, 45
Burke, Billie, 33, 112, 115
Burton, Richard, 2

Cagney, James, 166
Camille (George Cukor, 1936), 121
Card, James, 164
Carnegie, Andrew, 13
Carrington, Margaret, 16, 25, 28–9, 34, 51, 104
Casablanca (Michael Curtiz, 1942), 130
Cather, Willa, 26
Cavell, Stanley, 113, 122, 127, 171
Church, Hayden, 40
Clark, Marguerite, 15
Cohn, Harry, 172
Colbert, Claudette, 1, 102
Collier, Constance, 18, 21
Collier, William, 14, 18
Conley, Tom, 148
Conway, Jack, 77
Counsellor at Law (William Wyler, 1933), 159, 165, 179
Craig, Gordon, 25
Crane, William H., 15
Crawford, Joan, 83
Crosland, Alan, 99, 157
Cukor, George, 4, 7, 8, 33, 98, 101–2, 108, 109–22, 125, 127–8, 133, 179

Dane, Celmence, 32, 111, 125, 134
Daniels, William H., 83
Davenport, Guy, 2
Davis, Bette, 193, 195
Davis, Richard Harding, 14
Dawley, J. Searle, 15
Day, Marceline, 160
Decker, John, 1
Dempster, Carol, 37
Denny, Reginald, 37
Design for Living (Ernst Lubitsch, 1933), 75
Dickens, Charles, 103
The Dictator (Richard Harding Davis play, 1904 production), 14–15
The Dictator (Edwin S. Porter and Oscar Eagle, 1915), 51
Dinner at Eight (George Cukor, 1933), 4, 9, 98, 100–1, 103–7, 115–19, 133, 138, 145, 179
Dr. Jekyll and Mr. Hyde (John S. Robertson, 1920), 4–5, 13, 24, 26–8, 33, 38, 43–4, 48–9, 55, 59, 86, 105, 137–9, 144–5
Don Juan (Alan Crosland, 1926), 6, 30, 63, 71–4, 76–7, 79, 82, 83, 86, 145, 157
Double Life, A (George Cukor, 1947),
Doyle, Arthur Conan, 35–8, 41–5
Dreiser, Theodor, 26
du Maurier, George, 18, 25, 27, 85, 88
Dulac, Germaine, 35
Dyer, Elmer, 148

Eliot, T. S., 133
Eternal Love (Ernst Lubitsch, 1929), 6, 71, 74–5, 77, 79, 82, 84
Everson, William K., 45

Fairbanks, Douglas, 72, 74, 86, 109, 158, 160, 161
Felski, Rita, 150–1
Ferber, Edna, 101, 111, 115
Fernandel, 135
Fiske, Maddern, 15
Fitzgerald, F. Scott, 26
Fletcher, Bramwell, 87
Fortune Hunter, The (1909 production), 15, 25
42nd Street (Lloyd Bacon, 1933), 178–9
Fowler, Gene, 1, 132
Frankenstein (James Whale, 1931)
Freud, Sigmund, 5, 24, 27–9, 73, 99, 125

Gable, Clark, 147–8, 150
Galsworthy, John, 16, 18, 25

Garbo, Greta, 2, 6, 82, 83, 84, 101, 111, 118, 166
Gargan, William, 147
Garrett, Oliver H. P., 148
Garton, Joseph, 48, 55
Gielgud, John, 2, 22
Gilbert, John, 109, 166
Gish, Dorothy, 111
Gordon, C. Henry, 154
Goulding, Edmund, 4, 80, 98
Grand Hotel (Edmund Goulding, 1932), 4, 6, 8, 71, 79–82, 84, 98, 101–2, 133, 145, 147
Great Profile, The (Walter Lang, 1940), 9, 183–94
Griffith, D. W., 3, 4
Grot, Anton, 30, 32, 89
Gunning, Tom, 36, 39–40, 44

Hamlet (1922 production), 3, 22, 23–4, 28–30, 34, 38, 45, 48, 51, 56, 71, 72–4, 110, 112, 123–5, 127, 145, 157–8, 169
Hawks, Howard, 4, 9, 99, 169, 172–5, 177–82
Hayes, Helen, 111, 147
Hecht, Ben, 171–2, 179, 182
Hemingway, Ernest, 26
Henry VI (Shakespeare), 10, 21, 27, 104, 165
Hepburn, Katharine, 33, 112, 113, 128
His Girl Friday (Howard Hawks, 1940), 171–2
Hitchcock, Alfred, 79, 111
Hoffmann, E. T. A., 27
Hold That Co-ed (George Marshall, 1938), 184
Hollywood Revue (Charles Reisner, 1929), 160
Hopkins, Arthur M., 18–19, 25–7, 29, 32, 34, 73, 104, 111, 124, 192
Horn, Camilla, 77, 80
Hosea, Robert, 16
Hotchener, Harry, 88, 93

Ibsen, Henrik, 112, 117
Idol, The (1929 play), 30
If I Were King (J. Gordon Edwards, 1920), 157

Jelliffe, Smyth Ely, 27
Jest, The (1919 production), 19, 21, 26–7, 48, 50, 86
Jones, Robert Edmond, 18, 25, 29, 73
Justice (1916 production), 16, 18, 25

Kaufman, George S., 101, 111, 115
Kauffmann, Stanley, 133
Keane, Marian, 4, 47–8, 52, 158–9, 163–5
Keaton, Buster, 3, 36

Laban, Rudolf, 87–88, 90
Laemmle, Carl, 122
Lawrence, Florence, 122
Leisen, Mitchell, 102
Lloyd, Harold, 161
Lombard, Carole, 9, 169, 174
Lotus Eater, The (Marshall Neilan, 1921), 124
Love Parade (Ernst Lubitsch, 1929), 75
Loy, Myrna, 139, 147, 155
Luce, William, 132

MacArthur, Charles, 171–2, 179, 182
McGill, Barney, 89
Mad Genius, The (Michael Curtiz, 1931), 24, 30–2, 86
Man from Blankley's, The (Alfred E. Green, 1930), 30
Man from Mexico, The (1914 play), 51
Maltin, Leonard, 86
Man Who Came to Dinner, The (William Keighley, 1942), 193
Mankiewicz, Herman J., 115
Manon Lescaut (1892 opera), 158
Mansfield, Richard, 48–50, 56
Marion, Frances, 115
Mark of Zorro, The (Fred Niblo and Theodore Reed, 1920), 69
Marsh, Marian, 86–7
Mayo, Archie, 85–6, 88–9, 172
Melville, Herman, 59–60, 65, 68, 71
Mencken, H. L., 26
Midnight (Mitchell Leisen, 1936), 102
Moby Dick (Lloyd Bacon, 1930), 6, 24, 30, 32, 59–61, 64–71
Montgomery, Robert, 147, 150
Morley, Karen, 79
Mowbray, Alan, 1
Murder! (Alfred Hitchcock, 1930), 111
Murnau, F. W., 50, 179
Murray, John Tucker, 119
My Dear Children (1940 production), 189–92, 194
Myers, Carmel, 87, 91

Naremore, James, 112
Nietzsche, Friedrich, 129, 134
Night Flight (Clarence Brown, 1933), 8, 145–56
Nosferatu (F. W. Murnau, 1922), 42–50

Oelrichs, Blanche *see* Strange, Michael
Olivier, Lawrence, 22
O'Neill, Eugene, 26, 186

Pagnol, Marcel, 136
Paramount on Parade (multiple directors, 1930), 10
Parker, Albert, 36, 45, 48
Parker, Dorothy, 21
Peter Ibbetson (1917 production), 3, 18, 25, 27, 50, 168
Peters, Margot, 55, 131, 185, 193
Pezzaglia, Paola, 19
Pickford, Mary, 15, 168
Playmates (David Butler, 1941), 9, 144, 184, 193
Plummer, Christopher, 132–4
Poe, Edgar Allan, 3
Porcasi, Paul, 87
Porter, Edwin S., 3
Princess Zim-Zim (Edward Sheldon, 1911), 192

Raffles, the Amateur Cracksman (George Irving, 1917), 51
Redemption (1918 production), 18–19, 27
Rheinhardt, Max, 25
Richard III (1920 production), 13, 21, 26, 28–9, 38, 49, 51, 104, 132, 172, 190
Richard III (onscreen) *see Show of Shows*
Robin Hood (Allan Dwan, 1922), 72
Romeo and Juliet (George Cukor, 1936), 119–22
Row, Arthur, 104
Royal Family of Broadway, The (George Cukor and Cyril Gardner, 1930), 111

Schubert, Franz, 130
Sea Beast, The (Millard Webb, 1926), 6, 24, 59–71, 110
Selznick, David O., 33, 121, 125, 147, 148
Shakespeare, William, 3, 5, 10, 11, 19, 21–5, 27–9, 32, 34, 38, 48–9, 56, 73–4, 104, 109, 111, 120, 178
Shaw, George Bernard, 18, 48, 110, 115
Sheldon, Edward Brewster "Ned", 15–16, 18, 19, 25, 26, 27, 34, 51, 56, 192
Sherlock Holmes (Albert Parker, 1922), 5, 35–46, 48, 86
Sherlock Holmes Baffled (1900 film), 36
Sherlock, Jr. (Buster Keaton, 1924), 36
Show of Shows (John G. Adolfi, 1929), 9, 27–30
Slice of Life, A (1912 production), 25, 186

Smith, Winchell, 15
Smythe, Albert E. S., 27
Stanislavsky, Constantin, 51, 57–8
Star is Born, A (George Cukor, 1954), 109
Steiner, Max, 130
Stevenson, Robert Louis, 3, 44, 48, 86
Stewart, David Ogden, 115
Strange, Michael, 19, 99
Strunk, William, 119
Sullivan, T. R., 48
Svengali (Archie Mayo, 1931), 4, 6, 24, 30–2, 85–97, 143, 144, 172, 176, 179

Tale of Two Cities, A (Dickens novel), 103
Tell it to the Marines (George W. Hill, 1926), 68
Tempest (Joseph M. Schenck, 1926), 74, 76
Thalberg, Irving, 119, 121
Thin Man, The (film series), 80
Thing from Another World, The (Howard Hawks, 1951), 179–80
Thomas, Augustus, 13
Threepenny Opera, The (Brecht play, 1928), 159

Tolstoy, Leo, 18
Topaze (Harry d'Abbadie d'Arrast, 1933), 8, 135–44
Trouble in Paradise (Ernst Lubitsch, 1932), 75
Twain, Mark, 26
Twentieth Century (Howard Hawks, 1934), 4, 8, 9, 87, 99, 124, 138, 143–4, 145, 169–82

Veidt, Conrad, 160
Villon, François, 99
Vitaphone sound system, 24, 30, 157
Von Seyffertitz, Gustav, 36, 42–4

Welles, Orson, 2, 22, 33, 34, 191
What Price Hollywood? (George Cukor, 1932), 115, 119
When a Man Loves (Alan Crosland, 1927), 40, 157–8, 168
Wilde, Oscar, 27, 37
Woollcott, Alexander, 18, 48

Zanuck, Darryl F., 184, 190, 194

EU representative:
Easy Access System Europe
Mustamäe tee 50, 10621 Tallinn, Estonia
Gpsr.requests@easproject.com

www.ingramcontent.com/pod-product-compliance
Lightning Source LLC
Chambersburg PA
CBHW051058230426
43667CB00013B/2356